AWAKEN TO YOUR TRUE SELF

AWAKEN

TO YOUR

TRUE SELF

Why You're Still Stuck and
How to Break Through

ANDREW DANIEL

MetaHeal
Intentional Publishing House

Copyright © 2020, 2022 Andrew Daniel

andrewdaniel.org

All rights reserved. This book or any portion thereof may not be reproduced or used in any manner without the express written permission of the publisher or author except for the use of brief attributed quotations or passages. To request permissions for this book, contact the publisher at publishing@metaheal.com

Book and cover design: Andrew Daniel
Cover art source: "Flammarion Engraving" by Camille Flammarion
Previously published as: "Why You're Still Stuck" by Drew Gerald

The author of this book is not a doctor, and does not dispense medical advice, diagnosis, or prescribe the use of any technique as a form of treatment for psychological or medical problems without the advice of a physician, either directly or indirectly. These ideas are not a replacement for professional help. In the event you use any of the information in this book for yourself, the author and the publisher assume no responsibility for your actions.

Published by MetaHeal
188 Grand Street Unit #443
New York, NY 10013
metaheal.com

10 9 8 7 6 5 4 3 2

Publisher's Cataloging-in-Publication Data

Names: Daniel, Andrew, 1987- author.
Title: Awaken to your true self : why you're still stuck and how to break through / Andrew Daniel.
Description: New York : MetaHeal, 2022.
Identifiers: LCCN 2022933848 (print) | ISBN 9781953617033 (hardcover) | ISBN 9781953617064 (paperback) | ISBN 9781953617040 (ebook)
Subjects: LCSH: Mind and body. | Self-actualization (Psychology) | Mindfulness (Psychology) | Spiritual life. | BISAC: BODY, MIND & SPIRIT / Inspiration & Personal Growth. | BODY, MIND & SPIRIT / Mindfulness & Meditation. | SELF-HELP / Spiritual.
Classification: LCC BF637.S4 G47 2020 (print) | LCC BF637.S4 (ebook) | DDC 158.1--dc23.

First print edition December 2020: ISBN 9781953617002
Revision 20220222-4

For Granny, Grandpa, & Karl
my elders who have passed

"I know you're tired but come, this is the way."
RUMI

CONTENTS

PART II—MOVING FORWARD

INTRODUCTION

 know the pain of being stuck. Intimately. I've struggled most of my life trying to figure this all out, incessantly attempting to overcome the same struggles and plateaus, over and over again. I remember when a major company published me among the most prominent leaders in the field. It was validating, joyous, and a dream come true—I thought I had it made! And then... three months later I was homeless.

What's wrong with me? How could it be that I had such a success, yet couldn't even afford to live?

The perplexing thing was that this happened *after* years of self-help and being successful in business. I wasn't an amateur. Yet, it seemed that even after all of this work—in business and on myself—I still wasn't enough. I had been trying to fix myself for a decade, doing everything I could not to feel so resentful, trapped, hopeless, undesirable, and lonely. I wanted to be accepted, to be loved, and to feel fulfilled as a man. I thought improving meant being more valuable, which meant being more desirable and financially successful, which would ultimately lead to all the things that could make me happier: abundance, love, connection, actualization, and impact.

I thought self-help equaled self-happy.

I went as deep as anyone could go. You name it, I've tried it. I've removed blocks and cleared negative emotions. I've tried morning routines and building habits. I ate tonic herbs. I've been hypnotized and experienced qi gong. I've wrote affirmations on yellow sticky notes

1

throughout my house. I used a gratitude journal, healed generational trauma, did energy work, detoxed, tapped, and even tried plant medicines. Plus, all the acronym modalities you can think of, I've done 'em or something like 'em.

And you know what? They all *worked*; they were all *helpful*. I *improved* from all of it, and I would still recommend many of them for certain things.

...but I *still* kept getting stuck. None of these things quite *did it*.

I was learning the most incredible things, improving my health, healing my traumas, having all these breakthroughs—and despite all that powerful internal transformation—**my life, relationships, and bank account looked worse than ever.**

It baffled me. *What was I missing? Did I just suck at life?*

There wasn't a lack of work ethic, talent, knowledge, or capability, and there wasn't a lack of experience or success, either. I couldn't use these as a reason to justify my suffering because I had evidence that showed otherwise. Long before I became an author, I worked in the technology sector as a designer/developer turned entrepreneur. I began learning at fourteen, and then at eighteen, I built a physics and particle engine from scratch. I started this software company and ran it for seven years on my own. It served over 30,000 users, including many top brands you know and use daily. It was the first company and product I had ever created—proof enough that I was highly competent.

I applied myself the same way in my newfound teaching and coaching career. Gratefully, this led to that first publishing I mentioned. I was producing high value, life-changing content... so what caused such a catastrophic failure soon thereafter? How was it that after diving into therapy and spirituality and being of service—it seemed like I got wiser and wiser but less and less functional in the world?

Is that just how it works?

I chose not to accept that premise—there *had* to be a different way. I knew that others have prevailed, and so could I. It was clear that there must be something beyond smarts, talent, experience, hustling, connections, money, faith, spiritual knowledge, or emotional intelligence that factors into success and fulfillment. Something that wasn't stated in any of the well-known self-help or spirituality books. Perhaps a missing piece that escaped mainstream philosophies of performance, habits, mindfulness, healing, and success. An "elusive something" that makes all the difference.

My life quite literally depended on me figuring this out, and I was willing to do whatever it took to unravel the mystery and get unstuck. Not only from one situation, but unstuck in all areas of my life.

After many years of struggle and failure, I finally discovered what *it* was.

It changed everything for me, and its effect is felt in every word you'll read. Its identity revealed between the paragraphs of each chapter. Its source reflected upon every page. Its validity found in the publishing of this book. Its truth echoed through each choice this philosophy inspires you to make.

If you're still stuck despite all the work you've already done, this book will tell you why and how to overcome this plateau once and for all.

WHY YOU'RE HERE

Somehow, in some way, something is stuck in your life. Perhaps there's a problem or obstacle in your way that you haven't been able to crack. Maybe you've been struggling to penetrate the same pattern, cycle, or level for years. Or, perhaps you're on the path of spiritual awakening and are looking to move past suffering altogether and discover the truth of who you are.

You're reading this book because you have a desire to change. You want to know why you're still stuck despite all the work you've been doing and how to break through without additional struggle. You've been doing all of this "work" to change: to change a situation, a feeling, a cycle, a metric, yourself, or even someone else. To change from asleep to awake; from diseased to eased; to change from lesser-than to greater-than.

If you want to change effectively, you need to get clear on why things are not working and where to focus your effort instead of guessing. Your purpose in life is bigger than poking around in the dark for answers that have already been laid out for you to read. You don't have time to analyze two-hundred books only to find a few dozen "nuggets"—you need the entire gold mine, and you need it now. You don't have time to test dozens of theories over a decade to see what's legitimate—you need something proven, timeless, and genuine to commit to for lasting results.

I originally wrote this guide for professionals who have already studied personal development and spiritual concepts. Those who, despite years of work and healing, *still* aren't able to break through, wake up, and overcome stubborn struggles. These are the people who have dedicated their lives to mastery, growth, service, transformation, and sharing their gifts with the world. They've implemented and out-paced basic self-help strategies and concepts. They have a strong grasp on fundamental psychological, spiritual, and empowerment principles and need the most powerful, direct, and honest insights to reach their highest level of expression.

If *you* are one of these professionals who are self-aware and have already done "all the work" but have hit a seemingly impregnable block—**this book is exactly what you've been looking for**.

But what if you're *not* an experienced professional who has done a bunch of self-help work? What if you've never studied anything spiritual? Is this book for you too?

Yes, it can help you as well. There is no specific experience, religion, or career required to reap the benefits of these ideas. I've had folks completely unfamiliar with self-help concepts have realizations from me discussing the unconventional ideas and secrets revealed within this book.

However, there *is* a specific type of person who will get the most out of what's presented in this guide. It is most definitely *not* for the casual reader or someone looking for an effortless, inspirational book. I am not here to motivate or cheerlead you but to teach and demonstrate. We'll be doing real work during our time together.

If you are someone who:

- Is struggling to break free from destructive cycles, patterns, or relationships, or
- Is facing a plateau, block, challenge, or problem that you can't seem to get past, or
- Excels in a certain area of life but can't seem to "transfer that over" to the others

And who:

- Is ready to have a deep, honest look at themselves, take responsibility, and wake up
- Is open to grounded and applicable philosophical and spiritual insights, and
- Can take ideas and run with them, take action, and apply the ideas within this book to their own situation

...then this is *the* book to help you get unstuck and bypass years, or even decades, of more struggle and suffering. You are about to give yourself a gift—not only of healing and moving forward—but in the struggle, confusion, and wasted time you'll avoid.

If you've ever felt crazy or furious, thinking:

"I don't get it... I'm doing everything I can, and I'm still stuck. What the hell, I should be over this by now. This doesn't make any sense!"

I completely understand. You feel that, despite doing everything you "should" be doing, you ought to be further along than you are. It's as if, for some mysterious reason, there's an elusive something still missing—and you're always right on the precipice of discovering it. The inescapable struggle, endless fixing, and enigmatic cycles are exhausting. It can seem like we're doomed to keep repeating the same story year after year with no way out. It can feel maddening, confusing, and even hopeless at times... I get it.

Rest assured everything you've done is *not* in vain, and there *is* a reason why. However, despite your successes or failures, what got you *here* isn't going to be what gets you *there*. This guide will help you figure out exactly why you're stuck, how to break through the struggle, and even enlighten you to a greater Truth along the way. You'll discover what's *really* going on now **before you waste any more time, money, or energy on things that don't work.**

No matter what profession you're in, what culture you're from, what your circumstances are, or what in your life is stuck—this book will help. None of those variables matter for getting unstuck because your resolution is not in tactics, techniques, or advice. You're not stuck because you don't have the 33-step formula. You're not stuck because you don't know the magic words to land new clients or dates. You're not stuck because you don't have enough money or time. You're not stuck because of something much more fundamental and meaningful. This book offers you a brand new paradigm and approach to getting unstuck that transcends mundane self-help strategies and metaphysical mumbo jumbo.

WHAT YOU'LL GET FROM THIS

You have in your possession the most powerful, albeit *unconventional,* approach for getting unstuck in any area of your life. This is a comprehensive guide of great breadth and depth, offering everything you need to break through and genuinely awaken. It is not an entry-level book, and there is no hand-holding. Yet, it remains an approachable read for any sincere adult. Each philosophical and spiritual idea presented is practical and applicable to everyday living—though you may not see it at first. By practical, I mean they are not something that requires years of training, great expense, or esoteric powers—they are available to anyone. By applicable, I mean they are not only theoretical concepts, but things you can take action on while reading.

As you read, keep in mind that this material is *supposed* to be confronting. That's why it works. This is why it's called an "awakening". You will be stretched beyond your comfort zone. You may get offended or upset. You may flat out hate what I'm saying. You may not find the easy way out you secretly hoped I'd give you. You may dismiss or shun certain topics. You may find yourself triggered, angry, afraid, avoidant, or defensive. These are *good* things. See each of these as an emergency light illuminating the way towards the place needing healing. This is not *meant* to be an agreeable book. You may not like or agree with everything I have to say. Which is probably a good thing, or else why would you need this book? If nothing challenged or conflicted with what you already think or perceive, how could it possibly get you unstuck or lead to awakening?

Stick with it to the end. There's a reason you're here.

Not every chapter is intended to apply to everyone, in all instances; the reason you're stuck today may be different than tomorrow. Yet, if one idea, applied and embodied with genuine intention, transforms the way you relate to life—this book will have served its purpose. If you read the entire book while keeping an earnest, open mind, you will take away exactly what you need. Your life will only improve from applying the ideas within, even if you despise them. These pages cannot do it for you, but they can reveal what is hidden and offer new ways of being in the world. Everything you need to move forward is here, it is now, and it is within you and your ability to achieve.

HOW TO APPROACH THIS BOOK

This book is divided into two parts:

In **Part I**, I reveal 9 reasons why you're still stuck. *This is mostly the 'why.'*

In **Part II**, I disclose 9 ways to move forward. *This is more the 'how' and 'what to do.'*

We will dive right into our work in the first chapter and continue straight until the conclusion. I don't recommend this as a casual read; you're best served by committing to it. The book builds upon concepts as you go, yet each chapter remains its own topic: making the content digestible and dividable over readings. Early readers have noted that they get more from the book by reading a chapter or two per day in order to absorb it fully, rather than trying to rush through the whole book at once. This is not an informational book; it's an application book. You must apply the concepts and follow the instructions to unlock its riches. Read it in linear order: do not skip around your first time through. This book has been designed so that the more you re-read it, the more you get from it.

It is an honor to share these principles with you. May you use them sincerely and fruitfully on your quest for truth, freedom, joy, enlightenment, and your True Self.

Now, let's see *why you're still stuck.* 🍂

PART I

HOW YOU GOT HERE

YOUR STUCKY STORY

"All the world's a stage
And all the men and women merely players:
They have their exits and their entrances;
And one man in his time plays many parts."
— WILLIAM SHAKESPEARE,
Jaques in *As You Like It*

 hat you think is true is often a *story* about the truth. What you remember happening in your life is often a story about the events. What you believe about yourself now is often a story about what you decided about yourself long ago. Our interpretations of reality tend to be inaccurate. They are distorted, deleted, generalized, judged, and personalized by the filters of our ego. These jumbled narratives become what are called *stories*. These stories are then the justifications for our worldview and are defended by our ego at all costs. Our stories can be so stubborn, so sophisticated, so defensive—that they would rather keep us poor, sick, and struggling than stop and surrender to something greater.

Not only do we make stories from just about anything, but we also have overarching narratives that run us individually, familially, and culturally. These are called *mythologies*. Think of mythologies as the archetypal story and our personal stories as the specific manifestations of it. Our stories are interpretations with specific details and memories

13

from our own life, whereas our mythologies are the encompassing narrative force that underlies them. For example, if "the martyrdom myth" is running a person, they will likely have stories such as "people don't appreciate me," "nothing I ever do is good enough," or "every time I help my daughter I get taken advantage of." Myths are incredibly powerful and have a directing force of their own.

These stories and myths set our life stage from the core impressions of our childhood environments around money, love, worth, relationships, health, and anything else which may become part of our identity or define our lives. They also arise from the powerful driving forces in our genetics and lineage, perpetuating the same dynamics, values, beliefs, and socioeconomic status from generation to generation.

These initial conditions will be different for all of us. How we came into this world sets the stage for our autobiography.

Some people were born into loving environments at home with caring mothers and fathers. Some survived attempted abortions from a frightened single mother and were given away for adoption. Some people were born in sterile and cold hospital rooms via cesarean section, leaving the mother dead. Some were born from mothers who were healthy and clean, others from prostituting heroin addicts. Some people were born into wealth, others into poverty. Some arrived with lighter skin, others with darker skin. People get born into large supportive families, others into scattered dysfunctional families. Some of us were born from genetics that easily thrives in current conditions, others with genetics predisposed to health concerns. Some people arrived into cultures which value athleticism over intellect, others into cultures where sciences and math are dominant. Some were born into cultures that are community-focused, others where individuality is rewarded.

From the womb until this very moment, you have given meaning and made choices based on your circumstances. Notice in my description, I purely reported the data without any value judgment. *We* are the ones who say whether one side of the tracks is better or worse than the other. *We* are the ones who decide if we are less or more than others. *We* are the ones who interpret life events and determine what they mean about us. *We* are the ones who choose to take our parent's feelings and words and actions personally and make them mean something about us. *We* are the ones who decide which things are curses and which are gifts.

Even right now. Take, for example, your current stuck situation. You think you're stuck… *but are you?* What is "stuck"? Isn't your situation simply one that hasn't changed?

You decided it shouldn't be what it is and then chose to get frustrated by it because you made it mean something about who you are and your inability to change it.

This isn't merely word games—realize how none of our circumstances mean anything without our thoughts about it. You're stuck because you decided that's what is happening. Being stuck is only *one* perception. *You* are the one that defines it as "stuck." *You* labeled it, gave it a name, made it mean something. All you know is that your situation appears the same as it did before. You know that whatever you're doing isn't affecting it enough to change it completely. You know that you have a desire for it to be different. You know that it doesn't feel so good when you think about it. That's it—just the data. There's no story or justification when you look at only the data. There's no judgment, drama, or interpretation. Much of our suffering comes from our added meanings and projections that we superimpose upon what's real.

Here are examples of the stories we tell based upon each chapter:

1. "It's not a story I'm making up; this is really how the world works. I've seen it myself, and the facts show that people don't change."
2. "I can't just go out tomorrow and change how I live my life. That's not who I am!"
3. "No matter how hard I work or what I learn, I always wind up stuck right back where I started."
4. "If the world wasn't full of idiots, my life would be a lot easier. Even better if I didn't have to deal with people's feelings. I'd have a much better time relating to others if I could find people who matched my intellect."

5. "I need to work on myself more because I'm not good enough yet. It's depressing, but I'll put my happy face on and show the world my best parts because those are lovable."

6. "Once I learn the secrets to life, then I'll have the power to create the life I want. Once I find the right guru, he will be able to save me. Once I attain the next spiritual state, then I won't have to suffer anymore."

7. "You don't understand, the economy is bad, my partner left me, I was abused as a child, and I lost my job. I have to do this to cope... there's nothing I can do about it. It's not my fault."

8. "I can't do that; it makes me so anxious. I don't want to feel any of that if I don't have to. I'm not avoiding following my dreams... it's that it's too risky, and the thought alone makes me uncomfortable. I'm fine with my part-time job."

9. "I'm depressed because there's something wrong with me. But I'm working on it. Once I fix myself, then I'll be able to be happy! I just need to do this next course."

10. "My dating life is dysfunctional, but that doesn't affect my work. I'm a different person with clients than I am with people in my social circle."

11. "It's like the more I do good and the harder I try to be nice, the worse they treat me! Maybe if I were a jerk, people would treat me better."

12. "I don't need proof that I'm a wealthy or loved person. I don't care that only a few dollars are in my bank account, and I only have two friends. People don't get me; they only want to criticize my approach and offer their opinions."

13. "There's a reason I'm doing all this self-help work. I have to focus on my problems and get unstuck before I can even think about volunteering or helping other people."

14. "I hate all these negative feelings; they are useless! I want to feel good all the time and remove all the bad parts of me so I can be enlightened."

15. "To get to where I want to be in life, I have to do something more than what I'm doing now. I have to figure out what the secret missing tactic is in order to be fulfilled."
16. "I know I should be present with this person, but I really need to think about that project tomorrow, it can't wait. There's so much work ahead of us, and it can't be the mess it was three years ago."
17. "What does it matter how I show up in my body? It's just a meat-suit. My power is in my mind; I don't care how I move through the world physically. We're spiritual beings anyway."
18. "I shouldn't have to choose. I don't want to feel all that heavy responsibility. What does it matter if I keep doing it? It's not so bad. Stopping is going to be harder, anyway."

These may sound like typical, common statements about life—and they are—but they're all *stories*. So many people have normalized a way of life that isn't real. This is why it's so frightening. They are judgments, fears, meanings, dramas, distorted interpretations, or deceptions. None of them accurately describe reality. The more we repeat these to ourselves and others, the more we get stuck in illusion.

STOPPING THE STORIES

Ordinary self-help would say to redefine it. For example, it would reframe poor investments as: "you're spending money figuring out what doesn't work." Or reframe rock-bottom as: "you're in the perfect place before moving forward." Or reframe a failing relationship as: "you're exactly where you need to be."

These are *okay*. They're better *meanings*, better *labels*, better *stories* about the situation. It's a step up from being negative, surely.

The problem is, they're still *interpretations*. You're telling another story—except this time, you're spinning it positive. When we're giving meaning to something, even positive, we don't see it for what it really *is*. We are still distorting it to match our worldview—one that, while "better," is a lot less expansive and inclusive compared to what's *actually* occurring. It doesn't matter if any of your meanings are valid or not. Many of them may be. This work isn't about making your stories, meanings, struggles, or successes invalid—it's about stopping them altogether. We want to move past projected meanings and judgments outright. It's not "bad" if you're stuck, nor is it "good" if you're unstuck—it just is what it is.

Everything serves, even what doesn't.

I understand that moving past our meanings is easier said than done. But it *is* achievable, practical, and worthwhile to let go of the judgments. It's really just about stopping (which I will explain further as we continue). Resting peacefully in this truth requires surrender, faith, and hindsight.

One of my favorite ways to illustrate this concept of not being attached or giving meaning to what happens, comes from an ancient Chinese parable of the farmer and his horse:

> Once there was a farmer whose horse ran away. Later that day, the whole community came by to commiserate and show their condolences for him. They said, "It is most unfortunate that your horse ran away. We are sorry to hear of your bad news." The farmer replied, "We shall see." The next day the horse came back, with seven wild horses along with it. That evening, the townsfolk came back and said, "Aren't you lucky! What a good turn of events, your horse came back and now you have eight horses!" Again the farmer replied, "We shall see." The next day his eldest son was attempting to break one of the wild horses and was thrown off. The son had broken his leg. The community came around again and said, "What terrible news! How unfortunate." The farmer replied, "We shall see." A week later, war broke out. The army came through, recruiting all the men of the village. They

arrived at the farmer's son and saw he was not fit for
duty because of his broken leg. Again the neighbors
gathered and said, "Isn't that great? Your son is safe!"
Again the farmer replied, "We shall see."

We, too, can begin to get off the wheel of fortune and live from the same 'immovable spot.' It starts with stopping our stories, meanings, and judgments that we give to everything.

To see the world truly—not create a story about it—we need to stop exaggerating, distorting, dramatizing, and taking our experiences personally. At first, we will have to use our conscious willpower to stop our own 'noise' and see past the noise of others to observe only 'signal.' To do this, start by reporting the facts rather than sensationalizing your experiences. Communicate the data, not the drama. Strip out your stories and leave what's real.

Here are some examples:

- "I feel angry and violated" rather than "Frank is a jerk for stealing my girlfriend, and I'm going to kill him!"
- "No." rather than "Geez, you're seriously going to ask me to help you when you know I'm busy taking care of my dying cat? I'm offended!"
- "I asked him to lunch, but he declined" rather than "I like him so much, and I finally got the courage to ask him out, but I know he's too popular for me. I knew he was going to brush me off, and sure enough, he did."
- "Can you help me fix my car?" rather than "I'd normally never ask this, but I was late again and my car broke down. Would you be open to taking a look? I feel bad for asking, you don't have to fix it, but I don't have anyone else, so let me know if you can."
- "She liked my sweater" rather than "Wow, she's really into me, she gave me all these compliments about how I dress. I don't think it's my favorite sweater, though. I wish I had more money for a better one."

19

- "You are disrespecting me, and I will not tolerate it, please stop" rather than "You're really mean to me. I knew I couldn't trust you. All men are the same. I know I can't expect you to stop being a jerk, but boy, you better start treating me better or else!"

Can you see all the extra noise, drama, and stories that we unknowingly add to our communication and perceptions? All these projections, meanings, and judgments distort reality. Let me say it another way: these all obstruct your peace, joy, and success.

Start stripping away all but what is real.

As you do this, you will quickly discover how much of your experiences have been inflated. Some may scoff at this approach because it can seem like 'only reporting the details' is boring or dull. It may feel that way in comparison to making everything a, "Wow! Amazing! It was everything! Aren't you so excited?! Rah-rah!" hyped-up dramatization. Looking at my invitation through the perspective of this attitude, it feels like I'm taking all the fun out of everything, or I'm the old curmudgeon saying, "Get off my lawn, kid!"

But there's more here than meets the eye.

While much of this 'hype' can be positive and optimistic, it's still noise. It's not good or bad. However, much of it is psychological inflation to compensate for depression, fear, or an avoidance of feeling. Indeed, the hype can motivate, but it takes a lot of energy to sustain because it tries to overcome preexisting negative noise. It's not true inspiration; it's force. What-is is not good enough—it needs to be *more*. Inflation requires everything to become bigger, faster, stronger. If we are used to being hysterical, dramatic, and excited—without even realizing that's what we're doing—peace can seem like a real dud.

The problem is that anything that inflates must deflate. What goes up must come down. Those who are continually avoiding peace and the perfection of what-is will eventually swing in the other direction. What follows is not pleasant. If we dramatize the highs, we are going to do the same with the lows. This behavior gets folks trapped in their highs and lows, oscillating back and forth between excitement and depression. One week they're on top of the world, the next, rock bottom. If this sounds like the roller coaster of addiction, that's because it *is*.

Where we find peace and joy, there is no inflation or deflation. No excitement or depression. No exaggeration or downplaying. No drama, but not numbness either. No making up or leaving details out. We want to think, feel, and discuss what *really is* without making it into a story *about* what-is. This stopping of stories is not about becoming a robot devoid of flavor or feeling. It's about stopping all the dissociated things we do to avoid feeling.

What you truly feel is real. Joy is real. Feeling fear is real. Love is real. Arousal is real. Ecstasy is real. Feeling shame is real. These are all real feelings that we feel in our bodies. But going into our head, getting wrapped up in a fantasy of inflated ideas and working ourselves up into a stupor? That is not real—it's a story.

We are addicted to this noise. The silence makes us anxious. We're afraid that what-is, or who we are, isn't enough. We give things meaning and take things personally. We create fantastic explanations for why we can't have what we want—even talking about how much we deserve it can be another story of how we're not letting ourselves have it.

We must wean ourselves off the teat of noisy, inflated stimulation. Truth may not seem nearly as entertaining as our stories, but I promise you: within the quieter, stiller confines of Truth, there contains everything you're ever meant to have. I can write until my fingers bleed to convince you of this, but until you experience the peace within the silence yourself, the addiction to suffering will drown out the Truth.

It's like if you're used to eating junk food and then eat a wild cherry. You're so accustomed to the artificial flavors and saturation of sugar, grease, and salt that natural foods seem kind of bland. It takes a while to 'detox your taste buds' from all the junk food and get your palate reset. At first, they seem dull, boring, and not nearly as good as candy. You crave your old sweets. They were familiar, and you like them. They tasted great, and they weren't even *that* bad for you. I mean, you're still alive... right?

But as time goes on and you trust the process, you begin to taste more subtle, complex flavors in natural foods. These were flavors that were undetectable to you when everything you ate had in-your-face flavor. Eventually, you come to enjoy the depth and perfection of the cherry you once judged as bland. You notice how better you feel after eating it than junk food. You appreciate the delicious other fruits you had no idea even existed. You can always go back to the junk food if you want, but you have no good reason to do so with all this natural, flavorful food. Like with junk food, we must break our addiction to our stories if we wish to heal and enjoy the riches life has to offer.

A TRAGEDY OF STORYTELLING

Think about your own stories about being stuck and your meanings and judgments around them—all the shoulds, shouldn'ts, whys, why nots, and becauses. Do that right now. Feel free to write them down for this and any future exercises. You are encouraged to write exhaustively yet succinctly.

Take a look at your list. All these stories, dramas, explanations... what if you were to just stop telling them? What if you only reported the details instead of telling a story about it? What if you stripped away everything you thought was proof and evidence and focused on only the data?

Explore that now, and notice any urge to fight for their justification—to defend their validity. It's normal. We are all addicted and attached; our stories have been faithful companions for most of our lives. It can take seconds, or it can take years to stop.

Let's go a step further. After letting go of all of the stories of your struggle, success, stuckness, and survival, what if you were only left with the 'you' here in the present moment? A 'you' without any notion of who you have or have not been, and oblivious to who you should or shouldn't be. What would that feel like? Who would *that* person be? Don't go into your head and think about it; instead, look into your body and *feel* it.

For many, this is a terrifying question. It brings us to the edge of our identity and sense of self. It forces us to feel a sense of nothingness we've avoided most of our lives. It invalidates the decades of work we've done to improve ourselves. It approaches the shores of philosophy and can question the very nature of our existence. *"Who am I without my narrative?"* For some, it's also an illuminating one—for the exact same reasons.

> "When I let go of what I am,
> I become what I might be."
> — Lao Tzu

This is a place of possibility, a place of *liberation*. It's a place worth getting used to.

The more you can let go of your stories, the freer you are to do something you've never done before. The easier it is to get out from underneath the weight of "that's just how things are" and the mythologies of your family and culture. You are able to let go of the narrative that you use to defy and punish Love. We use our suffering to protest against our parents, God, the universe, Love, and life itself in an act of rebellion and vengeance and then use these stories to justify why we are unlovable.

The more you can associate with the *grand universal narrative* (Tao, will of God, Buddha Nature, etc.) instead of the one directed by your ego, the easier your life becomes. You let go of who you *think* you are and let life inform you of who you are. You surrender instead of fight. You *become* rather than defend. This leads you to partake as a functional part of life and the world, rather than an insurrection defying it.

THE AMNESIA EXERCISE

Here's a powerful thought experiment I use with my clients that takes the previous questions to their extreme:

Let's play pretend. Imagine you woke up tomorrow with functional amnesia. You could behave, speak, think, and move about the world fine—but you forgot everything that defines you. You forgot all

23

about your history, diagnoses, past relationships, jobs, achievements, etc. You never learned should or shouldn't, you know of no "ought-tos" or "cannots," and you have no recollection of what you or other people expect of you. You still have whatever you already had, and nothing else has changed except that you don't remember your limitations.

Reflect on the following questions:

- What would you do?
- Where would you live?
- Who would you meet?
- What would you say?
- What would you study?
- Where would you travel to?
- What foods would you try?
- How would you get around?
- What could you accomplish?
- Who could you have relationships with?
- Who would you be if you didn't remember who you were?

I'm not talking about a fantasy. I'm asking what you would genuinely, really do in tomorrow's world. If it's challenging to break out of the constraints of "you," remember this is *playing pretend*. You get to make it up.

Pay attention to the feelings and judgments that arise. Pay attention to where you're still restricting yourself and where you open up to possibility. Pay close attention to the voices that creep in and say things like "wait, you can't do that because..." or anything that binds you to your past self-definition.

Take as much time as you need to explore this amnesiac life. Like everything else, you will get out of this exercise what you put into it. Come back when you're finished.

Now the question becomes: how different is this from your current life?

If **it is not** much different, it's a good bet you either a) already love your life, or b) you're shut down from seeing what's possible for you. Both of which are essential things to become aware of.

If **it is** quite different, the question then becomes: *why?*

If the only difference between these two scenarios is your memory, which is essentially repeated and recalled thoughts, why do you keep these thoughts alive? It's one of the most important questions you could ever answer in your life: **"Why do I keep thinking things that prevent me from the life I truly desire?"** That is an answer only you know, and one that your life depends on figuring out.

This thought experiment also shows us how addictive these stories can be. It reveals how much we indulge in our suffering and how life-defining these patterns of thought are without us even realizing it. We don't want to give them up... even when we discover they're holding us back.

Stop, wait—I know what you're thinking:

"My thoughts are *not* the only difference. The other difference is that all my problems, responsibilities, relationships, and limitations *exist*. These things really happened to me. Forgetting about my life doesn't make it all go away."

Yes, that may be true.

It's easy to dismiss the practicality of stopping our stories when we don't see them as 'a story.' This happens when we use what's true about our experience to affirm the validity of the story. Yes, the real data and the real details found *within* your stories are valid. What truly happened *did* happen, and what's real doesn't go away when you create or stop a story. Truth itself is unaffected by stories, but our *perception* of the truth is absolutely affected. A story is never equivalent to its underlying experience. Your friend telling you about a movie is not the same as the movie, and the movie is not the same as its production. Reread the opening lines of this chapter. **Stopping the stories doesn't deny what's real; it denies what's *not* real.** It ends the interpretations, illusions, distortions, meanings, conclusions, and judgments that prevent us from seeing the truth. Without access to this truth, we constrain our perspective and become blind to the very information which would get us unstuck.

Your life might look starkly different if you were to stop repeating all the stories you tell yourself. For many things that keep you stuck, stopping the stories is all it would take. I'm not suggesting denial or to pretend your problems away. I'm suggesting that some of the things you *think* are real problems only persist because you keep beating the drum of their story. It's *these stories* which are pretend. This book is an invitation to stop telling yourself untrue stories that continue to cause your struggle and suffering.

Our stories exist because we keep telling them. We carry them along with us to the present and anxiously await their validation in the future. Sometimes we drag them along for so long, and we forget they're only memories from the past and drearily proclaim, "that's just the way it is." It's because of this that we have difficulty seeing *what really is* in the present moment. When we keep the past alive by reviving and resurrecting these stories repeatedly, they don't allow for *what-is* to be. We only see what is happening now through a lens of past experiences and meanings: a projection of our interpretations of the past onto the present moment. Our stories keep us bound to the past. They prevent us from having a direct experience of the present; they essentially keep us trapped in time. Your attachment to the past—an addiction to your stories—is what's keeping you stuck and suffering.

We are constantly invalidating what *is* with what *was*. When we stop making stories and giving meaning to what's happening, it allows us to see the truth. In turn, we get out of our heads and show up to deal with something new, rather than reenact old cycles. We carry with us the wisdom of the past but are not bound to its ignorant conclusions about life. This is *spiritual awakening*: emerging from the dream of a *perceived* reality and waking up to the genuine one. We are snapping out of the trance of unconscious conditionings and are beginning to see *what-is* with new eyes. We are awakening to the truth that's been there the entire time and become present to what's real.

This is how we arrive to *now* and get unstuck. 🌸

WHERE CHANGE HAPPENS

"You're always you, and that don't change,
and you're always changing, and there's
nothing you can do about it."
— NEIL GAIMAN, *The Graveyard Book*

 ne of the fundamental reasons you're still stuck is due to your approach to change. When we determine that we're stuck and want our life to look different, the first thing we think about doing is changing something. We either change something about our situation and what's happening around us, or we go inside and look at what we can change about ourselves. The fact that you're reading this reveals that you feel there's something about you or what you do that needs to change. If you could only figure out what that is and change it, you would get unstuck and become a better person in the process.

Think for a moment about how you typically go about that. Do you try different routines? Shift your mindset to a more positive one and get motivated? Work on your subconscious patterns? Associate with a new group of friends or join a mastermind? Do you buy new clothes and change your appearance? Heal trauma with a therapist? Study philosophy, religion, or partake in shamanism? Do you change what you eat—or do you change how you eat, why you eat, or with whom you eat?

Chances are, it's a lot of trying and doing. Attempts to make the pain go away, overcome an obstacle that's holding you back, learn something that will change your life, or try to improve yourself somehow. Some of it works well, and others, maybe not so much. This chapter will explore how people typically approach changing and the divergent philosophy this work presents.

WHERE SELF-HELP TYPICALLY FOCUSES

Let's look at how most of us approach changing from a meta-perspective. This is where nearly all self-improvement teachings and professional therapies focus, so it's a great place to set the stage.

Personal change happens on multiple levels in a hierarchy, which I call "The Hierarchy of Change." The top level holds the most cascading potential for change, and the bottom level affects the least.

- **Identity** — "Who I am" (*most*)
- **Feeling** — "How I feel"
- **Belief** — "What is true"
- **Attitude** — "Where I orient"
- **Behavior** — "What I do" (*least*)

Below we have each change-level and what four different situations' inner-dialog would sound like. We will go in reverse so you can see how each evolves into more powerful statements. Starting from the bottom of the list where most people attempt to change, and arriving at the top of the hierarchy, where people are least willing to shift. At each level, the situations stay in their respective order.

The four situations are:

1. A business that is struggling
2. An artist that can't sell their work
3. Difficulties in a romantic relationship
4. Low energy, poor health, disease

Behavior: I'll run different ads and promotions to get unstuck [1]. I'll talk to new potential clients with the latest sales script and improved presentation [2]. I'll take my partner out on a different kind of date [3]. I'll stop eating junk food [4].

Attitude: I'll start enjoying the marketing efforts I'm doing. I'll appreciate the clients I already have more. I'll change the way I think about how my partner takes care of the house. I'll find a way to enjoy eating healthier foods.

Belief: I believe my marketing efforts will work and provide a lot of value. I believe that I'm great at my craft. I believe that I'm kind, sexy, and supportive of my partner. I believe that a holistic and natural lifestyle will heal me.

Feeling: I can feel new people responding optimistically to my marketing efforts. I feel confident and abundant while signing on new clients for my business. I feel loved, cherished, supported, and safe in who I am regardless of what my lover says or does. I feel like I'm thriving and full of energy.

Identity: I am a successful entrepreneur. I am a world-class artist. I am a remarkable lover. I am a completely healthy person.

THE HIERARCHY OF CHANGE SUMMARY

The **behavior** level makes change through physical action. The **attitude** level makes change through the way we see and approach things. The **belief** level makes change through thought and the models of the world in the mind. The **feeling** level makes change through the body and emotions by way of symbolic experiences outside of rational, linear thought. The **identity** level makes change initially through "I AM" statements of the ego; of the persona.

When presented with the opportunity to change, the average person relies upon the *behavior* level. They are only focused on doing; finding new strategies and tactics to affect the world around them. It is outwardly focused, and the person is vastly unaware of the internal dynamics at play that influence everything. This can create immediate results in the world but rarely shifts anything lasting in the person.

HOW MOST PEOPLE GO ABOUT CHANGING

People look for strategies and tactics because, for a minimal investment, they can go out and do something immediately and get a new result. It gives them hope and immediate gratification. It can awaken them to the possibility that they aren't stuck with what's in front of them—that they have the power to change their lives, not merely deal with what's thrown their way. This is a beautiful thing. For some of us, that hope becomes an impetus to go deeper. **We realize that life doesn't only happen to us, but that *we* can also happen to life.**

So we search out ideas, books, modalities, or gurus that show us how to improve. We get into personal development because we relish the idea that we can change ourselves and our lives for the better. Most of this self-help advice focuses on changing behaviors, attitudes (states), and beliefs. These would be your typical motivational seminars, courses, viral videos, workshops, and inspirational events. They do a tremendous job at getting people out of depression and into the possibility of change and self-empowerment—yet rarely do they facilitate genuine transformation. Some of the more sincere ones do approach the identity level. However, unless they incorporate spiritual awareness, they only improve the ego-persona—hence 'personal' development.

Like anything else, the closer you get to the top, the less there is. There are fewer elite teachers and fewer students who want to try the intense, obscure approaches. As we go 'up' The Hierarchy of Change, fewer and fewer people are willing to face what awaits them on the ascent. It's easy to say, "Tomorrow, I'll drink more water!" and change a *behavior*—it's a lot more challenging to change an *identity* and face the pain, shame, anger, and distortions on the way to a completely different lifestyle.

There is nothing wrong with working at these varying levels, as they are all part of the whole system. Speaking to efficiency, however, the same energy applied at each level will yield exponentially different results. Change made from a single behavior will have little effect on self, whereas change at the identity level will trickle down and affect all levels of self below it. One changed behavior may not affect one's identity, but one change in identity *must* affect beliefs, attitudes, behaviors, and how we chronically feel.

A reason for your chronic stuckness may be that all your effort has gone to addressing things at the incorrect level for your problem. Some people focus all on their mind and feelings but never act, while others try all sorts of new actions but never address their flawed mindset. In this instance, I would suggest taking an inventory of what you've been doing to get unstuck and where each attempt falls in the hierarchy. *Do that now.* Write down everything you've been doing to get unstuck in a list, and then mark each item with the level of change it's operating at. Do it quickly and easily; you're simply looking to get a gist of where your efforts lie. You may discover a more efficient strategy by seeing what you're too focused on or avoiding.

THE LIMITS OF THIS APPROACH

This framework of The Hierarchy of Change is helpful. Perhaps the concepts of the levels are new to you. Great! The information is useful, and you need to be aware of it. It will benefit you to take some time to look at the things you've been doing and get proficient at classifying them, if only to grasp the premise.

Yet, this approach is basically what you've already been trying to do to get unstuck. It's generally how most people teach it and learn it, but it's a lot of fixing. It's a lot of information to cram into your head. Years and years of tedious fixing and improving. It works for a while, it can be incredibly helpful, and it can absolutely improve your life.

It's nothing to discount or abolish from our lives altogether. However, like training wheels, it eventually reaches an upper limit and becomes what holds you back. Even medicine becomes poison when taken longer than it should.

The purpose of the first half of this chapter was to give you context, not show you a way to get better at fixing yourself. Remember, what brought you here isn't going to get you *there*—so we have to look at change in a completely different way. It's taken me nearly a decade to figure it out, but I realized something is not quite right with this approach...

If you spend the next twenty years making lists of every belief, behavior, negative emotion you want to fix about yourself—and then go down that list and do some technique to eliminate it—you're not going to have a life. Ask me how I know.

If all this neurotic "work" is what you've been doing for years and your life isn't where you want it—then stop. **I invite you to stop trying to change every little thing you don't like about yourself.**

This approach never ends. It never realizes peace. More often than not, we end up secretly using this to bypass and avoid life. Since we often feel relief in the moment, it may not seem that way at first—but avoidance ultimately prolongs our suffering. We can spend decades waiting to be fixed before we feel ready to take on life, only to have our entire life pass us by.

This is not heroic—it's hell hidden in a hospital.

WHERE CHANGE ACTUALLY HAPPENS

Here is where this book begins to diverge. You are now crossing the threshold between all the self-help or spiritual work you may have done before this—and a radically different approach to transformation. It may *sound* similar, it may *look* similar, but I promise it's not what you think it is. Let's begin.

There is one more level which I left out.

After the identity level of the persona is the "True" identity, beyond self and ego—a direct experience of the divine. It is not the persona, or *mask*, we like to identify ourselves with. It lies outside of The Hierarchy of Change, as it also lies outside of time and space. It is that which is eternal, immaculate, and irrelevant to our notions of fixing.

The path to enlightenment requires us to drop the persona of the ego and connect with the **True Self**. To do so, we must go beyond wanted and unwanted, likes and dislikes, shoulds and shouldn'ts, comparisons, and judgments. This True Self lies beyond your personality, body, or mind, yet is still distinctly, uniquely *you*. It *is* you—eternal, unlimited, pure, whole, complete, and unconditional.

Other names commonly used for the True Self are *Atman, soul, who-you-really-are*, or *higher self.* The rest of the book rests upon this term, so make sure you associate whatever concept you prefer to use. The label is not important. The dogma of tradition is not relevant. What's important is your realization and experience of it.

To find your True Self requires no seeking, only stopping. We will be revisiting this premise many times throughout the book. Stopping our neurotic stories and thoughts provides a space to truly hear. This stillness and silence within ourselves is where we meet that-which-connects-us. It's this connection with our True Self—not more fixing strategies—that initiates 'true change.' It becomes an immaculate reference point for who-we-really-are beyond our stories, labels, words, meanings, judgments, beliefs, behaviors, and concepts.

Descriptions are but fingers pointing at the moon, not Luna herself. It is not an experience to be obtained from a book. It's not something to be grasped or understood. It's not something to attain or be obtained. It is not something for sale or to be given. It must be earnestly chosen and experienced by each of us. When we truly do experience Ourselves this way, the change it initiates within our normal day-to-day self is authentic and substantial. It is genuinely self-correcting because it *is* Self, not our ego's story of who we are or who we should be, which is oft tainted and astray. It's not "you, but perfect." It's also not "who you wish you were." It's beyond any concept of you that your intellect could conjure up.

THE PERSONA AND THE TRUE SELF

We thus have two reference points for facilitating true change: our *idea* of who we are in the world and the *Truth* of who-we-really-are beyond ego.

Here's an analogy:

Imagine you want to sell a tasty apple treat. This would be the difference between trying to formulate an artificial flavor in a lab, constantly changing and improving it with better and better synthetic chemicals—and simply using apples. But hey, the artificial flavor tastes pretty good, and your achievement wows a lot of people, and anyway, the apples are more expensive and seem to take a lot more effort to cultivate. So you keep going down this path. Most of the side-effects get engineered out, and ten years have been devoted to synthesizing a world-class apple flavor. It's quite impressive. You've made a lot of money, and a few people clap.

You did it, wow! There it is! The world's best *fake* apple treat.

And that's the rub: the best artificial anything will still never be the real deal. The Roboduck 3000 might look like a duck, quack like a duck, and even eat your bread like a duck—but it's still a replica robot duck. The best recreation is never going to be the genuine article. We sure try, though, don't we! We judge and dismiss Ourselves, then spend decades foolishly attempting to recreate ourselves—not in the image of the Godhead, but of a distorted ego. This is what was also meant by "Thou shall not worship false idols." This image—our persona—is a false idol we worship by feeding it with all our neurotic desires to improve it and become it. It's the ultimate form of self-betrayal and self-abandonment.

True change comes by dropping the pseudo-changes and being more like Ourselves. We stop investing and surrender our persona for the present, full experience of self.

We begin to align more and more with who-we-really-are instead of defending a persona or building a fantasy. We stop adding and start subtracting. We get more done by doing less. We reclaim all the energy we have locked-up in the tedious creation and upkeep of our masks. We become a better person when we stop trying so hard to be a better person.

It brings to mind one of my favorite chapters from the *Tao Te Ching*, by Lao Tzu. Verse 22 reads:

> *"If you want to become whole, first let yourself become broken. If you want to become straight, first let yourself become twisted. If you want to become full, first let yourself become empty. If you want to become new, first let yourself become old. Those whose desires are few gets them, those whose desires are great go astray. For this reason the Master embraces the Tao, as an example for the world to follow. Because he isn't self-centered, people can see the light in him. Because he does not boast of himself, he becomes a shining example. Because he does not glorify himself, he becomes a person of merit. Because he wants nothing from the world, the world cannot overcome him. When the ancient Masters said, 'If you want to become whole, then first let yourself be broken,' they weren't using empty words. All who do this will be made complete."*

When we do this in daily life, it appears to the world as if we have changed—and we have, compared to who we usually show up as. But internally, we are simply becoming less, which reveals more of who we already are. All of the things we used to assume were us, fall away. We are going for less distortion, not more improving. We let go of our character in the play and be as the actor himself. But to stop acting, one must first realize that they are acting. To get someone to realize that is a challenge because they have to value being an authentic, vulnerable, embodied human over living as a "safe" caricature. The majority of people don't. Can you blame them?

The great challenge of life is to be truly you.

THE VULNERABILITY ISSUE

To create profound change in your life, you require what nobody wants: *vulnerability*. Vulnerability is the nemesis of the ego. It is what all our masks, armor, personas, and walls are erected to eliminate, or at least mitigate. It can be so terrifying that some would rather die alone than to feel vulnerable. It's a big reason why public speaking is considered by some a greater fear than death itself. I see a lot of self-help strategies and spiritual techniques that say, "create a rejection-proof life" or, "here's a release or clearing method so you can eliminate the vulnerability."

Good luck!

The problem is not in the methods that make people feel less bad. It's that the reason for arriving at that point is fundamentally flawed. The presupposition that—feeling vulnerable and all the discomfort around it is to be avoided and eliminated at all costs—is entirely backward. **Vulnerability is not a bad thing.** Think about it: what's on the other side of this feeling? Probably something you want, something worth the courage and effort to get. Yet, how often are we told we need to betray ourselves and be something incongruent to have what we want—or at the extreme, to stay safe and alive? We're told to protect ourselves or fit in.

There's a reason this always fails in the long run. Despite what the media and culture parades and peddles—*life* craves the real, authentic, uncensored you. Not everyone, but those of us also participating in a heroic, fully alive life want to feel you completely. We yearn to witness you in all of your mess and insecurities. We want to know what you're *really* thinking. To celebrate you in your highest and most insignificantly seeming accomplishments. To hear your deepest secrets or agonies that keep you up at night. We want to experience you in your totality, including all of what you love and hate about yourself and the world. Even that awkward, raw, flawed you that lies somewhere between your facade and True Self is still lightyears more desirable than your best mask. The best version of your persona that you could possibly make—with all the right identities, beliefs, behaviors, feelings, and attitudes—will never approach the glory of the real you. Just as the universe sees itself through us, we want to see ourselves in you. We want to acknowledge our own experiences through yours. To understand that we are not alone or truly separate.

And so we surrender completely, standing naked for the world to either say 'yes' or 'no' to some or all of us. That potential rejection—or even total acceptance—when we have no more cards to play is terrifying. It is enough to make most people say, "Nah, I'll have the world's best fake apple treat instead, thanks." It is a perfectly fine path you can take... but because you're reading this, I think you know how it ends.

There is another road from here. One where you realize the divinity of the natural flavor of who-you-really-are the more you taste it, and are more willing to drop the artificial ego and its need for synthetic ingredients. One where you get to express yourself fully instead of conforming to a lie. A path that takes you towards yourself, rather than away from yourself.

You get to decide if you'd rather abandon yourself to avoid being hurt, or to open up to life and embrace yourself. It is always your choice. My job isn't to tell you what to do or what is better for you. All I can do is help you see in a new way; to see more truth than before. To remind you of what is already there in ways you've never considered. To illuminate a way of moving through the world that you may have never believed was worth it. 🜚

An Equation
for Suffering

"We can not solve our problems with the
same level of thinking that created them."

— ALBERT EINSTEIN

his chapter's opening quote from Einstein holds a secret for getting unstuck that you can apply directly to your stucky story. Have you ever noticed how hard it is to get unstuck from a circumstance when that's "just how life is"? If that's "just the way things are," there's not much we can do about it. At best, we have to make do with the limitations and find a solution that's possible with "the reality of how things are." From within these bounds, we look for answers or ways to compromise.

This way of thinking will keep you stuck forever. You will never move forward when you try to solve the stucky problem from within the constraints of the stucky story. You're merely solving the *story's* problem! Since stories are unreal anyway, nothing real happens. It's like being a child, and playing pretend, coming up with an imaginary game to win. Even if you win, it's all pretend; nothing real changes. You will never get unstuck because you are still playing by the rules defined by the stucky story—the same ones that got you stuck in the first place! You have to "solve the problem" from outside of the bounds and limitations of the story in order to get unstuck. The "solutions" you arrive at within the story wind up justifying and validating the very story you're attempting to collapse. The story *about* the "problem" is what's keeping you stuck, not your actual circumstance.

Your story is a filter of perception itself. It distorts what you see because you're looking through the world through the lens of the story. All the problems you see are seen through the beliefs of your story. All the possible solutions are seen through the worldview of being stuck. Trying to solve your problem through the perspective of your story only gets you more of the same. Your story can only produce results within the constraints set by the story. The rules are biased and only "true" within the story. This is why we need to stop the story altogether to get unstuck because any thought or action that comes from within a story can only create more of the story. Our stories—just as ourselves—can only create in their own image. As long as we are ran by them, what we create will be filtered by them and bare little resemblance to who-we-really-are.

Each of our stories adds another lens to our 'perceptual stack'; all slightly off-center, tinted, or warped. These stories act as filters that impose layer upon layer of distortion to the original image. Think about what would happen if you put five-hundred filters on top of an image. Can you imagine how different the final picture would be compared to the original? It would be a completely different image with little of the original data remaining. Well, this is what our stories do to our experiences! Our perception becomes more like a kaleidoscope than a transparent window.

When we are in our stucky story, it's like we are wearing green-tinted contacts without even knowing it. If I asked you to find something that was red, you'd have a tough time doing it because everything you see is a shade of green. But if you were to take out the contacts, you'd easily be able to find what was red—and blue and yellow and violet. All these additional colors are possible ways of getting unstuck, which aren't visible to you when you're looking through the "green contact lenses" of your story. Since you see everything as green—red and blue aren't possibilities—so of course they don't seem realistic to you. This is why it's futile to keep trying to solve your problems at the level of their story.

A PHILOSOPHER IN MATH CLASS

In our sciences and logic, we see things through the lens of "cause then effect." X happens which causes Y to happen; if X *then* Y. At a more existential level, this falls short where we see X is *because* Y. Our ordinary causal logic works for solving everyday physical problems but will keep you perpetually stuck when dealing with more metaphysical ones.

Look at the list below:

1. Positive + _Negative_
2. North + _____
3. Up + _____
4. Good + _____
5. Solution + _____

What did you do?

Did you mentally fill in the blank with its counterpart even though there was no instruction to do so? Most people tend to fill in the blanks with *south, down, bad, problem.*

Notice that each of these has a natural counterpart: an opposite built into the natural order of the universe.

Now look at this list:

1. Negative + _____
2. South + _____
3. Down + _____
4. Bad + _____
5. Problem + _____

The same natural counterparts from above would get filled-in here.

This is not a test; I'm illustrating how these dualistic concepts have polar opposites and how one can't exist without the other. This is not an esoteric philosophy. It's physics. When north is created on a magnet, south is simultaneously created. When there's a proton, there's also an electron. When a problem is created, its solution is also simultaneously created. You cannot have an up without a down, you cannot have a negative charge without a positive—and most importantly, **you cannot have a solution without a problem.**

The ordering of that sentence is the key to this entire chapter and getting unstuck. Let's look at this another way using elementary math.

Solve this equation: $1 + -1 = \underline{\quad}$

Okay, now this one: $-1 + 1 = \underline{\quad}$

You can see the order doesn't make any difference.

Now, answer for x: $1 + x = 0$ then $x = \underline{\quad}$

The answer is: -1.

Stay with me here. It'll all make sense.

BOB'S LADDER

Let's apply this formula to something practical:

If Bob took 10 steps up a ladder (x), then 10 steps down $(-x)$, how far did Bob move, and where did he end up?

The answer: Bob moved 20 steps and ended up exactly where he started.

"Who here feels like Bob? Raise your hand..."

Have you figured it out yet? What all this math has to do with being stuck? Nothing in Bob's life changed even though he spent 20 steps trying to arrive someplace else. All that time and energy, but nothing was different—he arrived at the same spot he started.

Now is the point during class when someone pipes up with, "Then what's the point, Bob's an idiot! If he wants to be at 0, why do all that walking?"

Bingo.

We create all these problems in our head (-1) and then spend all this time trying to solve them $(+1)$, just so we can be at peace (0).

We start at 0 (peace), exert a total of 2 units of energy to create a problem that didn't exist (being stuck/broken, -1) and then to solve it (personal development, $+1$), so we could be at 0 (peace).

And if we think our problem is enormous (-500), we're going to have to face such great odds and struggle to overcome it $(+500)$, using 1000 units of energy to get back to the peace of where we were before we made it all up (0).

Here's the kicker: **most people never fully solve the equation.**

They don't get the $+500$. It's more like a $+100$ in the form of entertainment or surface-level fixes, which keeps them in a perpetual state of having a lot of problems. Since nobody has only one problem, all of this starts to compound like debt. The most devout, really good self-helpers are perpetually fixing themselves. Have you ever noticed they're never entirely at peace? They never arrive. That has included me and nearly everyone I know that stays on this "path."

We spend all this time trying to fix ourselves but forget *we're* the ones who decided we were broken to begin with!

The more seeking we do, the more we validate the problem.

YOUR MATHEMATICAL BREAKTHROUGH

Why do we try so hard to fix, rather than stop and choose something else? Our cognitive dissonance makes us compulsive in trying to solve the equation we started. We make things into problems and then look for solutions to validate our initial judgment. We are compelled to be right, even if being right causes us to be miserable.

It's a losing battle that appears to be victorious. The very act of looking for solutions to unreal problems validates the problem's existence and reinforces the illusion. Where winning proves you were a loser. It perpetuates the stories; gives fuel to the suffering. Even if you *were* to find a solution to fix yourself, that would be the ultimate proof that you were indeed broken!

It's a desolating, enigmatic bind of the ego.

This is why we're using math. You can't get out of it; that's why they're called *proofs*. We're utilizing equations because they mathematically prove *implication*. If you have a 1 and an $=0$, it forces you to fill in a -1.

Trying to fix *implies* broken.

Looking for a solution *implies* a problem.

The breakthrough secret in the math is this:

Let's say $0 =$ peace (or joy, abundance, love, etc.). The more we look for the solution ($+500$), the bigger our problem MUST get (-500). If we no longer require a solution, then we no longer require a problem. We arrive at 0 without having to solve anything. There are now 1000 units of energy that were previously locked-up in struggle available for us to create what we want directly.

So, if trying to get unstuck implies being stuck... then what does it imply when we don't need to get unstuck? If necessitating a solution implies a problem, what is implied when we require there not to be a solution? What if all the searching and seeking, fixing and healing, was the *reason* why you had a problem?

Perhaps you're still stuck because you're fixated on finding a way to get unstuck.

NEVER GONNA GIVE YOU UP

You've got the theory, but what happens in real life? What happens for us when we stop looking for a solution to an unreal problem? Is it really that easy? What prevents us from applying this and stopping now?

When we do stop, it's not what happens that makes the shift, but what *doesn't*. All the stories, drama, struggle, suffering, meanings, judgments, reasons, and chaos that require a problem—no longer have anything to cling to—and so they vanish. Your suffering isn't actually about the challenge itself—it's about everything you surround it with in your mind. Remove the linchpin, and everything around it crumbles. What you do with the linchpin thereafter is up to you.

Finding peace can be that easy. I've seen it, I've done it *...but is it what you want? Are you ready for it?*

YOU MAY ACTUALLY WANT TO STRUGGLE

Have you noticed a tendency to self-sabotage? Have you seen yourself or those around you finding comfort in your misery? Are you ever eager to share about what goes wrong or how bad things are for you? Have you ever felt that, at some level, you derive a sense of purpose, power, pleasure, or profit from your problems?

It's entirely possible that you may actually *want* your problems.

Perhaps you've gone to school for it or made a career out of it. Maybe you've invested a lot of money or a lot of other people's money. Perhaps you've made incredible sacrifices in search of it. Maybe you've written a book about it, and that's what people know you for. Perhaps you're a masochist who gets off on pain and pity.

Or, like many highly functional clients I've worked with, maybe you feel like having problems is what you're *supposed* to be doing. You look around to see people flailing and suffering, complaining and moaning, and conclude that struggle is the norm. What comes to you so simply and easily doesn't to those around you. You think maybe there's something wrong with you. You've never quite felt "normal" anyway, so you make your life harder and create drama to feel "normal" and fit in.

Perhaps it feels like home. Or you feel like you deserve it. Maybe you believe your past guilt and shame condemn you to forever search—a life as Sisyphus. It could be your childhood religious beliefs that still run you. Or something you have not forgiven yourself for.

These 'secret reasons' are many. It is not my place to invalidate yours or convince you otherwise—but understand they *are* the stories that bind you. You may think (quite reasonably), "Nah, I'm certain I want to end my problem," but give this serious consideration. Make a choice to be completely honest with yourself while reading this. There is a reason why you're still stuck—and it could be that at some subconscious level, you don't really want to find the solution you're seeking.

SECONDARY GAINS

There are entire industries built around looking for solutions to problems, that if the problem were solved, thousands of people would be out of work. Billions of dollars would no longer be funneled to the cause once a solution was found. Uncountable assets and duties that would become irrelevant overnight. For some people, there is more incentive to *not* solve the problem than there is to solve it. These industries become "too big to succeed."

Detached and from the outside, we see how insane this appears. We are outraged by the shortsightedness, fear, and greed and can hardly fathom people would do that—but we are not so innocent ourselves. We play our own version of this where we choose to stay stuck. We are hypnotized by secondary gains.

Here are a few examples:

- The teenager who gets more attention from being in trouble than from getting along with everyone.
- The person who gets paid more on welfare or inheritance than from working.

- The person with a disease that has orchestrated all their friends, hobbies, and income around having a sickness that could be cured.
- The singer who keeps looking teacher after teacher for one who can help her hit that high note, so she doesn't have to show up on stage.
- The business owner who doesn't market their business because that would mean putting themselves out there, and it would imply getting more clients, which means they couldn't complain anymore or get pity from their struggling friends.

They all *think* they want to be good, work, get healthy, sing on stage, get clients—but subconsciously, the benefits of staying stuck appear to outweigh the solutions. It is entirely irrational to hold ourselves back, but that's how fear and comfort work.

There is always a benefit in staying stuck. There is a payoff in not moving forward at some level of our biology, chemistry, or psychology. There must be, or else we wouldn't do it. Humans only do what works, but we aren't always aware of *what thing* is working. That *thing* isn't necessarily in our best interest. The good news is that we are conscious adults and do not have to be at its effect. But first, we need to discover our *insidious incentives*.

Do that now. Make a list of how you benefit from staying stuck. What are your "insidious incentives?" What are the potential payoffs you are currently receiving from being stuck, playing the victim, or giving your power away? What do you get from having this problem?

The following list covers the big ones:

- Pity?
- Money?
- Support?
- Justification?
- Attention?
- Special privileges?

- Safety?
- Comfort?
- Righteousness?
- Pleasure?
- Unaccountability?
- An escape?
- Control?

As with anything, the only way to benefit from this is by being honest with yourself. It will do you no good to pretend or lie to yourself, hoping to cover up your reality with a sugarcoated ideal. It bears repeating: **this book only works if you tell the truth**.

Once you have your list, you will see the choices you've made to stay stuck instead of move forward. You will need to find something you value more than all these benefits in order to make a sustainable leap out of their gravity. You've been valuing their lesser benefits over your greater vision, and it's going to keep you stuck until you stop.

IDENTIFYING WITH OUR SUFFERING

Sometimes our problem isn't a situational thing but a significant life challenge. When we have invested years or decades of our life trying to overcome a problem, we easily begin to identify with it. It becomes more than a challenge; it becomes a way of life. After years of this, it is no longer merely a problem—it's who we *are*.

For example:

1. I have blood sugar issues > I have diabetes > I am a diabetic
2. I don't make a lot of money > I can't afford it > I am poor
3. I struggle to meet people > I don't have friends > I am a loser

As you learned from the last chapter, the identity level of The Hierarchy of Change carries massive weight. Who we are—what we follow "I AM" with—is life-defining. When this reflects our problem, we are writing our own destiny of struggle.

Look what happens when we reverse it:

1. I am a diabetic > I have diabetes > I have blood sugar issues
2. I am poor > I can't afford it > I don't make a lot of money
3. I am a loser > I don't have friends > I struggle to meet people

Recall our 'equation.' You can see that the order doesn't matter here. It makes sense in either direction you go. The identity necessitates results: a diabetic *implies* blood sugar issues; a poor person *implies* not making a lot of money; a loser *implies* not having friends. When we identify with our problems, it becomes a self-fulfilling prophecy. Our problems become "who we are" rather than us simply being "a person with a problem."

You see people raising awareness, making t-shirts, writing it in their biographies, introducing themselves with it—letting the world know how invested they are in being stuck, sick, or suffering. Of course, that's not what they *think* they're doing, but it is. **More often than not, they believe they are looking for results when they're actually looking to validate their stories.** The more they focus on their stucky story, the more it becomes the focus. The more they invest in the story and the seeking, the more power they give it. It becomes more about the *narrative* around finding a solution than actually solving it and finding peace.

We naively believe that our addiction to our struggle gives us a higher chance of solving it. You don't get what you *want*—you get what you *focus on*, consciously and subconsciously. If you're focusing on what you do not want—even to "create awareness" or fight against it—guess what you'll get more of? If you're looking into the world through eyes of rage, indignation, and suffering, guess what you'll see? It's not to say solving the problem is wrong or there are no good causes to support. It's that this particular approach doesn't get the intended result. There's a better way that leads to resolution, healing, and peace.

Imagine meeting someone who introduces himself as "The Hiccup Man," wearing a t-shirt that reads, "Ask Me About The Dangers of Diaphragms." He tells you all about his book on how to relate to people living with chronic hiccups and the legislature his group is trying to pass. He mentions all the lawsuits against restaurants that don't conduct hiccup prevention classes for employees. He shares about how much money he's invested in seminars and supplements. You can see how proud he is. He continues that, despite his investments, he still struggles with it. You learn that it has also ruined his relationships for the past twenty years. The person next to him places their hand upon his shoulder in pity. He hiccups. He ends by inviting you to his next meeting of Anti-Hiccups Anonymous, handing you his business card with the address. You feel bad for the poor fella, of course, and hope he gets better. Yet, you don't recall him ever talking about getting over it.

It's an absurd example, but this is what people do! They start with a sincere desire to get unstuck or help others—and I do believe that—but they become more invested in the problem than the solution.

Unwittingly, they get lost along the way. They only want to talk about the problem and the problems surrounding the problem. But when it comes to solving it and getting on with their life, there's always an excuse. They are complainers (or what a mentor used to call "crap magnets"). The struggle and drama are more important to them than the solution. They don't want to get on with their life; they want to make their life about struggle.

> "It is difficult to get a man to understand
> something when his salary depends
> upon his not understanding it."
> — Upton Sinclair

Again, our 'equation' applies. The 'fight' or 'search' for a solution sustains the problem.

I can hear the most passionate say, "But justice! Change! Cures! Inclusion! Helping people! The good fight! Spreading awareness! Changing the world!"

I hear you, and right now, my focus is on *you*. How to help *you* get unstuck, find peace, allow more beauty, experience deeper intimacy, feel more pleasure, thrive, and get out of your own way. To help *you* break through and awaken to your True Self. To help *you* realize why you're still stuck and how to move forward in a new way. To demonstrate that *you* can live a life that stands for joy, beauty, humor, love, growth, compassion, responsibility, and truth.

If your identification with your problem is genuinely keeping you from those things or otherwise causing you to suffer—despite whatever apparent benefits it's giving you or others—it's not worth keeping. I don't care what cause, disease, religion, party, career, or relationship it's based on—it, or your interpretation of it, is no longer serving you. This book is not about changing the world—it's about helping *you* finally stop suffering and wake up.

> "Utopia must spring in the private bosom before
> it can flower into civic virtue, inner reforms
> leading to outer ones. A man who has
> reformed himself will reform thousands."
> — *Paramahansa Yogananda*

Keep in mind that these 'identities' are what we associate our existence with—they don't usually go without a fight. It is natural to get triggered or agitated by what I'm saying. It may seem as if I'm a bigot, or mean, or unjust, or lacking compassion. It can feel like you're being invalidated—but whatever feels invalidated is not *you*.

Anything that gets defensive is not who-you-really-are. That's how you know when you're defending a lie. The truth requires no defense.

I'm not here to make you wrong or take anything away from you—but I'm also not here to support you in your war or to tell you how to get better at suffering. I'm here to help you reclaim your grace and find peace.

CONFRONTING YOUR IDENTITY

To reiterate, I'm referring to a particular situation in which we identify with our struggle and use our problems to define ourselves and those around us. Where our problem is no longer merely a challenge or equation, but the title of our story.

When we stay with friends or join groups that are identified with struggle, we end up trading who we are for a sense of belonging—belonging to a culture of suffering. We get to meet new people, be a part of something, get validated, and feel understood in our struggle. This route is seductive. It's an easy-out guised as 'progress.' But it is an illusion. We are actually exchanging peace, freedom, and joy for a false sense of righteousness, acceptance, and meaning. We are surrounded by folks like us, and to solve the problem for ourselves would mean no longer belonging.

The identification with the problem *becomes* the limitation.

If we take this road and then come out a few months later with a solution and get on with our lives, great. But that's not usually what happens. We become invested, get comfortable, and create familiarity—all fine things—except when they hold us back.

Let's imagine for a moment what happens when your problem does end. I know this won't be how everyone responds, but play along. Imagine if, all of a sudden, the problem goes away after all that time, energy, and investment. What would happen to your identity? Who would you be after five, ten, twenty, fifty years of struggle, rallying against, and fighting—no longer with an enemy? If your sense of self-definition is based on that problem, who are you without the problem?

We are back to the first chapter's definitive question: "Who would you be without your stories?"

It would feel disorienting and uncertain, surely.

Now imagine someone came to you and proved that you were mistaken the entire time. It wasn't solved; the problem wasn't real to begin with. All that effort, investment, blood, sweat, and tears for nothing. You invested twenty years into a life that was based on something that wasn't even real. What would that feel like? Devastating, crushing, incomprehensible? Pointless, wasted? Would you feel angry, depressed, suicidal, or defiant? Would you be in denial?

It's a disruptive realization to face and not a happy situation for many folks. So, society plays along with it all to keep the gears turning, to keep the industries running. We 'keep the peace' trying to avoid being shown our denial. We are doled out diluted and weaker advice and teachings that aren't as confronting or liberating. We do not like these feelings, nor do we like having our sense of self ripped away from us. What I'm saying in this book can feel like that, and some of it actually *is* that. I am inviting you to let go of the identities that you're attached to that are based on unreal problems. The ones that you have invested decades of your life into under the illusion of validity. This is the same invitation I gave to let go of your fabricated stories in the first chapter, "Your Stucky Story."

How do you respond to the invitation to let go of who you *think* you are?

A DESPERATE, CLINGY EGO

When I'm working with clients, this is one of the final barriers to their transformation. They feel as if I'm trying to take away who they are, so we help the client see it's not really *them*. We demonstrate that an identity, belief, or behavior they *think* is helping them—even around healing and spirituality—is actually keeping them stuck.

It's a tough one.

It's like telling an addict that loves their addiction that it's not good for them, and they quip back with, "But I feel great!" ...while their life around them is falling apart. That's precisely what it is. We are all addicted to our stories and notions of who we are, even if they are ruining our lives and the lives of those around us. This is the desperate ego. Our egos are attached to these identities. We defend, fight, and justify. Our egos act out in all sorts of insane ways when they are threatened. We begin to defend our limitations and justify why we should keep suffering. We get paranoid. We distort real love and concern into danger and bigotry (more on this in the later chapter, "When Wrong Works").

Now you see why it's so hard for us to give these identities up, and why so many of us fail to make these changes and finally stop suffering. Even in the face of undeniable proof, there is so much cognitive dissonance that we implode. It invalidates *everything*.

It's a form of ego death.

When someone or some idea comes along and challenges our identity, it forces us to reevaluate the validity of our previous behaviors, attitudes, beliefs, and feelings based upon that as well. This is because a shift at the identity level affects all five levels of The Hierarchy of Change. It can be a lot of life to surrender. We must ask ourselves: *"Is giving up my struggle and suffering worth letting go of everything I think I am?"*

Is having everything you truly want (not your ego, but who-you-really-are) worth letting go of all of this?

I'm not asking you to stop doing what you genuinely love and be someone you're not. If you're seriously stuck—that's what you've already done. This is not about acquiescing or turning into a blob void of personality and passion. This is not about never solving problems either. I'm not suggesting that you don't solve *real* problems for yourself or others—that's one of the best ways to be of service in the world.

This entire chapter is an invitation to stop chronic patterns of struggle where you're wasting your life and energy trying to solve a problem that doesn't exist while under the illusion that it *does*. It's time to get off of Bob's Ladder. To stop wasting your life on things that aren't even real. It's time to make your life stand for something beyond yours or another's suffering. ✺

WHEN INTELLECT SLOWS YOU DOWN

"The man who asks a question is a fool for a minute, ✗
the man who does not ask is a fool for life."
— CONFUCIUS

he intellect is incredible. It's what separated us from animals and exalted human beings to outer space. It brought us out of caves and into sprawling metropolises. It allows us to solve complex problems and imagine things that have never been done. It allows for logic, reason, and analysis—all things that ushered us out of the dark ages.

The intellect is a defining feature of mankind.

But what exactly is the 'intellect'? Before we go further, it's imperative that we are using the same definition of intellect.

Throughout this book, you will notice that my definitions for certain terms aren't necessarily how they'd be typically defined. Words like *intelligence*, *suffering*, *feeling*, *narcissism*, and *mythology* are used a bit differently here than their colloquial use. My choices are purposeful and precise. Their use may sound a little odd initially, but trust that these nuances are only for your benefit. Grasping the subtleties of meaning is crucial for benefiting from this work. Our words define our world, and deliberate use can change your reality. You wouldn't believe how many clients say things like, "Oh! *That's* what you meant! I've heard you say that word five hundred times and it didn't hit me until now. I thought I knew it already, so I never actually listened."

Back to the word 'intellect.' I am using the term intellect to mean the use and reliance on the brain and mind. Intellect is the raw brainpower and mental swiftness; it is all about *thinking*. In this book, an intellectual isn't merely someone who is super smart and aspires to higher thinking fields; it's someone who relies predominantly upon, and interfaces through, their logical, reasoning processes of thinking.

In essence: intellect is human thinking functionality.

We use the intellect to do things such as:

- Organize and govern
- Solve complex problems
- Plan and comprehend time
- Perform logic and reason
- Philosophize and hypothesize
- Analyze information

These are noble pursuits and skills worth developing.

As a civilization, we've built quite an ego around our mental prowess and the technology it has ushered in. Yet, as much as it serves, the intellect isn't the end-all-be-all epitome of human greatness. Being the *smartest* one in the room doesn't mean the most *successful*. If it did, IQ or academic performance would directly correlate with income, sexual satisfaction, health, status, social life, and general happiness. If it did, the smartest students should end up with the best lives.

But it doesn't. It can surely benefit us, but it's not everything.

Intellectual people make a lot of money *and* little money.

Intellectual people have high status *and* low status.

Intellectual people have a lot of sex *and* no sex.

It may even seem that some of the most hyper-intellectuals have difficulties because of how smart they are and how much they rely on thinking their way through everything.

Why is that?

If you're someone who's been told "you're too smart for your own good," "get out of your head," or if you find yourself stuck despite your brilliance, past success, or talent—then this chapter is for you. If you've found yourself struggling with things that you think most other people have no trouble with, this chapter will help you understand why. Your fast intellect or astute logic may be the very thing that's slowing you down.

Or, perhaps you don't see yourself as an intellectual, but you still have a greater vision for yourself. You've seen countless people without degrees or superstar talent do incredibly well in life, so there must be another way. Maybe you've heard of or experienced the benefits of meditation and are looking for its practical application. Perhaps you've gone deep into shamanism or mysticism and are looking to integrate these realms of awareness into daily life. You know there's another way to live besides thinking all the time, but aren't quite sure what that would look like. This chapter reveals what that other way is.

INTELLECTUAL TYPES THAT STRUGGLE

Now that the power and value of the intellect has been well-established, let's explore some of its weaknesses. To first illustrate how our dependence on intellect can slow us down, we will look at what happens when the intellect gets out of control. You will begin to see how an over-reliance on thinking can get in our way.

The following are examples of certain types of people who, despite their incredible intellect, struggle using that same strategy elsewhere in life. I will give some indicators of the behavior, where it may 'work' and where it may not, and how similar behavior may be keeping *you* stuck.

THOSE THAT OVER-ANALYZE EVERYTHING

These types collect data, facts, and figures and use this information to run through every possible outcome and validate their views. They compare and consider all available options after diligent research. They base their decisions on the best or worst scenario, usually to avoid failure.

Really good for launching rockets; really bad for going for the first kiss and ordering lunch.

Why It Can Keep You Stuck

When you're over-analyzing everything, you leave the present moment and rely on past data to play out future scenarios—none of which are real. You abandon *now*. You forget that facts can change at any moment with one new piece of data, which can crumble your expertly built-up narrative to the ground. Instead of ready, aim, fire—you're ready, aim, ready, aim, ready, aim... It's hard to take the shot quickly because you want it to be perfect, and unluckily for you, you're so smart you might actually be able to do it.

THOSE THAT KNOW IT ALL

These kinds have read hundreds of books, studies, and newspapers, and perhaps have even written them. They are up-to-date on current affairs. They've taken all the courses, have all the certifications, and studied with all the names. They have all the authoritative qualifications. They pipe-in to correct you when you're wrong and need to add more when you're right. They agree and disagree, rather than take it in with wonder as a child would.

Really good for Jeopardy and scientific journals; really bad for dinner parties and unlearning a lot of things that don't work.

Why It Can Keep You Stuck

When you think you know it all already, you don't take new information in; you compare it to what you already know. You're not *really* listening; you're assessing to accept or reject. Your cup is too full for anything more to be poured in. You're prone to skipping over what you think you already know, which can be the essential parts: the basics.

> *"Sell your cleverness and buy bewilderment."* ∜
> — Rumi

THOSE THAT ACT SUPERIOR

These ones are simply smarter than others—either verifiably measurable or in their own minds. Their brilliance is a tool used to surpass others. They may have been publicly praised and awarded for their vast intellectual superiority through the work they produce. Their way of thinking is the best one—and they can prove it. They may be judgmental towards lesser religions (or all), the indigenous, uncultured, uninitiated, unlearned, or unapproved. They show signs of elitism, all the way to megalomania.

Really good for winning individual sports and competitive business; really bad for nearly all healthy relationships, teamwork, and human compassion.

Why It Can Keep You Stuck

When you think you're superior, you are playing the 'levels game.' It necessitates others that are 'less than' you—but it also necessitates there are those that are 'greater than' you. When we act superior, it's almost always in reaction formation to feeling inferior at some point, in the same way. It creates blocks to intimacy and feedback since you are always on guard against being made to feel inferior. It is inherently a pushing away, exclusive energy that tends to isolate emotionally or relationally.

THOSE THAT REJECT FEELING

These are the ones who try to understand emotion through logic, and it doesn't compute. Feeling is overwhelmingly uncomfortable—they don't 'get' its value, often seeing it as a weakness. They consider the mind to be superior to the body. They are effective at their jobs because they don't get caught up in illogical drama. They value stoicism and physical evidence over fully feeling and the metaphysical. They prefer to keep interactions at a distance by keeping them at the intellectual level.

Really good for programming computers; really bad for sex, intimacy, spiritual connection, empathy, and intuition.

Why It Can Keep You Stuck

When you are out of relationship with your body, feeling, emotions, intuition—a lot of things in your life don't work. You live in a little box cut off from life in something that resembles a head. It's almost always a reaction to trauma, which doesn't have to be dramatic or extreme. It can simply be from growing up with parents who were also cut off, who never modeled emotional intelligence.

ON INTELLECTUAL TRAPS

While these are extreme generalizations, they are helpful illustrations showing why intellect alone won't free you. If any of these seem like you, understand that I'm not making you wrong. I'm revealing the booby traps of the mind and another possible reason why you're still stuck. Hearing that our brilliance is limiting us can be a tough one to face, especially when our livelihood and sense of value is based upon it. I know it was for me—I was a software programmer for fifteen years, for heaven's sake! You are free to fight it, but I can tell you from experience it's a losing battle. You're only fighting against what you truly want.

These examples are not invalidations of intellect altogether; it is not an 'either-or.' It is not 'be intellectual or be a heathen'—I'm not asking you to throw intellect away and become an ape. Being intellectual doesn't make us smart, and not being one doesn't make us dumb. This is not an invalidation—it's an *invitation*. An invitation to a life that's not only lived in your head. A life that doesn't pass you by like a film. A fully-experienced life that moves through you, rather than an eight-decade-long computational program installed in your brain. **It is entirely possible that what's holding you back, is in fact, how good you are.** How smart and clever you are. How talented you are. How successful you've already been. How developed your persona is. How you're the best at what you do. How powerful your thinking is. Your intellect may have got you here (and what a blessing!), but it won't get you *there*. In my decade-plus of working with clients, I've never found a single one struggling because they weren't thinking enough. I've never, ever had to say, "You need to be *more* in your head!" *More* is rarely the solution. I'm inviting you to give up your addiction to thinking. Yes, 'addiction' is often *precisely* what it is.

Here are some ways relying more on intellect can slow us down:

- Thinking more means we are sensing and feeling less— which translates to less intuition, pleasure, love, real-time data and awareness, and direct experience of life
- Thinking more means we are less connected and aware of the world around us—which translates to being absent-minded, clumsy, isolated, disconnected, and afraid
- Thinking more takes us out of the moment and makes us less present—which translates to limited depths of intimacy, empathy, and emotional access to and from others
- Thinking more means our communication lacks feeling— which translates to monotone speech, rigidity in presentation, 'academic writing,' and an uninspiring message that lacks passion or zeal

- Thinking more means our problem-solving ability is capped based on preexisting knowledge—which translates to lack of innovation and creativity, or products and art that seem like the same ol' same ol'
- Thinking more means more mental stimulation and noise—which translates to more stress, anxiety, complication, fear, and poor sleep and focus

These all result in struggles in leadership, innovation, relationships, intimacy, physical health, empathy, and self-expression. Even in highly technical, scientific, and mathematical areas, significant breakthroughs often occur when the person is engaged in unrelated activities. We've all had the experience of being in the shower without focus and out of nowhere an idea or breakthrough comes to us. It's almost as if taking a break from all the thinking allows something else to occur...

THE ADVANTAGES OF NON-INTELLECT

We've covered the limitations and problems that occur from over-thinking, relying too much on the intellect, and being in our heads. Now let's see what happens when we stop that. Children are a great example of this. They are naturally less in their heads because their intellect hasn't developed yet. Yes, this means they are limited and ignorant in many ways, but it also means they are *less* restricted in others. I am not implying the solution is ignorance or regression; however, there are many things we can learn from these tiny teachers.

Here are some ways in which the intellect hasn't yet slowed them down:

- They're not capable of analyzing twenty bits of data at a time and playing out a hundred scenarios—so they go with their instinct, which can be more in tune with nature
- They're not thinking about what people think about them and don't even know that what they're doing 'should' be embarrassing

- They don't realize what they're doing is considered risky, so they just do it
- They don't have the smart answers, so they're willing to ask the dumb questions
- They don't have a lot of knowledge, so they take things in like a sponge without assessing everything
- They don't know there are other ways, so they make do with what they know
- They're not censoring what comes out, so while they may say inappropriate comments, they are more often speaking the truth than adults
- They're not aware of, thus not concerned with, the grand problems of the world, and so they address the relevant issues in their own life
- They don't have sophisticated terminology to describe the workings of life, but they're in life having a direct experience of it

Children have many limitations, and yet, some of their most natural ways of being can demonstrate what we as adults have lost, as our stories and intellect erect their own limitations.

We assume in our culture that a bigger intellect is better, and less of one is inferior. We think that thinking more and harder gets us there faster. In actuality, this idea is an elitism. It is a perversion of the ego, a misidentification of self-power. Many people who would never be considered 'intellectual' by our society move powerfully through the world and live abundant, productive, creative, successful lives. There are other paths of high functionality and problem-solving that don't rely on being in our heads thinking through seventy pieces of data each moment of life. Ones that require trust in something greater than what we already know.

TRUSTING A
GREATER INTELLIGENCE

As I've alluded to throughout this chapter, there is something beyond our intellect we can tap into and rely on. Something that doesn't require us to revert back to children or abandon our brains. Some other way of moving through the world that doesn't require us to always be in our head thinking about everything all the time.

This 'something' is what I refer to as *intelligence*. It is the source of *intuition*.

It is not a synonym—intelligence is *not* the same as intellect.

There's a difference between intellect and intelligence. Noise propagates the former, silence the latter. Intellect is inherited; intelligence is inherent.

Our **intellect** relies on our brainpower, mental strength, education, experience, and reasoning. It requires us to leave the present moment and go into our heads to use conscious will to figure it out. It requires great effort, energy, and time. It is individualized to each of us.

Our **intelligence** is built-in, arises from and manages our entire body without effort, doesn't require years of study to utilize, and is available and fully operational since birth. It informs us in the silence; we don't force it. It works in real-time, and is present in and part of the space. It is a singular source we all have access to because we are *of it*.

This distinction lies within us, between the mind's intellect and the intelligence of the body. It is the difference between thinking and feeling, and of thought and intuition.

It's this distinction that illuminated a way of getting out of my head and into the mysteries of life. I've had experiences of knowing and intuition that didn't make any rational sense, knowing things I shouldn't have been able to know. I was able to see things in ways I was never taught. I was able to sense and feel things around me. I was able to tell things about people without having to ask them—I just *knew*. Without realizing it, I was tapping into another way to 'process' things.

I eventually came to find out what that was: **I could *feel* my way through the world rather than *think* my way through**. I could operate from a feeling-based awareness instead of an analytical awareness. I could trust my gut 'knowing' rather than spend hours or weeks gathering data to prove to myself what I didn't trust.

The body has an innate intelligence that keeps us alive, doing millions of things our conscious mind has no idea how to do. It's the same intelligence behind the plants, the animals, the atoms, and the forces of nature. It's the same intelligence behind the spinning of the celestial spheres and the evolution of all life on Earth. It is the intelligence behind the math that makes geometry and music beautiful. It is the same intelligence that governs the microcosm and macrocosm as holographic mirrors. We can ignore this intelligence and think our minds are superior, or we can trust it and let it be the wind beneath our wings.

What makes tuning into our innate intelligence powerful is that it's already there—it's built-in. This intelligence is in-tune with the natural rhythms and order of nature and isn't hindered by the stories that bind the mind. It has direct access to what's happening around us without the ability to give it meaning. This intelligence doesn't filter or distort, or justify or prove. It doesn't require time or understanding to work or make use of. It's pure direct experience, which makes it *symbolic* in nature, not rational.

For an abstract concept such as this, it can help to compare a bit more so you can understand—or rather, get a *feel* for—the difference between the two. Here are some further comparisons between intellect and intelligence:

↯ Intellect

    i.   It can be described with words such as: *thinking, mind, head, figure out, understand, contemplate, theorize, thoughts, rational, logical, airy*

   ii.   It is limited; confined to the person's head, one's own knowledge, perception, and experience

iii. It requires will and conscious understanding; familiar and dominant; easily taught and tested

iv. Reading, watching, or listening to someone show up from this place can feel: *heady, shallow, lackluster, noisy, avoidant, fast, witty, exciting, trying to prove, intellectualized, empirical, imposing, informational, or academic*

Intelligence

i. It can be described with words such as: *feeling, body, knowing, inside, universal, intuitive, a gut feeling, hunch, unconscious, subtle, symbolic, nonlinear, grounded*

ii. It is unlimited; it is inclusive, runs all living things; the same intelligence that has evolved from the first subatomic particles of the Big Bang to the first amoeba to us

iii. It's built-in, but these instruments atrophy when we rely more on intellect; it requires trust, silence, surrender, attention to subtle awareness; non-obvious and intangible

iv. Reading, watching, or listening to someone showing up from this place can feel: *resonate, deep, quiet, empathetic, inviting, boring, captivating, genuine, slow, eternal, stating what is, relational, or anecdotal*

It's essentially thought versus intuition, being in our head versus in our body, and rationalizing versus feeling.

"AM I IN MY HEAD OR FEELING?"

Now that you understand the difference between being in your head and being in feeling, you will learn some basic ways to determine which you are operating from. It can be a challenge to self-analyze, especially when we're like fish trying to figure out if we're in water or not, but this section will get you started in the right direction.

Below are some indicators that may help you determine when you're in your head or not. They are not absolutely indicative, and different activities and situations may cause you to respond differently, but I have found them to be reliable guideposts for myself and my clients.

From Your Head (Intellect)

i. You look up into your head to figure stuff out or think about it
ii. Talking extremely fast in a sort of 'verbal vomit' where the other person is overloaded, and you're going so fast you skip over the feeling
iii. You go and search for words or answers
iv. You tend to overthink, analyze, and complicate simple things
v. You are prone to excessive daydreaming, anxiety, panic, boredom, escapism, and distraction
vi. You speak from what you know and have a myriad of facts, figures, and authoritative citations to back it all up
vii. You must ask others how they feel and try to figure it out and understand
viii. You live from a control room in your head, filtering life through your mind like a movie, and your body seems below you as a machine remotely operated
ix. Your body tenses or pulls upward toward your shoulders, neck, head; you are easily distracted, and you feel 'airy' and don't take up make space with your presence

From Feeling (Intelligence)

i. You look down into your body to feel what's real and true in the moment
ii. You talk slower and feel each word as you speak it, connected to the other person and aware of how they are receiving it without having to ask
iii. You let the words and answers arise and come to you

iv. You trust your intuition to get you where you need to go while also being aware (but not caught up in) the potential consequences

v. You are comfortable being still and silent, sensual, slow, and savoring

vi. You trust what you feel and speak from your own truth

vii. You don't need to ask others what they feel because you can feel them

viii. You are in relationship with and can feel all parts, limbs, and aspects of your body

ix. You feel grounded, centered, stable, and 'plugged-in' to the Earth and space around you

These indicators point to where you're coming from. They also show you *how* to come from either your head or from feeling. The more you operate from the body, while feeling and trusting in the greater intelligence, the less you will be stuck in your head. This leads you to be less anxious and less prone to overthinking and overanalyzing. The more you begin to feel yourself, the easier it becomes to feel others and the space around you. This connection with others and the space subconsciously informs you. You receive symbolic data that would otherwise be invisible while in your head. If you've never experienced this, it may not make any sense, but if you *have*, you know exactly what I'm talking about. You can't get this from a book—you must have the direct, embodied experience yourself. Otherwise, this may seem like gobbledygook nonsense.

Another way to determine if we are in our head or in feeling is through the words we use. As I've mentioned earlier, our words define our reality. By listening to others and observing our language, we can begin to paint a picture of how we move through life. Here are some common phrases that illustrate the differences in approach.

See if you can tell which are relying on thinking and which are more based on feeling:

• "The data shows that people are like this."

- "I'm thinking about what that felt like."
- "I sense a lot of anxiety in the room."
- "I'll have to think about it."
- "It feels as if you don't trust yourself."
- "I don't know how I knew; I just did."
- "Your feelings are irrelevant. The facts prove it."
- "What? That doesn't make any sense!"
- "I have a bad feeling about this."

Notice some of the peculiarities, such as "thinking about feeling"—how we fool ourselves!

Consider your own life, the words you use, and the way you approach solving problems, creating, and relating to others. Which do you *think* or *feel* you tend to operate from primarily? Is one more overdeveloped than the other? Do you have any judgments about intellect or feeling? Any judgments about people who operate differently than you? Do you struggle with appropriately using intelligence or intellect?

Reflect on your relationship between the concepts of intellect and intelligence. Reflect on your relationship with both of these throughout your life.

THE EGOIC INTELLECTUAL'S PAIN

After experiencing trauma or hurt, it can be a big step to begin trusting again; to feel safe in our body, in the world. It is not something we can force or rush and must be a choice that comes from within. However, it is an essential part of the process of healing, transformation, awakening, and getting unstuck. There is no way around it: coming home to our body and beginning to feel again is central to this work.

We all have our unique ways of disconnecting, dissociating, and defending against life. We have developed strategies to cope with the traumas and pain we've experienced, usually subconsciously. Everyone has experienced some form of trauma, even if you don't call it that. These coping strategies have allowed us to stay alive, remain somewhat functional, and get through hard times. Humans are incredibly resilient and are designed to survive. These psychological and energetic configurations serve us for a while, but eventually, what has kept us safe becomes the very thing that keeps us stuck. But surviving is not the same as thriving, and this book is oriented towards helping you thrive.

One of the most common strategies we use to dissociate is to be in our heads and rely heavily on intellect. Even without trauma, it is the default way most of us escape from life... without even being aware we're doing it.

The work I do specializes in helping people get out of their heads, drop into feeling, and develop genuine intuition. I work with a lot of smart, successful folks who struggle with being in their heads. They've reached a point where they can't get any further being how they've been. The biggest challenge high-intellectual people tend to face when starting to embody their body is their judgment against feeling. It takes months for the stubborn ones (or years for people like me) to begin to see the real value of it. When they finally experience it for themselves, everything begins to open up in their lives and career.

One of the superficial reasons for this judgment comes from our association with the word 'feeling.' *Feeling* is not the same as "our feelings." As used in common parlance, the word 'feelings' is often used to label our emotional reactions, opinions, and superficial attitudes. We see this when someone talks about "their feelings" from a dramatic, hysteric, reactive place when they are feeling hurt, e.g., "You hurt my feelings!" or "I don't care about your feelings." Most of the time, these people aren't really *feeling:* they're *acting out* what they won't feel. We also see this used interchangeably to refer to someone's emotional charges, meanings, attitudes, and opinions about a topic, i.e., how they "feel about an issue." When you ask somebody "how they feel about something," rarely do they drop into their body, go into what they truly feel, and report *that truth*. Usually, what comes as a reply is an amalgam of views, beliefs, and emotionally reactive opinions.

None of that is what I mean by 'feeling'! Of course none of *that* can be trusted or depended on. Of course none of *that* is superior to facts, data, and rational thinking. But *that* is not what I am referring to when I say "feeling." When I say feel, I mean *feel*.

THE FIGHT OF THEIR LIFE

The Egoic Intellectual does not go down (into their bodies) without a fight. The scorn and superiority against the consecration of feeling are from those who are completely out of relationship with it. They hide behind perverted stoicism or logic, finding emotions and feeling weak, flawed, and unnecessary. In truth, it is useless to them because it is *painful*. Nobody shuts off feeling because it feels wonderful and trustable; they shut down because it feels awful and unsafe. Being in our head cuts us off from our body, and as a consequence, we become dissociated and desensitized.

This is not usually by accident, as the head is a great place to avoid feeling, life, and other people. Buried below are stories about when they once trusted feeling, and it led to tremendous pain. These were the times when they were innocent and genuine, loving and open, and those around them who were suffering shut them down. At some point, they started taking it personally and began to hate themselves for it. They hated their beauty, love, and innocence because they mistakenly took it as the cause of their suffering. Thus, they retreat to the superiority and numbness of their mind to never feel such humiliation, hurt, and betrayal again.

These are all defense mechanisms to avoid feeling because the Egoic Intellectual doesn't trust feeling itself.

We are not in control of intelligence or intuition. Its nonlinear and symbolic nature lends it to be considered unreliable and nebulous. For both reasons, our ego doesn't trust it. Our intellect seems like a safer bet because we are in control of it. It seems safer to us. Our ego does not like to feel out of control. Why? The ego's entire existence is built upon its promise that it can provide us safety through control. This is the grand seduction of intellect in our world: the allure of

71

control. This is the connection between the ego and intellect. It is a deal with the devil.

The ego is jealous. It is tiny, isolated, and powerless compared to the omniscient intelligence that permeates all-that-is. The egoic intellect is but a frozen drop of water in the vastness of oceanic intelligence. The Egoic Intellectual *must* be envious, as he has cut himself off from spirit and his True Self. He hates himself because he chose to disconnect and now punishes himself, defending against love with justifications to rationalize his self-betrayal. He is terrified to stop and face the guilt and pain his avoidance is protecting himself from. For if he were to stop and begin to feel, he would—after the layers of discomfort and pain—inevitably reach unconditional love. A love that would invalidate everything he prides himself in dismissing and being superior to, and the image of who he's built himself up to be.

It's Love that the ego can never provide, no matter what deal or sacrifice is made. Everything besides Love is a consolation prize, and the ego does whatever it can to keep you from seeing the Truth. It will offer superiority to overcome the pain of inferiority. It will offer riches to overcome the pain of emptiness. It will offer lust to overcome the vulnerabilities of intimacy. It will offer entertainment to overcome the renunciation of creativity. It will offer attention to overcome the void of affection. It will offer noise to overcome the discomfort of self-abandonment. It will offer all these things as easy outs from immediate pain, but without reading you the fine print that states it cannot offer you healing or authentic resolution. It offers you short-term escape in exchange for long-term suffering.

The ego can *only* offer you illusion because that's all the ego is. None of these offers solve anything. None of them are loving. None of this heals, for only Love and Truth can heal. The ego doesn't love you; it *can't* love you. Hence everything the ego does to 'help you' is designed to prevent you from seeing that it can't truly help you. Thus, the Egoic Intellectual finds that his only possible salvation is by surrendering to his nemesis: *feeling*. It's only by feeling that we heal, love, and experience our True Self, and it's only by getting out of our head and into our body that we can begin to feel.

AN INVITATION TO TRUST

The words in this chapter may feel like a threat—but they are not a threat to *you*. They are a threat to the illusions of your ego. If you have trouble coming to terms with this, my biggest suggestion is to *surrender*. Not to me, my words, or these concepts—but to an intelligence within, greater than your intellect. In surrendering to that *something* greater than yourself—whatever name you wish to give it—you will derive your true power. This act of letting go will push you to the edge, asking, "In who or what do you trust?" If the answer is only in yourself, your ego, your mind—then you shall continue to live a life far less than what you're capable of.

The world's most innovative and revolutionary acts, products, and art weren't a result of more and more thinking, but intuitive sparks of madness—also called genius. The most awe-inspiring, timeless masterpieces weren't contrived by an ego. They were manifestations of Beauty that came forth into the world through man. That's why there is no scientific strategy—this intuitive insight is a spontaneous, emergent force. It is to be fostered and allowed, not forced. It is to be listened to, not willed. It is to be accepted, not overcome. It is an intelligence beyond our ego, and therefore beyond our control. The more we trust it, the more we are *en*trusted. It only asks that we listen and act.

This is how we begin accessing our intelligence. It's also referred to as developing our intuition or learning to trust our gut, hunch, or feeling. The occurrence of this in day-to-day life happens instantaneously, and until cultivated, seemingly at random.

How To Begin Accessing Your Intelligence

Anytime you're facing a problem, being creative, meeting someone new, empathizing, making decisions, speaking, or looking for answers—you can start to rely on your intelligence instead of your intellect. Although intuition itself generally happens in an instant, we can break it down into steps for clarity:

1. Stop thinking and quiet your head noise. It requires an *inner* silence and stillness, not necessarily some meditative position.

2. Get out of your head, and drop into your body and being to feel. Intuition always starts through feeling. It may lead to mental thought, but its origin is felt.

3. Listen to the silence and wait for data to arise. Relax into it. Drop expectation and attachment. Let *it* inform *you*, don't go working and seeking.

4. You will feel it, sense it, see an image, or hear it. At first, it may be subtle, obscure, seemingly irrelevant. Follow it, trust it, see where it leads you. It will be symbolic, not rational; it will be a feeling, not a thought. Do not confuse this with getting carried away in thought or minutes and hours of meditation. Intuition is *insight*, not technique.

5. Once you have the feeling or symbolic awareness, you may wish to then translate it into something your conscious mind can understand or communicate with others. There may be no words for it. That's fine. Intuition is symbolic and feeling-based, and so it cannot be rationalized. It can only be felt and *then* translated internally to words or thought.

6. Trust it and act upon it. Feel gratitude for it. If you hear it but don't listen and heed its call, you are subconsciously telling yourself that you don't fully trust it. You must begin to act upon the impulse and rely on it, for what appears to you as "better or worse."

At first, it is an act of faith. It may take a while to regain your relationship with this aspect of yourself, so like any other skill, don't blame it because it led to something your ego *thinks* was a failure. There are layers and layers of stories, myths, and filters between you and this voice. Until you begin to purify and penetrate these, the message—like the game 'telephone'—has a high chance of getting distorted along the way. It's never the intelligence that fails us, but our *interpretation*. **Feeling is the most real and reliable thing**. It's decades of 'gunk' that distorts, filters, and imbues the chaos which impairs our perception; it's not a fault in the mechanism.

This intuitive intelligence is our birthright—it is not something you must 'acquire.' We are being informed all the time, but we have tuned it out or discarded it as nonsense. Much of our head noise drowns out its whisper. Much of our judgment shoots it down. We are quick to blame and resent it. Despite our arrogance, it remains, as it always has and always will, even after we're gone. We never lose it; we simply lose touch with it.

The way to regain access to this power is to be willing to trust in something greater than that intellectual supercomputer in your head. High intellect and deep thinking are gifts and should not be ignored, and like any other tool, it needs to be used appropriately and put in its proper place. This requires you to make the leap and begin relying on feeling as your default once again. To find a rhythm with the same force that has managed to keep all of nature on this planet thriving for billions of years without human intellect. It asks you to drop into the physicality and intelligence of your body. You must let whoever you *think* you are be dismantled and let who-you-really-are shine through.

If you're able to empty your cup, surrender, and trust—you will discover the grace and intelligence of life guiding you. It may not make sense logically—and you may never fully understand it—but are those worth giving up in order to have peace, connection, intuition, and true power? Is your intellectual superiority worth surrendering over to Love and all its riches? Is being protected and disconnected in your head worth giving up in order to know your True Self? 🌿

THE MOST
IMPORTANT PERSON

"As he stooped to quench his thirst
another thirst increased.
While he is drinking he beholds himself
reflected in the mirrored pool—and loves;
loves an imagined body which contains
no substance, for he deems the mirrored shade
a thing of life to love.
— OVID,

Echo & Narcissus in Metamorphoses

he great thing about self-help is that you don't need anyone else. There are no universities, therapists, doctors, professors, classmates, or institutions required, only your learning materials and a willingness to be taught and grow. It's faster and less expensive compared to university and available to most people in the modern world.

As an autodidact, I have spent over a decade as a student and teacher in the personal development world, and it has been the cornerstone of my adult life and career. I attribute much healing, growth, knowledge, and transformation to the plethora of self-help materials from which I have learned from. I have immense respect and gratitude for this genre in which I am in some way entangled. I have come to know its strengths—and its limitations. I have seen life-changing transformation, healing, and spiritual awakening—and I have also seen the charlatans, loveless products, and dishonesty. Like any other field, it has its own booby traps, distortions, addictions, and seductions that no 'guru' dare expose about his livelihood.

You're here because you've been doing all this work on yourself and you're still stuck. The cause may be found in the DNA of the work you've been attempting. This trap is so obvious, it's spelled right in the name: *self-help, self-improvement, personal development...*

We are focusing on our *self.*

Working on ourselves can be a path to both liberation and self-centeredness. It doesn't *have* to be self-absorbed or selfish, but self-help's inherent nature is about *ourselves.* This makes sense because we are the only ones we can control. This comes from the truism that, "I am the only one I can change, and you are the only one you can change." We can't force anyone else out there to change or make our lives better, so we feel a lot more hopeful and empowered taking improvement into our own hands.

The 'self' part isn't wrong or bad. It is fair to make it about us and own our needs. It's noble to handle our trauma before projecting it all over others. Doing the inner-work ourselves before teaching or expecting others to do it keeps us steeped in integrity. Going inwards and being alone in our healing or creativity is necessary. There is tremendous value in healing ourselves and showing up in new, more functional ways.

Yet, the line between self-help and self-obsession can be easily blurred in the name of "healing." We can easily mask our narcissism or self-indulgence with a false narrative about needing to "take care of ourselves" at the expense of our responsibilities to others. We can reach a point where doing the inner-work all ourselves becomes our new stucky story.

NARCISSISM

We often think of a narcissist as someone who cares too much about how they look, who's in love with themselves, and who's superficial. They take vast amounts of pictures of themselves and talk about only them. At the extreme, we see someone who is abusive and manipulative or consumed with vanity. These people only care about the most important person in the world: 'me.' We don't want this type of person around us because they can be maliciously charming, seductive, and destructive.

But most of all, we think of a narcissist as anyone else but *us*.

Nearly nobody thinks *they* are narcissistic, even if they are. It's tricky because the admission itself is an attack on the narcissistic image, which a narcissist identifies as self, and so defends. Just as most people aren't going to say, "Yes, I'm a bad person," most people don't consider themselves narcissistic.

I sure didn't.

I would have never imagined I was narcissistic when I was younger. I didn't think I displayed any of *those* qualities. I didn't feel like I was abusive, selfish, in love with myself, uncaring of others, manipulative, or staring at the mirror, making kissy faces all day. Nobody in my relationships told me they thought I was vain or into myself. I didn't spend three hours getting ready to leave the house. All these stereotypical, overt signs of narcissism never landed for me—and I was open to hearing it.

It wasn't until I saw myself on video and kept getting feedback from my mentor that I finally saw the narcissism. The funny thing was, it didn't *look* like what we'd typically consider narcissistic behaviors. But as I explored the concept from a bit more spiritual and psychological perspective, I realized that's *exactly* what I was doing. I had the idea of it completely distorted. It was like being blindsided by a baseball bat; all this dark, uncomfortable, 'unlovable' shadow material erupted from my subconscious for me to look at. I got to see the truth of how

I had been showing up over the past decade of my life—a truth I had been in complete denial of.

It took a few years to penetrate, heal, learn, and rewire what was underneath that behavior. There was scarcity, fear, lack of trust, undeservedness, rejection, not-enoughness, and feeling undesirable. I had to face all the things I was using self-help to avoid. I had to feel vulnerable, exposed, and intimate—which was terrifying. I got to see how I was objectifying everything around me, including women, clients, and myself.

It felt awful taking accountability for all of that. It sucked, but it was necessary. Without seeing and owning these behaviors, I would have remained a victim to them and created suffering for others and myself.

This 'mirror' was held up to me in order to see an accurate reflection of myself. I got to see the truth of how I had embodied and presented myself in the world, which looked starkly different than how I imagined. This mirror helped me see past my denial, delusions, and fantasies of myself that shrouded the reality of who I actually was being. I was exposed—all this 'bad' stuff about me was available for everyone to see. The persona I was using to cover-up the lies I believed about myself was revealed. I had put a 'nice person' mask on to hide my subconscious narcissism because I judged it, which itself resulted from a bunch of stories and ideas that weren't true.

What I saw in my reflection was not the Truth, but my distortions. By penetrating these distortions, I was able to see everything I believed about myself that led to narcissistic behavior. I saw the stories, traumas, and judgments that validated my distorted reflection, but more importantly, I realized they were not real. My reason for being narcissistic was based on a lie. The illusion dissolved, and I saw who-I-really-was, collapsing the mythology that enabled the narcissism.

The difference in me after these few years was tangible. You can even see the change in my face in photos before and after this process. Looking back, I can see it plain-as-day in my smug mug, but I had no idea while I was in it. Without a group of people that loved me enough to tell me the truth, and a commitment to make truth the most important thing, I would have stayed stuck until the end of days.

I'm not here to tell you if you or anyone you know is a narcissist or not. These concepts are not based on psychiatric definitions or stereotypes. This is not a clinical diagnosis. Rather, I am sharing non-traditional revelations on narcissism that will help you see where you or those you know may fall into this trap. The behaviors I will mention aren't all *inherently* narcissistic. Things like wanting to be alone, taking care of ourselves, having few friends, or being self-reliant aren't themselves narcissistic. It's what's *underneath* the behaviors and attitudes that determine the pathology. Everything is contextual, and I'm purposefully painting a picture with broad strokes to illustrate my point.

LOVING OUR IMAGE

The following paragraph from Alexander Lowen, M.D.'s book, *Narcissism*, offers a perspective about narcissism which allowed me to relate to the term much easier:

> *"Narcissists do show a lack of concern for others, but they are equally insensitive to their own true needs. Often their behavior is self-destructive. Moreover, when we speak of narcissists' 'self' love, we need to make a distinction. Narcissism denotes investment in one's image as opposed to one's self. Narcissists love their image, not their real self. They have a poor sense of self; they are not self-directed. Instead, their activities are directed toward the enhancement of their image, often at the expense of the self."*

Narcissism is the denial of our Truth in exchange for a lie. It is an act of self-betrayal in exchange for a fantasy. It is the rejection of Beauty in exchange for a fixation of lust. It is not a self-obsession; it's an *image-obsession*. What the narcissist fixates upon is their *narcissistic image* (a persona).

Narcissists don't actually love themselves—they are in love with their *image*. What we're often doing in self-help is improving our image. This is because, fundamentally, our True Self is not 'improvable.' It (who-we-really-are) is not broken, lacking, or bad. Nevertheless, we are addicted to suffering and think that fixing and improving will alleviate us. We don't love and accept ourselves, so instead, we put all our love into our image—investing in our "self" trying to make it "better." We judge all of the things that make us real, human, and beautiful—and become obsessed with something less real, less genuine, and less whole. We deny who-we-really-are in an attempt to construct a simulated avatar that's 'better than us' to live through. We invest all this effort into 'working on it,' thinking that something more than ourselves will make others accept and approve of us. We hope that filtering the flaws out and presenting only the highlight-reel will somehow 'trick' people into loving us.

But it never does. It can't. It is only self-betrayal.

It is self-betrayal when we make this work about building a better persona instead of being a more real us. Self-help becomes self-abuse when we use it to bypass and avoid life, our shadow, and our divinity. The perversion occurs when we use the healing arts to stay stuck. We can grow and heal from a place of purification and unconditional love, or we can do it from a place of judgment and rejection. We can use spirituality to find Truth or use it to make up our own distorted 'truth' and live there alone. Like any tool, self-improvement work can be used to help or hinder—but unlike other tools, the guise of 'improvement' and 'help' cloaks our self-deceit. When any of this work leads to more suffering, we have distorted its purpose.

Doing personal development work isn't "bad" or "wrong." Many of us need to start with all of the improving because anything that brings us out of depression, pain, or suffering is helpful. These approaches serve us for a time, and like training wheels, they then become what holds us back. We end up trapped behind a distorted idea of "being broken and improving our image." These approaches got you here, but they won't be able to get you *there*—to your True Self. That's because your egoic image is an illusion, and nothing unreal is truly lovable.

BEING UNLOVABLE

That's what we secretly want, though, isn't it? *To be unlovable?* Why else would we continue down a path that only validates our stories of suffering? Why else would we keep doing the things that proved there's something wrong with us? We believe we are broken, not enough, undeserving, inadequate, undesirable, lacking, flawed—that, in totality, we are unlovable. We embark on a never-ending quest to fix and improve ourselves until we're perfect, remaining unlovable until perfection is reached. But it's unreachable, and at the deepest level, we know it's a futile quest.

That's why we never stop—it's not an impulse towards being lovable, but towards being *unlovable*. We never stop 'working on ourselves' because we are addicted to being unlovable. If we were to stop and accept ourselves fully, it would mean that we were lovable exactly how we are—and that terrifies us.

We think, "All these horrible, painful, flawed, shadowy, bad things about me are lovable too? Yeah, no thanks." And so we build a narcissistic image as a stand-in to hide behind. We don't want to think we are enough as-is because our images would be invalidated—and we don't want to invalidate what we are in love with because it means their destruction.

We feel like it's never enough—and it's not. Our narcissistic image *isn't* enough. It *isn't* worthy. It *isn't* lovable. It never will be, no matter how much we improve it. But we are not this image. When we feel attacked, defensive, and threatened, it is the illusion of our persona that is threatened, not us. I know it may feel this way when you are identified with it, but I am not trying to take away who you are—it's who you are *not* that needs to go. The confusion between these two is what makes us cling to our image and suffer. This image is what Narcissus fell in love with—and ultimately drowned in. It wasn't another person or even himself, but rather, a vapid reflection.

Giving up the addiction, dropping the image, and allowing ourselves to be unconditionally lovable feels like death. The narcissistic behavior is the ego protecting itself against love and death—and it *is*

83

death. The death of the lie, the addiction, the suffering, the persona, the isolation. In order for who-we-really-are to have a life the narcissistic image must die.

Underneath that image is the real you, your True Self. And *that you* is lovable.

Speaking to that you, not your persona: You are lovable. You are lovable without having to prove anything. You are lovable without 'dancing for your dinner' (having to 'earn it' or by 'selling yourself out'). You are lovable without having to do or be for anyone else. Your lovability is innate.

MEETING OUR OWN NEEDS

"Why rely on someone else if I can do it myself?"

Anyone who's been in business or leadership knows the dangers of this statement. We simply cannot do everything ourselves, and if we try, we quickly become overwhelmed, stressed, and scattered. We become the bottleneck in our business and stunt its growth. We think this way because we make delegating mean something: a loss of control, inadequacy, more management, or scarcity. It is not true: delegation is really freedom and wealth.

When it comes to meeting our own needs, this thinking is equally limiting. We think we're being independent, self-reliant, and strong. We act like we don't need anyone to love us, care for us, touch us, nurture us, help us, protect us, or witness us. It can be that in the worst of times, this attitude helps us stay alive. Yet, when this becomes our modus operandi in the world—coming from pain, fear, resentment, betrayal, and abandonment—it is an arrogant, stubborn act. We wear our burden like a badge of honor as if somehow we're more respectable if we are less human, less helpable.

But the only thing we're wearing is armor. Our only reward is loneliness.

"Love is our true destiny.
We do not find the meaning
of life by ourselves alone
we find it with another."
— *Thomas Merton*

Due to the pride surrounding this behavior, it can be tricky to see, let alone admit. Here are some common phrases that *may* allude to this behavior:

- "I don't need love from anyone else. I can love myself."
- "People always let me down. If I only depend on myself, that won't happen."
- "I know how to do everything, so why would I hire someone?"
- "I am good at introspection; I don't need anyone's input."
- "I am an introvert. I don't like people."
- "I'm strong, and I'm a survivor. I don't need anybody."
- "People lie and cheat. I don't let anyone close to me."
- "Only I can know what feels good. Men are clueless; I'll pleasure myself."
- "Women are crazy, I will never understand them, and don't need the drama anyway."
- "I don't need a man."
- "If you want it done right, you gotta do it yourself."
- "I'm bad at receiving."
- "Nobody cares about me."

Are you surprised at how often you've heard these phrases? People say them all the time. They will use pride to shield themselves from both others and their own pain. It's a coping mechanism, not a superpower. What we're doing with this behavior is trying to meet all of our own needs. This is narcissistic.

"Wait, I thought we're supposed to take responsibility and not be codependent? Now you're saying it's bad to take care of ourselves and not need anyone?!"

It is right and good to be happy by oneself. If we cannot make ourselves happy, how can we expect anyone else to? This is not about making someone else responsible for our happiness or do the work for us, nor is it about having someone 'complete us.' We are whole, complete, and sovereign—and still, we are also humans that depend on other humans for many things. Being self-sufficient doesn't mean we never need help. Being independent doesn't mean we have to do it alone. **We can be *interdependent* without being *codependent*.**

The self-righteous independence displayed in the above list is often a reaction-formation to trauma or unpleasant experiences. We've been disappointed, betrayed, let down, hurt, rejected, abandoned, heartbroken, and humiliated. We are left feeling resentful, fearful, and in pain. We no longer feel safe, nor can we trust others or our judgment of them.

"Never again!" we proclaim as we protect ourselves.

It's a logical response. Even *without* some sort of trauma, it's hard enough letting ourselves have needs and asking others to meet them.

Sometimes our choice to meet all our own needs comes from an avoidance of feeling needy. We may have previously been codependent, needy, clingy, or desperate in the past, and after a lot of work, we overcame those traumas and stories. Or, we've been with someone who was like this in the past and remember how gross it can feel. Or, we could have been neglected in the past and feel we don't deserve to have our needs met. Thus, when we arrive at a feeling of reliance, dependence, surrender, allowance, asking, and needing—it reminds us of our prior insecurities or experiences, which we want to stay away from.

This is what I did.

Anything that reminded me of being a teenager and being needy, desperate, and rejected was something to avoid. Any experience that reminded me of being in scarcity or poor, I'd be afraid it meant I was slipping back into destitution. So I tried to find ways to get my needs met without needing them. *Yes, it was insane as it sounds.* I did this because 'needing' felt like lack, and I didn't want to feel that again. But getting our needs met is the only way to be in abundance—again, it's the opposite of what we think. There is something deeper at play, which we will explore in the later chapter, "When Wrong Works."

I still catch myself going into justification with myself and others, trying to defend why I should be able to have what I need. Have you ever done that? Have you ever, at some level, felt guilty and started to explain why you should have even your most essential needs met? That's a story about something that isn't true. When we feel undeserving, we feel compelled to justify our needs. But we don't need to justify or explain our needs! There is no explanation required for requiring basic necessities, love, touch, intimacy, safety, and respect. There is no manipulation, convincing, prostitution, abandonment, negotiating, or justification necessary. They are universal; there is no need for shame or guilt whatsoever. If we experience these feelings, we must know they are not based on genuine needs but our distorted stories.

We are allowed to have our needs met or ask others to acknowledge them. We are not entitled to anyone meeting our needs, but we are entitled to our boundaries and standards.

The meanings we give to 'needing' creates unnecessary duality. We can have needs without being needy. We can ask for what we want without desperation. We can be vulnerable without being a weakling. We can be supported because we're doing something so much bigger than ourselves, not because we're pathetic and incompetent. We receive easily not because we are lacking, but because we are grateful and loved. We can ask for advice because we are brave enough to try something we've never done, not because we're idiots. Having needs is not a weakness; it's needed to live.

LETTING OTHERS HELP

What does 'needing' have to do with narcissism? We have distorted what receiving means and made it all about us. Again, we've got it backward. **Letting others help you is not about you.** Allowing people in to meet your needs is also about them and their sense of purpose, joy, gratitude, intimacy, expression, and love. People want to be generous and feel like they're useful—contributing and making a difference in your life. When you shut people out, deny, reject, dismiss, or close-off from this, you are making it all about you.

You know the wonderful feeling you get when you give someone a gift, and they light up with delight? It's wonderful, right? It feels joyous to give someone a gift. You *both* feel grateful and pleased. Well, how do you think *they* feel when you dismiss, downplay, or decline *their gift* to you? Do you not think they want to feel likewise when giving to you? You are robbing them of the same joy of giving. They may even feel rejected, despite your kind decline. Neither person experiences gratitude. Now replace "gift" with love, gratitude, compliments, or money.

We don't realize how selfish trying to not be selfish can be.

When you don't let others in, and you try to meet all your own needs, you are robbing people of the gift of helping you. You think you're being humble, protective, smart, safe, or whatever—but you're actually self-absorbed in your own suffering, insecurities, and judgments—unwilling to share the beauty of your vulnerability with others. We don't see it this way when we do it, but it's a complete avoidance of intimacy. It is arrogant, self-centered, and cowardly. It is false pride and fake humility.

We are shut-off from the resources of others when we live from this place. We don't let people in, so wherever we find a gap in our needs, we fill it ourselves. Any leak of data to those around us about our needs or vulnerabilities, we plug up. Where is there room for anyone else in that? There isn't. How can there be any intimacy? There can't. It's an isolated world where "me, myself, and I" are taking care of each other.

This is what makes it narcissistic.

Our values are skewed towards fear when we move through life this way. We wind up valuing perfection more than allowing someone to learn from their mistakes, valuing isolation over the unpredictability of human connection, valuing protection over the pleasure and affection of touch, and valuing rejection over the vulnerability of intimacy. Sure this whole game 'works,' keeping us 'safe' or 'unhurt' to a point—but ultimately, it only leads to more suffering.

SELF-CONSUMED

When we are caught up in our self—such as our insecurities, our negative emotions, our problems, our stories—we are so inwardly focused on our own issues that we often forget there are other people in our lives. The clients, customers, friends, and strangers who are *real* people, with *real* feelings and *real* lives. We get so consumed with our suffering and struggling that we make everything about us and dissociate from the world. These things become numbers and metrics on the way to our goal.

Your actions affect other people. What you do is not only about how *you* feel but the impact you have on *others*. This is not about worrying what other people think of you but being completely aware of your impact on the space. It's about getting out of your head and into the world. Not only do we need self-awareness, but we need *other-awareness* too. This is an awareness of others and the environment around us. How do they feel, what are they thinking? What needs do they have? How is our presence affecting them? How are we relating to each other? Is it through our trauma, stories, manipulations, or through truth, joy, and play?

We do this through *presence*, not heady analysis or compulsive asking. Become aware of how you relate to the space around you and how it relates to you.

Pay attention to:

How your presence influences other people's thoughts and emotions; how you treat and interact with objects in the environment; how you orient and move through the material world; what your relationship is with the walls, floor, ceiling, tables, chairs, doors, windows, trees, grass, roads, etc.; how you leave the space once you're done, and how others do.

Ask yourself:

Is your world safe, or is it conspiring against you? Do the people in the room light up or ignore you when you enter? Do people remember your presence ten years later, or are you forgettable? Do you leave a trail of chaos in your wake or peace? Does your place feel fit for a king and queen, or do you not even pay attention to how people will feel when they arrive at your home?

These can all be boiled down to these questions: **does the space around you feel supportive, or does it feel threatening? Do you feel like you are a part of the space or separate from it?**

This answer alone may tell you everything you need to know about why you're still stuck. We will explore this further in the later chapter, "Your Life Is Not About You."

AN EXAMPLE

Let's say Bob acts out and disrespects someone, and they feel hurt. The other person enforces their boundaries, calling him out on the misbehavior. Bob then feels guilty and bad about what he did. Bob starts crying. He begins to indulge in his stories about messing up like this many times before and how he can't ever do anything right or make anyone happy. Bob feels even worse, creating a dramatic scene, apologizing profusely. He continues down this downward spiral, self-consumed with emotional reactivity. The other person then helps Bob with what he is going through, which then becomes the focus.

Here are some of the narcissistic dynamics at work:

1. The other person was the one who was wronged and felt hurt by Bob, but then Bob made the entire thing about himself. Now all the attention is on Bob and his story of how 'bad and worthless' he is.
2. Bob is competing with the pain of the other person, creating drama for attention.
3. Bob's guilt has manipulated the other person out of *their* pain and what *they* were feeling (due to Bob's initial behavior) and into the suffering of Bob.
4. Bob has no room left to feel, support, or empathize with the other person he hurt because he is self-consumed with his own issues.

5. Bob's profuse apologizing becomes a way to not be held accountable to stop the behavior, as it is almost guaranteed to happen again. Bob knows it's a repeat of his past, hence all the guilt.

6. The other person may even feel guilty themselves, thinking that *they* made Bob upset. This is how an abuser *transfers* it to their victim. It's an easy-out for Bob to avoid feeling his initial guilt and taking true accountability. If the other person is codependent, they may try to 'rescue' Bob from his pain while ignoring their own. This is a destructive game.

When we get this wrapped up in fixing ourselves and our problems and are so consumed with how bad we feel—to the point of making everything that happens about us or taking it personally—we are being narcissistic. When we are in overdrive dealing with internal noise, we have no bandwidth to feel into another and see how they are doing. When we are in survival mode, trauma response, or feeling scarce, we revert to self-preservation. We cannot actualize or be of service from this place. Our self-generated noise blocks our empathy for others in that moment.

This narcissistic cut-off is another way we avoid feeling.

When you read something like "Bob manipulated" or "Bob abused," it could be either that he did it consciously, or it was an unconscious behavior.

We're not always doing these behaviors on purpose—nor are we always innocent, as you'll discover in the upcoming chapter, "The Victim Trap." We often have layer after layer of distortions that obfuscate the reality of our intentions. Most of us don't realize this is what's actually happening, let alone readily acknowledge it. We don't consider these things manipulation, codependency, or abuse, but much of the time, that's what they are. Yet, at some level, we know what we're doing—even if we hide it from ourselves.

NARCISSISTIC SUPPLY
& OBJECTIFICATION

There is a difference between being worried about what other people think about us and caring about how we affect those around us. The first is taking others' perceptions personally, giving it meaning, and making it about us. We are narcissistically concerned about our image. The second is empathy and connection, where we take responsibility for how we show up in the world and affect others.

To the narcissist, it's as if there's no other person in the space but him. He doesn't feel a part of the space and thus has separated himself and objectified it. What were once other real people are now *objects*. People become objects because objects don't have needs or feelings, which the narcissist would otherwise have to consider because, unlike a sociopath, he *is* able to feel. As he seeks to fulfill his needs, the narcissist doesn't find much use for a person as an actual person because he is unable to empathize, relate, or be intimate with them. But an *object* can be used: they serve their user, giving them purpose. Everything in the now objectified space is classified as either 'useful' or 'not useful.'

The narcissist does not actually let others meet his needs: he uses other people to fulfill his own needs.

This is one of the ways this behavior is covert and deceptive. The narcissist still has other people in his life to fulfill his needs, but *they* aren't the ones to fulfill them—he is. He objectifies others and uses them as *'narcissistic supply'* to meet his own needs and reinforce his image. This includes using others to suffer and abuse himself (like Bob did). To maintain control, nobody else can help him. Instead, he uses others to help and hurt himself.

The narcissist *appears* to be letting others help him, but they are merely another *thing* between him and what he wants. They leave their interactions with him feeling *less* rather than *greater*. There is a confusion, emptiness, or feeling of being taken-from after helping a narcissist, rather than a feeling of joy, gratitude, contribution, and fulfillment one would generally feel. This is because the other person is the *supply* for what the narcissist thinks he needs. Deep down, he longs for others' unconditional love but will only trust himself to take it conditionally.

This narcissistic abuse can be seen in the following examples:

- A parent who uses or forces their child to live out their own fantasies: such as determining the child's career, steering them with shame and guilt or financial control.
- A parent who sees their child as a source (supply) of entertainment, validation, or affection: making their child do things like dance, act, perform, say sweet things, or give affection—while withholding basic needs, love, affection, and approval from the child unless they perform.
- A speaker who uses their audience to validate themselves: There is no intimacy with the audience because to him, they are not people, but objects. He uses the 'metrics' of his audience to enhance or diminish his self-image.
- A partner who demands the other to be their source of happiness: "Don't you want to make me happy?" or "Entertain me!" withholding sex, love, affection, or money until they get it.
- A person who sees their partner as a 'trophy': The classic 'trophy wife' (or similar) who is primarily there to supply money, attention, validation, or status.
- The philanthropist who donates for their own gain: The money isn't about helping people in need, but feeling good about themselves for giving, achieving status, or pretending like it's not only for a tax break. Volunteering can be used in the same way.

Everything relates back to the narcissist, even his helping of others.

"The most loving parents
and relatives commit murder
with smiles on their faces.
They force us to destroy
the person we really are:
a subtle kind of murder."
— Jim Morrison

The world revolves around him. He is constantly justifying his cut-off by asking, "What does that have to do with me? How is that my problem? What's in for me? Why should I care?" Even if the narcissist obliges, there is not a sense of grace or joy, but martyrdom or resentment. He has an agenda, an ulterior motive, because he is expecting something for himself but being dishonest about his needs. All of this reinforces the story that people merely want something from him—a projection based on how *he* uses others—solidifying the desire to be isolated further. It is a self-contained, self-created, self-governed, and self-consuming world—and he wants it this way.

How can you feel disappointed if you don't depend on anyone?
How can you be screwed over or blamed if you do it all yourself?
How can you feel betrayed if you don't have to trust anyone?
How can you be abandoned if you don't let anyone in?
How can you be rejected, hurt, or attacked if you're not vulnerable?

The world of the narcissist is a world of protection, not intimacy. It is one of having to take, not of trusting that it will be provided. It is a world where only he can meet his own needs, yet they're never able to be fully met. It is one of fear, not of faith in something greater than himself. Narcissism is truly an insane barter between suffering and suffering: the hurt 'from others' and the pain 'without others.' The narcissist chooses between the lesser of two evils, picking isolation as the better of the two, simply because it makes him feel in *control*. Again, it's another form of suffering.

The remedy to this calls for *absolute surrender and faith.* It is the antidote to a toxic ego. Sadly, it's a pill few are ready to swallow. To the narcissist, *more* trust hardly seems like a better option. It feels more dangerous, irrational, stupid, and vulnerable. Even the upsides are no longer enticing, realistic, or important due to his past hurt. Most people don't want to stop protecting themselves from what they perceive as danger, even if that protection is what's causing them suffering.

This constant justification and denial make it hard for people to admit, want, and seek help. Now you see why narcissistic behavior is one of the top causes of being stuck!

CONCLUSION

You may still be stuck because you are dealing with someone like this, or you may unknowingly be doing some of these things yourself like I was. Self-help is the perfect breeding ground for narcissistic behaviors for reasons I've already made apparent. If we get too self-consumed with our own struggles, we may find ourselves on a slippery slope towards some of these behaviors without realizing it.

If you see yourself in these words, it doesn't mean you *are* a narcissist. Feel whatever you genuinely feel, and have compassion without making it mean anything. I've done everything I write about in this book—it doesn't make me a bad person, nor does it make you or whomever you know bad. We don't know until we know.

You *can* beat yourself and others up and use this information to suffer more if that's what you want. *Or,* you can use it to free yourself and others.

I understand this topic may be heavy and particularly confront-ing—and it's also essential if you are sincere in waking up. I remember how eye-opening and freeing it was to see these things in my behavior, as I hope it will be for you, too. Now you can be aware of these behav-iors in yourself and others.

If you are ready to try something new, I invite you to:

- Surrender, not defend.
  Example: When you feel like someone is making you wrong, listen instead of fighting back.
- Be intimate instead of isolated.
  Example: Work with clients one-on-one or in small groups in person, rather than virtually from your house or on a stage.
- Be vulnerable instead of comfortable.
  Example: Join a group or club doing something you are completely clueless about rather than sticking to what you excel at.
- Choose Truth instead of illusion.
  Example: Ask for feedback from past partners rather than assume you were the perfect lover.
- Trust instead of seeking protection.
  Example: Share your ideas openly rather than squirreling them away or forcing your friends to sign nondisclosure agreements to talk.
- Let others in, all the way, completely.
  Example: Tell your partner your greatest fears, insecurities, and weaknesses.
- Give without attachment, agenda, or control.
  Example: Gift one of your pieces of art to a stranger without having to publicize it or look for recognition or thanks.

These are simple everyday examples. You can take these invitations and go much deeper. There are no shoulds or shouldn'ts, musts or mustn'ts. *You* get to decide if you'd rather keep your persona or let yourself embody and fully express who-you-really-are. 🐝

The Spiritual Path
Is Failing You

"Life has no meaning. Each of us has meaning
and we bring it to life. It is a waste to be asking
the question when you are the answer."

— Joseph Campbell

re you suffering? Perhaps you're seriously struggling in life or are facing tragic circumstances. Maybe you've been stuck for a long time, and it is ruining your life. To that, it may be easy for you to say, "Yes, I am suffering." But what if you're making great money, you have a good relationship, and are in good health? If your family is safe, business is running smooth, and you're living in a beautiful home? Could it be that you, too, are suffering? What if you were to dig deeper than worldly success and happiness—much deeper. Are you suffering and not even realizing it?

When people hear the word "suffering," most tend to imagine something tragic and terrible. They think of great physical pain, emotional trauma, or mental anguish. They relate it to profound loss, depression, poverty, despair, tragedy, or disease. It's something so severe the pain is palpable: we can see when someone is suffering because they're going through something horrific. They lost their home to a fire, a family member died, they got into an accident, they lived through war, they were cheated on, they're homeless, or whatever else our society deems "a terrible thing." All of those events are painful; unquestionably they hurt. We will all experience our own tragedies—there is no avoiding that.

From this perspective, it's apparent why when we hear the famous quote from Buddha, "All life is suffering," it may sound bleak or depressing. Some relate as cynics and say, "Yeah, life sucks." Others reject it and say, "That's so pessimistic." However, both of these approaches are incomplete and biased on the wrong side of 'cause.' Buddha did not say, "Life *causes* you to suffer, the end, you're forever stuck."

Consider the following questions: Can we experience the great tragedies of life without using them to suffer needlessly? Must we suffer when tragedy hits, or is that part optional? Is suffering equivalent to pain and being hurt? Can we move through the world in a way where we no longer suffer? Is there anyone who has experienced great tragedy and pain who has not used it to suffer?

Pain itself is not suffering. Tragedy itself is not suffering. Getting sick itself is not suffering. There are veterans, cancer patients, trauma victims, prisoners of war, and disabled persons who have not used their circumstances to suffer. They may have endured great hardships, pain, and sufferable conditions—but they refused to use it as a reason to *suffer*. If those who have faced tragedy don't *have* to suffer, this shows us suffering is not forever inevitable. Many people suffer despite not facing great tragedy, circumstance, or pain, revealing that tragedy is not a requirement for suffering.

This all leads us to a pivotal understanding of what the Buddha meant. Its premise that, when fully grasped, will lead to your liberation. It is this: **Pain is unavoidable, yet suffering is optional, with or without it.**

> "Everything can be taken from a man but one thing:
> the last of the human freedoms—to choose one's
> attitude in any given set of circumstances, to choose
> one's own way."
> — *Viktor E. Frankl, Man's Search for Meaning*

WHAT IT MEANS TO SUFFER

There is the feeling (the pain, hurt), and there is the reality of what actually happened—that's it. Everything else we do *around it* is the suffering. We think that it's the great tragedies we face and the pain we encounter that cause our suffering—but they don't. They are terrible, awful, and undesirable. They are an unavoidable source of anguish. Yet, it's not for these reasons alone that we suffer.

Suffering isn't the pain, hurt, or heartbreak itself—it's bitterness, numbness, dissociation, fear, and anger. Suffering isn't the loss itself; it's the pain from the attachment and the meaning we associate with it. Suffering isn't the failure or rejection itself; it's the pain from the story we create about it and continue telling ourselves. Suffering isn't the reality of our situation; it's the fantasy we build around it to avoid facing the truth. Suffering isn't the tragedy itself; it's the drama, noise, and hysteria we create about it.

When we are in the midst of the pain of being stuck, it is more than the situation that takes us out of joy and peace. Suffering includes the addictions and choices against who-we-really-are that lead up to pain (before). Suffering includes the pain we indulge in, the anger that erupts, and the escalation we partake in during the pain (during). Suffering includes the meanings we give it, the stories we create, the reaction-formations we take, the feelings we numb, the resentment that we build, and how we use it to define us (after).

This is how we suffer.

HOW WE SUFFER

Let's take a look at the practical ways we do this in daily life. We suffer when we:

- Don't let ourselves have what we want or need
- Compare ourselves to others
- Judge anything or anyone, especially ourselves

99

- Put something (time, money, people) between us and joy
- Try to fit in or are incongruent with who-we-really-are
- Seek specialness or superiority
- Are addicted to anything, even "positive" things
- Avoid life and reality, avoid responsibility and accountability
- Feel sorry for ourselves or look for pity to continue our stucky story
- Achieve or acquire what we desire by betraying our True Self
- Avoid, reject, or repress feeling
- React to, or take personally, criticisms or compliments
- Get defensive, attack, seek revenge or justice, or refuse forgiveness
- Withhold love, our gifts, authentic expression, and the truth
- Manipulate or act dishonestly to get what we want, or our needs met
- Resist what-is and refuse to accept what's real
- Abandon, martyr, or punish ourselves and others
- Explain, justify, convince, rationalize, defend, or lie
- Try to fix and improve ourselves while denying our True Self
- Seek validation, approval, or acceptance by self-abandonment or self-betrayal
- Protect ourselves from intimacy, love, connection, vulnerability, or being seen
- Put a mask, facade, or persona on, or live through a narcissistic image
- Go against or reject the natural order and flow of the universe
- Seek perfection and are afraid of messing up
- Desire and long for things
- Give meaning to things that aren't real
- Hold on to, become attached to, or cling to any outcome, thing, time, or person

These are a few of the ways we suffer—there are many more.

These seemingly insignificant acts of suffering form the underlying currents that influence your choices, results, and responses to life. None of the items listed may look catastrophic. Few of them seem like they'd ruin your day, let alone your life. Yet, allow a tiny crack in your hull while in the harbor, and in enough time, you will have a leak: sinking your ship while far out in the ocean. **It's not the first annoyance where resentment is seen, but it is the foundation whereupon resentment is built.**

You may overlook the suffering when you choose to close off from love at that moment, but over the next ten, twenty, forty, sixty years of a hardening heart—you will be destroyed by it. You may overlook the suffering when you choose to see yourself as a failure, but over the next five-hundred ideas you want to attempt but decide against—you will be impoverished by it. You may overlook the suffering when you choose to stop playing your instrument because it's not a realistic career path—but on your deathbed after a life working a job you didn't care about, you will be consumed with the regret of it. That one choice of self-betrayal, that one belief about who you are, that one choice to not share your gift—these choices will cause you more suffering than any individual circumstance.

Do you see yourself doing any of this? Take a moment and see the ways you suffer without even realizing it. It may not be apparent at first, so take as long as you need to. Your ability to get unstuck and wake up depends on your willingness to see how you choose to suffer, both consciously and subconsciously. Once you see how you're suffering, consider what would happen if you stopped? What would you do with your life without your suffering? How are you using your suffering to justify staying stuck?

The behaviors in this list do not cause us suffering because of their associated physical, mental, or emotional pain. The secret to understanding why these are detrimental to your joy, beauty, and peace is this: all of these choices are a denial of the Truth and of your True Self. *That* is why you suffer. Not because of pain or being hurt, but because you deny who-you-really-are.

POSITIVELY SUFFERING

As counter-intuitive as it sounds, we can suffer even if we do what's considered "positive." Positive stories, positive meanings, positive desires—all of this is still suffering. Yes, you read that correctly. It does not matter what the quality of a story is: a story is not real. It doesn't matter what quality a meaning has: it's not true. It doesn't matter what status you desire or if you achieve it or not, as either outcome still validates the lie that you need to prove yourself. It does not matter what the quality of your suffering is or if it has a valid justification: it's still suffering.

The ideas of positive psychology tell us to be more optimistic and focus on the good, which is undisputedly better than being oriented negatively or pessimistically. I do not argue that; we know that we get what we focus on. However, many people who apply these concepts wind up suffering further, knowingly or unknowingly. Why is that? Instead of stopping the negativity, they sugarcoat and continue denying reality. It happens like this: they first deny reality by giving it an untrue negative meaning, they then deny that distortion with a positive meaning, and then create a new happy story to encompass it all. Unfortunately, none of it is real—not the negativity *nor* the positivity. It's merely noise replaced with better noise. It's a bastard child of the "Equation for Suffering."

You cannot turn suffering positive in order to arrive at peace— you can only find peace by stopping suffering.

One of the ego's tricks is to get us on a path of seeking happiness. It says to us, "Look, you're in pain and unsatisfied. Why don't you look for ways to be happier?" But what the ego provides us is superficial. Does it provide us with pleasure, happiness, and ease from our pains? Yes, it does—but we confuse distractions, escapism, and momentary happiness and pleasure with the cessation of suffering. What we see out in the world that we think will resolve our suffering will only reinforce it. By obtaining the sex, the toy, the approval, the outfit, the money, or the status which the ego says will complete us and make us happy—we only further validate the lie that we are not enough.

Even if it does make us happy, we cling to that happiness and are sad when it leaves us moments later. The ego handles this by promising that "just one more thing" will bring us to peace and fulfillment. This happiness-seeking will always fall short because we are chasing a *state*. The ego equates 'happiness' with 'the antidote to suffering,' which is terribly flawed. The antidote to a life of suffering is not trying to be happy 24/7. Happiness is temporary, and our attachment to something ephemeral will eventually lead to suffering. It's why making happiness our goal in life often leads to narcissism, misery, and a meaningless life. We can't be happy all the time, and we wouldn't want to even if we could.

"You will never be happy if you continue to search for ✖
*what happiness consists of. You will never live if you
are looking for the meaning of life."*
— *Albert Camus*

Instead of seeking happiness, we want to choose joy. Joy is eternal and comes from within—it cannot be obtained outside of us, nor can it be lost to time. There is peace in joy, and joy in peace, and neither requires suffering, seeking, or getting unstuck.

You cannot suffer your way to joy. You must enjoy yourself to joy.

THE FEAR OF ACCEPTANCE & CONTENTMENT

This book is about getting unstuck, which means ending your suffering. 'Stuck' is really just another word for 'suffering.' Once we stop suffering, no matter if our circumstances have changed or not, we are no longer stuck. Recall from the first chapter that 'being stuck' is a story. It's a meaning we're giving. We established that it's not about telling better stories or giving them positive meanings, but stopping them altogether. Once we stop making our situation mean we're stuck we can start moving forward. We accept what-is without having to give it an improved meaning or fight against it. This resistance to what-is and our attachment to meaning is at the heart of our struggle with suffering. The way out is through surrender and acceptance.

"But if I surrender and accept the situation, or if I stop suffering, won't I still be stuck? I want to move forward and change, not accept what-is."

We may be afraid that stopping our suffering will stop our reason and motivation to get unstuck. We are afraid that if we no longer have our suffering, we can no longer use it to justify our choices. We use our suffering and our stories to avoid taking responsibility and being accountable for our actions. We give our power away to our suffering to avoid taking ownership of the fact that it was us who chose to suffer—a choice made consciously or not. Our suffering becomes what we use to suffer. We create an inescapable cycle of suffering and justification. It's the "Equation for Suffering" at play once again. We are trying to suffer our way out of being stuck. It doesn't work.

> "If you try to change it, you will ruin it.
> Try to hold it, and you will lose it."
> — Lao Tzu, Tao Te Ching

All of this is due to a misunderstanding of what 'acceptance' is. Accepting is not settling, defeat, or unchanging. In reality, it's the opposite: acceptance is the only way we can handle change. Everything is changing, always. Fighting the changing nature of the universe is futile. When we resist this change, that's when *we* stop changing. Ergo, being stuck and suffering can only occur when we do not accept what-is. The only way we can change *is* to accept what-is. When we accept, we stop our internal and external resistance towards reality, not creating an invitation for more of it. When we stop resisting what we *don't* want, we are also ending the resistance to what we *do* want. When we open up, our life opens up. It's the opposite of what we fear. When we fight, resist, and reject what-is and go out into the world from that place—we are met with struggle, resistance, and rejection.

What we resist, persists

When we fight the universe, it fights us. When we yield to the universe, it yields to us. When we accept ourselves as-is, we accept the universe as-is. When we accept what-is, we have peace.

Don't seek for a later peace; accept the not-peace now, and you will have peace. Your unwillingness to accept what-is now and the resistance to reality is what creates your suffering. It's this suffering that keeps what you desire away from you. You cannot find joy by seeking happiness. Seeking happiness leads to, and is based upon, suffering. Why? Because it's projected onto a later date. You suffer *now* because you're waiting for a happy *later*. This is not hoping—this is suffering. You must choose to be joyous now if you're ever to be joyful! When we put obstacles, such as time or money, in between us and our peace, we are choosing to suffer. We won't let ourselves have it *now* because of some story and justification about why we can't have it now. We place our joy, love, and peace at a distance, forever putting off what is here already.

Practically, this all means that we make it impossible for us to ever have what we want or stop our suffering.

THE SPIRITUAL PATH

We know that ending our suffering is not impossible, and many people further seek to end their suffering with more seeking. One way humanity attempts to relieve their suffering is by embarking on 'the spiritual path.' This could be one of the traditional quests towards enlightenment, nirvana, ascension, or heaven. It could be fervent personal development and self-help. It could be stoicism, intellectualism, or militant environmentalism. It could even be scientism or technological transhumanism. We may begin with good intentions, but sometimes things go astray. The path becomes a spiritualization of our suffering, rather than the cessation of it. We want to 'beat' our ego. We want to 'eliminate' our shadow. We think that if only we could permanently remove all dark, evil things about us or the world, then everything would be wonderful for everyone.

Mythologically, we are seeking to get back to the time when we were in 'The Garden of Eden.' We are trying to go back to ignorance and its proverbial bliss. We want to go back to paradise and irresponsibility. We want to leave the planes of suffering and return. But we can't. We have already experienced good and evil—there is no undoing that. Trying to 'get back' to anything only leads to suffering. Now is all there is. There is no 'back.' Those attached to the utopian ideals are trapped in this dynamic.

While there is no going back to ignorance, we can move forward to reclaim our *innocence*. We can let go of the stories, illusions, meanings, judgments, and justifications that keep us from Truth and bound to suffering. We can arrive to the eternal now and find peace in the stillness and silence. We can see past duality and "be one with the Father," which brings us to "the kingdom of God within us and on Earth." Unfortunately, the practical process of this has been perverted and distorted. Rather than a reclamation of innocence and a cessation of suffering through responsibility and choice, it becomes a game for greater power or a way to escape.

Often, but not always, these 'spiritual paths' are used to justify a story about becoming superior to the human experience, rather than a full expression in and of it. We are already out of touch with our own humanity and think that by bypassing it, even more, we will somehow find peace, bliss, or utopia. We think that by being less human and more of something 'higher' we can eliminate our suffering. This path of seeking often becomes more about avoiding and denying than it is about a heroic journey of humanity or a genuine divine illumination.

This is a sophisticated scam of the ego—another genuine ruse. **Only the insane would try to end suffering with more suffering.** This is because an avoidance of being human *is* suffering. It's what you're doing when you're playing the spiritual versus materialistic game. It's what you're doing when you're playing duality. It's what you're doing when you're trying to fix yourself. And it's what you're doing when you're acting superior: trying to fix, change, and save everyone and everything. You're trying to usurp Truth with a "better truth." This can only occur in an insane mind, not in reality. What could be more true than what's already true? What could be more fixed than what was never broken? What could be more beautiful than Beauty? What could be more spiritual than what's divine?

Nothing. No wonder we get stuck!

The ego says to us, "There is something wrong with you, you are not enough, you don't have what you need—see, here's proof. Let me help with that; I can fix you, improve you. You need me." The ego is really saying: "I'm distorting reality to create a problem that isn't there, and then offering a solution to a nonexistent problem, so you have a reason to keep me around. This will only create more suffering because it revalidates the problem the more you improve. As I make and develop your better persona, it will distance you and the world further from your True Self."

And then, for some of us, we eventually get the shiny, upgraded "spiritualized ego" model. You know the one: the ego that knows all the spiritual or religious jargon, or attended the schools and has the official rankings, or that has lineage with a certain guru or shaman. The ego which says, "Hey, you know what, they're right, egos are bad. Let's become spiritual so we can be superior to all those unawakened humans. We'll suffer a lot less once we know the secrets that help us not be affected by those lowly, normal people problems." This can be even more dangerous because the ego and suffering are still there, but now they're hidden under the cloak (or *illusion*) of being awake. Insidious.

That is the ego. It can *only* be insane. It can *only always* be stuck.

Many of us, including myself, have fallen into this trap. It's incredibly seductive. Who wouldn't want to be above the human condition or become 'special'? The seeking is addictive. The lie—the biggest. The promise—the ultimate. The prize—superhuman.

The problem with all of this is, you *are* human.

YOUR DIVINITY

Spending our lives seeking to be something other than who we already are is defiance towards Spirit itself. This game we play trying to 'ascend' from the human condition doesn't work. It fails because it's about rejecting that which makes us human. It's a pseudo-spirituality that is made in the image of the ego. This 'spiritual' path is directly in opposition to our true spiritual nature. When we find ourselves stuck, struggling, and suffering more the further we walk down this road—perhaps it's because it's not the path we thought it was. When we are caught up in this well-intentioned but misguided undertaking, we get hoodwinked by an illusion. An illusion that only *appears* as if we are seeking the divine. And that seeking would be a grand, noble thing—if it wasn't hijacked by a phantasmagoria of delusion.

> ✹ "The meaning of life is just to be alive. It is so plain
> and so obvious and so simple. And yet, everybody
> rushes around in a great panic as if it were
> necessary to achieve something beyond themselves."
> — Alan W. Watts

You see, *it's a rigged game.* This spiritual path is a trap because its very purpose is untrue. How can you find what was never lost? How can you reach for what has never left you? How can you become something other than your nature?

You can never get there from there because **your humanity *is* your divinity.**

We are running away from ourselves trying to find ourselves! We are looking for the divine everywhere else *except* for in the most divine place! We are playing spiritual hide-n-seek as both the hider and seeker. We blame both the hider and the seeker for our pain, refusing to admit the game itself is what's causing our suffering.

Sit with the implication of the phrase, "Your humanity *is* your divinity." The Truth behind this phrase—not the words themselves—invalidates your suffering. Meaning, you cannot suffer when you are fully accepting and present to what it implies. It unmasks the impostor spiritual path and delivers peace. It is the revelation of the 'man behind the curtain'. It is the antidote to seeking. It is the unveiling of the Grail. It is the completion of duality and the reunion with non-duality. It collapses separation and fosters compassion for all. It makes the divine Beauty of every single thing and circumstance apparent.

This understanding of the innate divine nature of humanity has been stated throughout the ages in various ways. Jesus said, "I and the Father are one." In the Upanishads, it states, "Tat tvam asi," literally, "Thou are that," translated from Sanskrit. 'Tat,' in essence Brahman, or the ultimate reality, or even 'God'; and 'tvam,' in essence the Atman, or the self. The book of Genesis states, "God created man in his own image." In Buddhist philosophy, the concept of 'Buddha-Nature' nudges us towards a similar realization. The Hermetic principle, "As above, so below," also points at the same realization.

But we need not look to ancient religions in order to see this Truth for ourselves.

You can see it in the crusty bark of trees and feel it in the breeze of their dangling leaves. You can hear it between the chirps of crickets and in the echo of yells across a canyon. You can feel it in the roaring of a truck's force, reverberating in your chest as it plows past. You can see it outlined in the moonlight shadow of a pack of hyenas hunting in the Sahara.

You can feel it under your feet on the dance floor, in your legs and arms as they rise, fall, extend, and contract—all to the varying lengths of sound and silence. You can see it in the eyes of a prisoner—and in his maniacal expression too. You can see it in the rotting flesh of roadkill and the mortal grin of a buried skull. You feel it in the power of a jet engine as you take off from the airport upon millennia of innovation and dreams.

You can feel it building as heat in your loins and in the rush of ecstasy as you climax. You can smell it in the decaying leaves, in the campfire smoke, and in the pine air after an early autumn rain. You can sense it when you pray, and perhaps, even more, when you foam at the mouth in vile rage. You can feel it when you get a handmade gift and when you give a stranger a tender, vulnerable hug.

You can see it in the mushroom cloud of a nuclear bomb being tested, in villages being raided by soldiers on the news, and in emaciated children homeless on the streets. You can taste it in grandma's warm apple pies and while eating prosciutto with aged wine and cheese in a Tuscan vineyard. You can see it the smile of a baby—and in its diapers too. You can hear it in the adoring applause after a riveting performance on stage. You can feel it when you bathe, you can smell it when you sweat, and sometimes you can even taste it when you cry.

Life itself reminding us of our very nature. It's you whispering to yourself. It's as if the entire cosmos is trying to tell us in each moment, "Don't you see? *You're it!*" 🪷

THE VICTIM TRAP

❉ *"Most people do not really want freedom,
because freedom involves responsibility, and
most people are frightened of responsibility."*
— SIGMUND FREUD

here is a certain allure to the victim mentality. It would
appear that not being blamed, not having to take responsibility, not having to change or make choices, and not
being the one who gets punished or has to fix things—is
a super deal. We think, "Why would we ever make ourselves at fault
or have to be the one to do something if we didn't *have* to?" On the
surface, life sure looks a lot easier this way.

We don't even realize that we're in victimhood when we do this;
it just seems like an easy way out of a situation. Perhaps, it's the best
path we think we have. We are taught that blaming others, not taking
on responsibility, and not holding ourselves accountable is a way to
play it safe—or even stay alive. We may learn that the world treats
us special when we are victimized, that we get more attention and
privileges, or people will do things for us. Maybe we notice that we
get more sympathy and pity when we are seen as innocent than we
do when we're seen guilty. We see that fault comes with blame, shame,
guilt, and punishment ever since we were children, and see the same

in society's laws as adults. The easy way out is enticing, from infancy to old age.

And you know what? This way of life may "work." Adopting a victim mentality *may* do a lot of these things. It *may* keep us safe, bestow pity and attention, and get others to do the heavy lifting for us. It *may* prevent us from having to take responsibility or be held accountable for anything. It *may* even allow us to avoid making a new choice and change. At least... for a while.

While it may "work," none of this comes without great cost. Just as stories bind us to a nonexistent past, victimhood binds us to *powerlessness*. **Victimhood is the definitive 'stucky story' for one simple reason: it doesn't allow us the possibility of getting unstuck ourselves.**

When terrible, unfair, or incomprehensible things occur in our life, we must find a way to deal with them. These things happen to *everyone*—we are not alone in the universal hardships of life. There are many ways to deal with these, and none of them are 'right' or 'wrong.' Yet, some work better than others to bring us joy and peace. **When we're in the victim mentality, we exchange the momentary discomfort of responsibility for the lasting 'comfort' of powerlessness.** We give up our freedom for helplessness. We avoid accountability and lose fulfillment and satisfaction. We sacrifice our sovereignty for dependence. We take on anger, resentment, misery, or despair—and lose authentic joy, gratitude, and peace. And it is understandable. We may have every reason and right to, and we want so badly to cling to our justifications. I know I sure wanted to!

Like a deranged wild animal, we defend our stories and attack anyone who dares to take away what little we have. We snarl at the one who offers peace if we were to give up our anger. We hiss at the one who offers freedom but asks us to take responsibility. We claw at those who dare to question our innocence and demands for justice. We bite anyone who attempts to proclaim that we don't *have* to suffer. We kill and devour the person who even implies we are not helpless and powerless and that our choices have led to our situation.

It's not for the pain or agony of the situation, but for this *attachment* that we truly suffer. As you learned in the last chapter, it's our addiction to these stories—not the hurt itself—that causes us to suffer.

In my work, I experience this often. I help people see that they are more powerful than they think and can choose to improve their lives—and what do they want to do? Argue with me that it's not true. They tell me that I'm mean and "don't understand." They insist that they *have* to suffer because of a laundry list of reasons and stories. That things *can't* get better until somebody else fixes them or the problem, or that they can *never* get better because they're broken, not enough, or undeserving. They get off on the story that nothing works for them. They attack me because I see through their comforting illusions and invite them back into their true power. They are fighting for their limitations.

This is the insidiousness of victim mentality, where we become righteous and justified, defending our limitations and stucky story until the bitter end. The victim mentality is a delusional prison—one that is unknowingly self-made. The reason you're still stuck may be that you are giving your power away without even knowing it.

OUR INTENTION FOR THIS CHAPTER

Before we go any further, it's important to clarify that this topic is not about "victim-blaming." Throw this thought out the window immediately. This chapter is about 'victim' as an *identity:* someone who goes through life, blaming everyone and everything for their problems. We are not referring to the label we give to someone when a misdeed occurs against their will, such as in a disaster or crime. **When I say 'victim,' I'm referring to the identification of someone who lives from a place of victimhood.**

This book has one focus: helping *you* get unstuck. We cannot change or control anyone else, nor can we change what happened in the past. While I acknowledge that there are many terrible corrupt systems in place, monstrous people in the world, and atrocities that occur, we can't do anything in this book to remedy it—except by helping *you* empower *yourself*.

Everything you will read in this chapter is for *your* benefit and will only empower you to create a better life for yourself and those around you. This is high-level work—it is not about being nice, or what seems fair, or being socially or politically correct—it's about getting you aligned with the highest order of what *actually* works, not the trends of what society wants to believe.

I respect that this topic may be sensitive for you. Be advised it may be confronting, especially if you've experienced trauma. With that said, I want to invite you to use whatever may trigger you—whether you think what I'm saying is right or wrong—to go inside and see what that's really about for you. Find a way to let this heal you instead of being outraged and further solidifying your suffering.

I know how this works because I've been there myself. Getting out of the victim mentality has been the critical factor of my success and transformation. I am forever grateful to have recognized it and learned about it when I was twenty-one. I had lived my entire childhood as a victim, and I had every right to—I was bullied and dealt with varying kinds of traumas. It took remarkable levels of honesty and stopping. It was incredibly confronting, but I broke through. It is a true awakening, and I've only owned more as I've grown in maturity. I can promise that whatever you are afraid of losing by surrendering the victim mentality, it pales in comparison to the love, peace, freedom, power, and riches you will gain.

The victim mentality is the primary cause of suffering that I see most people in society struggle with. **If you cannot accept that you are responsible for your life and what becomes of it, you will struggle.** This book *will* help you get unstuck, but you must be willing to listen, be honest with yourself, and follow the instructions. If this chapter drives you crazy, makes you irate, or sounds preposterous—keep rereading this book until it doesn't. I don't care if it takes years—if you're playing the victim, getting out of this mentality needs to be your number one priority in life if you're ever to truly get unstuck.

WHAT IS A VICTIM?

A victim is someone with a victim mentality, who feels that life happens *to* them rather than *from* them. They are at the *effect* of the world rather than at *cause*. They have surrendered their sense of agency to extraneous circumstances. They feel powerless and helpless and believe that somebody or something outside of themselves is responsible for their suffering—and their happiness. It is never *their* fault. They blame to avoid taking responsibility and accountability, both of which can subconsciously feel annihilating. They justify their chronic struggle with stories of unfairness, reasons, oppression, and things outside their control. They may be ran by guilt, shame, and anger. Or, they may feel hopeless, despaired, and depressed.

It's not always about oppression and trauma. Nothing necessarily has to have *happened* to them to adopt a victim mentality. They can be a victim to the economy, their feelings, the people around them, their sickness, their debt, their excuses, and anything else they could possibly objectify as the cause for their suffering. It doesn't have to be some evil, terrible thing that happened to feel victimized; they just need a reason to not take responsibility.

The victim operates in a land of guilt and punishment, blame and shame, and righteousness and justification. It is an inherently narcissistic world, where they are at the center of their strife and are powerless until circumstances change in their favor. The victim appears to be at the effect of circumstances out of their control. It is this lack of control that the victim persona attaches onto for dear life. It is here they find pity, support, attention, and justification for their refusal of responsibility. This victim role has a certain social currency, which is often used pervertedly to garner sympathy and status, but ultimately only serves to keep them in suffering. When you see a culture prizing and valuing victimhood and fear, watch out! Things are about to get ugly.

The victim may attempt to fight to regain their power from another or pray to be saved. This is where the victim gets it backward. They have effectively inverted the hierarchy of control and surrender. They try to control and change what they cannot (others, situations, the world) and refuse to control what they can (thoughts, behaviors, choices, perspectives). Instead of surrendering and accepting what is outside of them, and changing what they're responsible for, they blame and punish. Unbeknownst to them, this blame and punishment is a projection of their own guilt—even if it's directed at themselves.

The victim remains stuck until they face what they're avoiding: responsibility and accountability.

DEFINING IDEAS

The words we use to discuss victimhood are imperative to understand accurately if we wish to navigate such a muddied terrain. We use words willy-nilly without grasping the weight or meaning behind them, creating confusion. You may use the words found in this book differently in your daily life or profession, so it's essential that you ensure our definitions in this context match. We are not discussing criminology, social legislature, or academics, but ways of seeing the world which are the most empowering. What will lead you to a better life is not necessarily what the culture's consensus is. Often, it's usually not.

> "Whenever you find yourself on the side of the
> majority, it is time to reform (or pause and reflect)."
> — Mark Twain

Victim: One who has identified with the victim mentality (see description above).

Victimhood: The pathology of victim mentality.

Ownership: Taking ownership means we make a claim to what is ours as the rightful owner. We embody a sense of possession, belonging, or duty to the circumstance, problem, idea, or behavior. We take ownership because we can only change what is ours, and what is not ours is out of our ability to control. We have no right to change or control what we don't own.

Responsible: Taking responsibility means that we take ownership of the situation, our part in it, and how we respond to it. We accept ourselves as the source, agent, or cause of our results in life without value judgment. We hold ourselves and each other accountable to the truth. We own our role in all circumstances we are a part of, however minute it may be.

Accountable: Holding ourselves accountable means that we are willing to face whatever the consequences are for our thoughts, behaviors, and role in a given circumstance. This can be reward or punishment, or it could be love and support. When we are afraid of facing the actions of our consequences, we don't allow the support that will teach us, love us, and help us grow. Think of responsibility as owning the choice and circumstance, and accountability as owning the *consequences* of the choice.

Blame: Blaming points the finger and projects guilt upon something *without* taking responsibility. It is used to avoid admission while implying guilt. It is an attempt at *transference* from one party to the other. Blame has a defensive, judgmental quality to it.

Fault: Being at fault has an implication of guilt or wrongdoing and is used with blame to hold someone accountable. It is also used to 'admit,' as in "It's my fault," which tends to carry guilt. We often look for who's at fault to know who to blame and hold responsible for fixing it. Fault also doesn't necessarily carry a sense of ownership and responsibility, as one can be at fault without taking ownership.

In this chapter, both the words 'blame' and 'fault' are used with implications of feeling guilty, accusation, projection, or wrongness. They are often used interchangeably with 'responsible' and 'accountable' in common usage, but this is inaccurate and sloppy. It's safe to assume that when someone is blaming or saying it's anyone's fault, there is victim mentality at play.

You don't have to have guilt to take responsibility, and you can feel guilty without being responsible. You can blame yourself or another, but that blame is in opposition to responsibility. Genuine responsibility and accountability expands and empowers while blaming and fault carry guilt, which contracts, distorts, and disempowers. The latter of these are tools used by both victim and victimizer to control and avoid, not heal and tell the truth.

Feeling shame or guilt is a normal reaction to something we've done that goes against our morals. It is a useful indicator that we're "off course." The problem occurs when it's inappropriate, projected, avoided, or remains unresolved and runs us. Many things we feel as adults are unconscious reactions to past stories or traumas, not responses to what-really-is in the present moment. As we wake up, mature, and grow, we need not rely on shame and guilt to steer our conscience. We do not need to rely on training wheels once we've emotionally and spiritually matured. The more we align with our True Self and not our shadow, the less we need to be shamed and guilted into behaving rightly.

DESCRIBING THE VICTIM

How do you know if you or someone you know is 'being a victim' or operating from a victim mentality? The following lists paint a picture of the characteristics, feelings, distortions, and phrases typically seen. Each is not a requirement, but a variety of what may indicate it.

Here are the qualities of someone in a victim mindset:

- The attitude is that of "poor me" and pessimism
- The 'locus of control' is externalized
- The behavior is to blame, complain, and justify
- The worldview is that "life happens *to* me"
- The belief is that "I am helpless"
- The avoidance is punishment, power, and responsibility

- The body lacks presence, potency, and ownership
- The energy is lethargic (despair) or fiery (anger)

The victim may feel that:

- They are disadvantaged; things are stacked up against them
- They have little to no power or control; there is little they can do
- They are special for the same reasons that they are preyed upon or targeted
- They are helpless to the "bad" oppressor or perpetrator, who are 'bad'
- They are not responsible for what is happening
- They, or others like them, need to be rescued
- They are entitled to the pity, help, and generosity of others
- They are proud and wear their suffering like a badge of honor
- They are on the righteous side because they're worse off than others, or because the other side is "bad"
- They are justified in their anger or revenge

They have a distorted perception of reality in which they:

- Replace empathy with pity
- Replace compassion with shame
- Replace accountability with justification
- Replace responsibility with blame
- Replace logic with emotional reactivity
- Replace possibility with pessimism
- Replace nuance with absolutes
- Replace cause with effect
- Replace facts with distortions
- Replace reality with fantasy
- Replace context with universal generalizations

The most common victim phrases:

- "He made me do..."
- "She made me feel..."
- "I can't because..."
- "...happened to me."
- "You don't understand. It won't work because..."
- "People like me aren't able to because..."
- "They won't let me..."
- "That wasn't my intention. See what happens!"
- "Somebody else will take care of it."
- "I don't feel that way, so you are wrong or bad!"
- "I don't have any choice."
- "It's their fault. They're the ones who..."
- "Yeah, but the problem is..."
- "Why (not) me?"
- "These oppressive structures prevent me from..."
- "It's not fair. I shouldn't have to be the one who..."
- "I'll feel better only when they change..."

Saying these things doesn't make someone a victim, but they are things people with a victim mentality tend to say. The greater occurrence of these in an individual, group, or society, the more likely they are identified with victimhood. This identification can be conscious, as with the "Poor me, you must pay!" victim, or unconscious, as with the "Poor me, why is my life so bad?" victim. Neither recognize their part and what is truly going on under the surface.

STRATEGIES OF THE VICTIM

There are a few core strategies the victim employs to sustain their victim image. This will round-out our picture of the victim persona.

Not all victims respond to the feelings of powerlessness and helplessness the same. Not all respond to accusations the same.

Understanding how the victim responds to life can help us identify these disempowering behaviors in others and ourselves.

Keep in mind that most of the time, these strategies are unconscious. The victim mentality has distorted truth, and so most people who do these don't see what they're *really* doing. Quite often, the victim will employ the very strategy that you illuminate to react to your feedback. Great compassion and discernment are required. We are doing the best we can with what we know—and, we all are still held accountable for our choices, despite our justified intentions.

Defensiveness — *"It wasn't me!"*

When the victim *feels* accused, attacked, or blamed, they immediately go into defensiveness. Justification is also a symptom of this. They feel the need to explain, excuse, and justify everything they're doing; they are compelled to give a 'why.' It can become so automatic that even if they *aren't* being blamed, attacked, or asked, they perceive it as such. The ego distorts and filters the experience to match their narrative of being made wrong or that people are always against them. Everything becomes combative because everything seems like a threat to their innocence. Each conversation needs to be defused from becoming all about 'the blame' or 'the attack.' They are ran by an underlying sense of guilt and shame, also because they themselves blame and attack, especially when defending. We know that the truth requires no defense, and so we know that what the victim is defending is a lie. That lie is that who-they-really-are can be destroyed, wrong, broken, unworthy, or unlovable.

Despair — *"Poor me!"*

When the victim feels victimized and hopeless, they may submit and indulge in it. Often times they play the "poor me" card. This is when everything is about how oppressive and unfair life is, how terrible people are to them, how they can't ever get ahead, how everyone is against them, how they're such a good person yet they have disease and suffering. They are looking for pity and sympathy to validate their victimization, not solutions to empower themselves. They play the "see, no matter what I do, everyone treats me like..." game, defending their intentions rather than looking at their own dysfunctional behavior. They tend to gather in groups with other victims who are complaining and enabling each other. They never take a look at what they're doing to cause people to treat them a certain way or what they can do to change their situation. They are in despair; nothing they try would help.

Indignation — *"How dare you!"*

When the victim feels powerless *and* wants to do something about it, they are fueled by indignation to reclaim their power. This rage, anger, and ire is a reaction to feeling like their power was taken away, especially if unjustly or unfairly. The victim uses this energy to attack an 'object of hate' that represents what is responsible for their misery. Oftentimes it's not even the original cause but something that represents it. They use this anger to take their power back, thinking that if they can tear down the 'object,' they will rise and reclaim their power. This is often through force and intolerance to opposing views, blind to their hypocrisy by a veil of righteousness and moral superiority. Unfortunately, any victory is short-lived since the act of suppression, stripping down, or destruction of another does little to create true joy, peace, or happiness in the world or in oneself. Instead, the victim has become the very thing they despise—an oppressor. Unwittingly despising themselves, they further play the victim role, projecting layer after layer of their shadow upon the world and continue to rage against that superimposed image.

Bullying — *"You will pay!"*

When the victim is in pain and they feel powerless, resentment and anger build. This eventually needs an outlet. They may seek retribution and revenge, or they may look to control and bully others. Hurt people hurt people. There are no victimizers who were not victims themselves.

There are no victims who are not themselves victimizers. In victimhood, one becomes both victim and victimizer, prey and predator—if not to others, at least to themselves. Both roles feel powerless and attempt to reclaim power by taking it from another. They both have been hurt and seek retribution in their own ways. This is the reactionary cycle of bullying and abuse.

Blame — *"It was their fault!"*

Blame is about "passing the buck" or "pointing the finger" at someone or something else to project fault away from themselves. It is the typical, go-to victim response and is easy to spot. If you're blaming, you're being a victim. This behavior can also manifest as someone who: looks for things to use against someone or builds up 'ammunition' over time, capitalizes on circumstances, looks for ways to "get out of it," or spends more energy on excuses than just doing the thing. Blame is not always externalized; it becomes self-blame when pointed inwards. However, as we will learn in the following section, this is still not taking responsibility.

Rescuing — *"It's not your fault!"*

The victim tries to protect another *perceived* victim from the "threat" of responsibility and accountability. Since they are victims themselves, they see these two virtues as attacks and want to protect the other victim. Why? Because the person is helpless and powerless, and so "it's not fair." It doesn't matter if the perceived victim actually is or isn't. The victim sees the other as helpless because that's how they see *themselves*. Despite this, the victim thinks they can protect or save another—but they can't. What they're actually doing is reinforcing the belief that the person is helpless! They unknowingly become a sort of victimizer themselves. Instead of empowering them—which is what responsibility and accountability do—they deny the other "victim" the opportunity to grow and become self-empowered, for the victim secretly can't stand to see others they perceive as victims stop the mythology they themselves won't. They find their sense of purpose in rescuing others, which is robbed when someone refuses to play the role of victim. This strategy is not about real help. It is quintessentially codependent, selfish, and is really about holding everyone back.

Martyring — *"I'll take the fault!"*

The victim who martyrs is essentially victimizing both the person who's responsible and themselves. They are attempting to take away the sovereignty and power of another because of arrogance. They appear to be benevolent by 'taking the fall' for another, but what they're really doing is acting superior or attempting to regain their power through sacrifice. It is not a true sacrifice, but martyrdom. This is because it only results in further disempowerment for both. They are doing it out of contempt of power. They think they can take the blame better or have the power to save or protect another from rightful accountability. Another reason can be that they are doing it out of self-loathing. They are subconsciously addicted to guilt and shame and thus seek punishment. They think that "everyone always blames me anyway," and so they can strengthen the 'poor me' narrative, potentially using it against others in the future.

THE BLAME GAME

Out of all the strategies, blame is the victim's best weapon and defense—it is also their worst poison. Like hate and revenge, blame cannot be used against another without detriment to oneself. If it's ultimately harmful, why do we blame? We blame in order to avoid. We blame in order to avoid getting punished or accused. We blame in order to avoid ridicule or embarrassment. We blame in order to avoid feeling what we don't want to feel and to avoid facing what we don't want to face. We blame and point the finger at others to avoid having to look at our own shadow. Blame is a projection of our own fears, inadequacies, guilt, shame, self-loathing, cowardice, and perversions that we refuse to acknowledge willingly.

We blame in order to avoid responsibility and accountability.
One of the reasons some people struggle with taking responsibility is that they associate *fault* with it. When something goes awry, they are so accustomed to being made wrong, attacked, judged, and ridiculed that they need to protect themselves whether or not they did anything wrong. This builds a painful subconscious narrative (a *story* about being made wrong), causing us to detest and avoid anything that resembles it. What resembles it? Taking responsibility and accountability, of course! So they defend against the guilt and shame of being made wrong, ignorant to the fact that taking ownership has nothing to do with that. They think that taking responsibility will come along with the same pain of being judged, ridiculed, and hurt. Thus, they blame to protect themselves against their distorted idea of accountability.

It's common to hear phrases like:

- "It's the economy's fault."
- "It's the government's fault."
- "It wasn't me; she did it!"
- "My boss didn't tell me it had to be done, so it's not my fault."
- "I'm sorry that wasn't my intention, something happened and I..."
- "Sorry I'm late. There was rush hour traffic."
- "I have no idea what you're talking about. How was I supposed to know?"
- "I said no, but he made me do it. Blame him!"

These are all phrases that blame and avoid taking responsibility. At each opportunity, the victim seeks to deny, ignore, or deflect to avoid being held accountable for their choices.

I used to live in Los Angeles, CA, where the traffic was truly horrid. It could take two hours to go a few miles, so you had to plan your day around it. While this was a real factor, what so many people did was use "traffic" as an excuse for their disrespect. You'd have an appointment, and people would show up thirty minutes, even an hour late, and stroll in like it was no big deal. They never owned the fact they were caught up in their own world, that they made poor choices, and arrived late. There was always an excuse or an apology to avoid taking responsibility. It is narcissistic and a victim behavior that does not respect their own time or others. Not only did I deal with this for many years, but I did it myself. How easy it was to hold others hostage, disrespect the time of both people, and then use traffic as a (somewhat) valid excuse for being late. It was only after I moved away and got a wake-up call that I saw this was not a functional, healthy behavior.

> *"Wrong does not cease to be wrong*
> *because the majority share in it."*
> *— Leo Tolstoy*

What happens when you call this behavior out and enforce your boundaries? Blame! They tell you to "take it easy" or "relax and go with the flow" (blaming you). Or they may lash out, "I apologized already, I said I was sorry! What more do you want? It wasn't my fault!" (blaming others and you). Or they go into a 'poor me, don't hurt me' strategy, "I know, I'm so awful. I'm sorry I suck." (blaming themselves), looking for pity. It's all a manipulation and a way to not be accountable. It's a projection of their own shame and guilt, and a refusal to stop.

From the victim persona, most of the "I'm sorry" responses are automatic defenses, and most importantly, they are an excuse to keep doing the behavior.

Yes, they do say they're sorry... each time they repeat the behavior. You can tell when this person does not own it when you hear that "sorry" once again. They're really telling you they plan on doing it again. You know someone is truly apologizing and sorry when they stop doing what they were doing.

To the victim, it's not about being sorry and making a new choice— it's about an addiction to guilt and punishment. How many times do you hear a person say, "That wasn't my intention!" or "I didn't mean to!" or "I'm so sorry!" ...over and over again, each time with excuses and justifications? They are not taking responsibility for it; they do not own their choices or decide to relate to you in a more respectful way.

How often do you hear someone respond to being late with "I was late because I did not manage my time, and I don't respect myself enough to set a schedule. I understand this behavior holds you hostage and inconveniences many others, and all I worry about is the guilt and shame I feel, how I beat myself up with it each time, and don't really know how you feel. Thank you for making me aware. I will be on time from now on."

You may never have. But this is mature and self-aware; this is what adults do instead of saying "sorry." They accept feedback and the enforcement of another's boundaries. They own their mistakes and make a new choice going forward. This is the level of accountability to hold yourself to if you want to get unstuck and be highly functional.

There's a saying that sums up blame perfectly: "When you point your finger at someone else, there are three fingers pointing back at you."

SELF-BLAME

For the victim, there's always someone to blame, even if it's themselves. Blaming ourselves for something bad that happened to us is also a victim mentality. Do not confuse self-*responsibility* for self-*blame*. Responsibility implies an ownership; blame implies a guilt. One is factual, the other judgmental. One is expansive, the other contracting. **Blaming ourselves is not taking responsibility!**

Self-blame not only arises from immense guilt, self-punishment, judgment, and further disempowerment, but fosters more of it. None of this helps. Blaming ourselves makes us a victim because we feel helpless about how bad we are, how stupid or careless we are, how much we deserve bad things, or how there's something wrong with us. The 'object' of blame is not a separate *external* force or circumstance in the world, but a separate *internal* one. Self-blame seeks to find fault and guilt about an aspect of oneself, which is a form of dissociation. To the victim, it is not "I who made the choice," but it's "something about me did or made me." The cause, even though it was within their person, was not *them*. Here it becomes a dissociated internal aspect. This behavior can become a manipulation for pity or a way to shift focus away from ownership. All of this is what allows the victim to remain 'innocent.'

More self-abuse will only reinforce the guilt and validate the victim mythology—and blame is abusive. You want to stop *all* blame, especially the type pointed at yourself! Judgment and guilt are what got you in this mess—they won't help you out. Creating a different story about the blame won't help you out. Looking for more evidence to prove your stories right, or even wrong, won't help you out. Stopping the blame used for justification, assuming responsibility for where you are now, and making new choices—is what will help you out.

All blame—along with justifying, projecting, and avoidance—keeps us bound to victimhood. These reactive patterns prevent ownership, accountability, and responsibility—which are required to have freedom. This triad is the rectifier of victimhood. They are liberators of the disempowered. Our sense of power is not found in demanding handouts, nor from pity, nor through riots and rage—but in owning our circumstance and taking responsibility and accountability for it. Ending the enabling is loving because that is what liberates. Free will *must* be loving because it is the nature of the universe. Freedom and self-empowerment are kind; codependency is what is cruel.

As long as we blame and justify why and where we're at, we remain slaves. And make no mistake: it *is* slavery. We are indebted until we grow up and learn what it is there to teach. We can con and connive all we want, but this game we play never acquits us—we are always ultimately held responsible. There is no escaping the consequences of our thoughts and actions.

THE ILLUSION OF INNOCENCE

The only way a victim can sustain their identity is by being *innocent*. The victim must be innocent—or believe and rationalize in some way their innocence—in order to avoid being responsible. This is because responsibility is the opposing waveform to victimhood, and owning the circumstances would collapse the victim narrative. At the very least, they must be *far* more innocent and 'good' than who or what they are blaming. It is the linchpin that holds their entire narrative together.

This is the fundamental premise that enables the victim mentality, which means that it is flawed at its core. The victim believes they are helpless and powerless to their circumstance, that there is nothing they could have done differently or are able to do about it now. In order to believe that, the victim *cannot* own it because it would imply that they *do* play a part—which means they are *not* helpless victims.

When something unfavorable is occurring, it doesn't mean the person afflicted *must* accept their victimization. They can accept that the action is taking place without abandoning their power or going into denial. They are able to surrender and accept it: not that it is right or fair, but accept that it *is*. There are those who have been perpetrated against or have been affected by worldly conditions but refuse to be victims of it. They refuse to feel sorry for themselves or blame anyone, but instead choose to do something about it.

If there is real wrongdoing underway, it is true and righteous to stop and end it. Those who refuse to be victims and take responsibility for everything that happens to them are the ones who vanquish evil. Those who play the victim role are those who enable the behavior, and by consequence, validate the necessity for the victimizer role. They are also more likely to perpetuate the behavior in the world than someone who refuses. After a resolution, someone *without* a victim mentality will feel gratitude, have likely partaken in the stopping, and get on with their lives. Someone *with* a victim mentality will feel entitled to the help and the ending of the oppression, hold on to the rage and resentment, and then shortly move on to the next 'bad' thing. This reveals that the circumstance is not what makes someone a victim, but how they respond to it.

It is the person who refuses to be a victim that stops the cycle.

We can be this person for ourselves and as an example for others. We can stop the cycle in many ways. We can refuse to play the victim and leave, we can stand up and enforce our boundaries, or we can not submit to the oppressive mindset or circumstance. For example, if we are in an abusive relationship, we get up at that moment and leave the relationship for good without compromise. If there is a bully, we stand up to them and refuse to take any more teasing. If we are in a job surrounded by gossip, negativity, jealousy, and ridicule, we either rise to the top with kindness or quit and find a place that treats us well. We are only destined to repeat the cycles and stay stuck as long as we keep putting up with the same treatment.

"But it's not my fault! I can't just leave! I can't just fight back! I can't just quit! You don't understand."

I do understand—and this narrative is why you're still stuck.

KEEPING THE LIE ALIVE

This brings us to the question: does the victim arise from the circumstance, or does the circumstance arise from the victim?

Let's go back to the idea of duality and what we learned in the chapter, "An Equation for Suffering." If there is a north, there must be a south. If there is a solution, there is a problem. If there is a predator, there must be prey. If there is a search for a solution, it must necessitate a problem. Thus, if there is a victim, there must be a victimizer.

If there is no problem or victimizer... is there still a victim?

A victim *must* have a problem. They *are* a victim—it is their identity. Recall how powerful identities are from "Where Change Happens." If the victim does not have one, they will cease to be a victim, and so they must look for a victimizer to sustain the identity. This can be a person, event, circumstance, ideology, system—whatever can be objectified as 'the cause.' It can even be directed internally, blaming or fighting against themselves. It's not always some evil monster; the victimizer could be something as nebulous as 'the government,' the weather, 'people,' 'Mondays,' or life itself.

Remember that the antidote to victimhood is responsibility and accountability, but to the victim, it looks like poison. They must sustain their victimized persona to avoid having to face both of these. The victim continues to convince themselves and others that there really *is* a perpetrator and that *they* are innocent of any wrongdoing.

The victim mythology won't allow them to imagine anyone would choose to suffer or that anyone could manipulate others into victimizing them. *They must refuse this notion, or else it would mean they too made a choice that went against themselves.* The ability to 'choose against ourselves' invalidates the entire notion of helpless innocence. It collapses the story that the victim uses to avoid taking responsibility. It would force them to feel and change themselves and admit whatever they feel guilty of. The humiliation and humility required to break this pattern feels like a greater discomfort and pain than their chronic suffering, misery, ire, and resentment.

Thus, the victim usually keeps up the role and proceeds to blame. If the victim succeeds in convincing the world they are innocent, then they (temporarily) avoid responsibility and accountability. Though, even if they 'get away with it,' the truth hasn't changed. The acquittal is all but an illusion.

This is when we realize... **we are not that innocent.**

No, "not being innocent" doesn't automatically imply that we are guilty, at fault, or wrong. No, "not being innocent" doesn't mean others aren't responsible for their misdeeds. No, "not being innocent" is not victim-blaming. No, "not being innocent" does not imply we 'deserved it' or 'had it coming to us.' "Not being innocent" means that blame is unreal. It means that we cannot truly blame anyone else for being stuck and that we recognize we had a part in it. It has nothing to do with anyone else's choices and what they're responsible for doing—it's about *us.* **This is how we reclaim our power and how we stop victimizing ourselves.** Seeing that we had power in creating it means that we also now have the power to *uncreate* it.

Realize that we are not innocent when we...

- Feel like we deserve to be mistreated

- Feel unworthy and choose destructive relationships
- Eat a terrible diet and get sick
- Devalue ourselves and allow continual attack
- Do not have established, clear, enforced boundaries
- Instigate and play dumb
- Abuse ourselves
- Do not prepare or make uninformed choices
- Keep choosing the same things
- Look for evidence to sustain our victimhood
- Manipulate others without realizing that's what it is
- Watched and chose to do nothing about it

This is not at all about blaming ourselves, taking fault, or excusing the actions of others. It means that when we are in this victim mentality, there is no such thing as "helpless innocence." Without this premise being true, we can no longer weasel out of responsibility. Go back to the phrases victims say at the beginning of this chapter, and you will see how much we use the plea of innocence to defend against fault.

TAKING OUR POWER BACK

Once we realize that it's never *only* somebody else's fault and that we played a role in our own circumstance, the next thing to uncover is what that role was. If we can see what choices we made, what stories were running us, and what subconscious patterns led to our stucky story, *we can then truly do something about it within ourselves.* This is where everything in your life can change, and you begin to wake up from suffering.

It takes some effort to uncover what we're really up to—and there's a lot we're up to. The work is getting through the layers of stories, distortions, traumas, and conditioning that muddy up the waters. To get to the bottom of it, we must start taking ownership of our shadow, and stop pretending like it's not there.

Victimhood is a mindset, not the condition of a circumstance. Living as a victim is a *choice*, not a requirement. It is a choice to be helpless and give our power away, as it is a choice not to. We all have instances where we feel helpless and powerless. The difference between being a victim or non-victim is what we do with it. Do we look for evidence to support our helplessness or for evidence that we are not helpless? The victim looks for ways to feel sorry for themselves and hopes to be rescued. The non-victim knows that, while they may not have caused the situation, they've made certain choices that led them there, and it is their choice to be a victim or not in response. The classic victim rebuttal to this would be: "But I didn't *choose* to be a victim!"

You can see where that line of thinking arises from and ends up. It's what we do in the face of circumstance that determines if we are victimized, not the situation. The perpetrator or circumstance does not determine that for us, we do!

> "Do not pray for an easy life, pray
> for the strength to endure a difficult one."
> — Bruce Lee

Can someone *take* your humor away? Your confidence away? Your kindness away? Your gratitude away? Your thoughts away? No. They can make your life hell against your will, but they are powerless in *taking* it without your compliance. They cannot also give you these things; you must feel and cultivate them from within. There is no pill that can bestow these upon you.

The victim does not have their power *taken* away; it is *given* away. This epitomizes the illusion of innocence.

Have you ever had someone you love suffering intensely, and all you wanted to do is take their pain away, and you did everything you could to comfort them... but ultimately, you knew that you couldn't? They had to go through the process themselves; they had to make their choices themselves. Likewise, nobody can make a choice for you. You have to do it. *Even* if someone puts a gun to your head, *you* have to make the choice to comply or die. Granted, it's not much of a choice and is a total violation of will, but it is *technically* still a choice you have to make yourself. We must be able to take this to the extreme if we are to know it is true! And it *is* true that you have free will.

Nobody can *give* you your power, and nobody can take it away from you. It is your choice.

If you can accept this to be true, you will have to face many belief systems, stories, and shadow material that conflict with this. This statement invalidates the victim mythology, which is terrifying for the victim who wants to remain one. Yet, to the one who no longer wants to be a victim, it offers True Hope. The victim despises this, but the empowered individual will find great solace in this.

This truth goes against everything the victim has built their image and narrative up to be, and it appears to be an encounter with death— and it is a death of the 'victim image.' For those who have based businesses, communities, political movements, and income upon it, this empire of stories can seem like too much attachment to give up. But for the ones ready to awaken to something so much more joyous and grand, this disillusion of the victim mythos only marks the halfway point. Passing the threshold, they behold the unwavering knowledge that nobody can ever take their power away again.

The veil of helplessness is lifted. The true source of inner-power is within reach.

Your inner-power is this: to be secure in the Truth that nobody can ever threaten who-you-really-are—even if your life is threatened. It is an embodied *knowing* that nobody can take anything Real away from you. This is the **strength** of the warrior; this is the **freedom** of the revolutionary; this is the **hope** of the hero. These things are what the victim is trying to reacquire from outside of themselves through their strategies. But this gift is already yours: all you have to do is surrender your illusions of powerlessness.

You are who you've been waiting for. Nobody will fix you, save you, or do it for you—nor can they.

It may seem daunting to make the choice now if you've spent a lifetime in the victim mentality. As victims, we didn't *have* to make the choice; someone else (like an "authority") did it, an unconscious aspect of us did it, or the victimizer did it for us. The invitation here is to become the authority yourself. That sounds well and good to become empowered, but it may also be frightening. This chapter's quote by Freud on freedom and responsibility summarizes it impeccably.

It is quite a responsibility indeed, and perhaps that's why we so easily relinquish it. In the opening section, I talked about the allure of the victim mentality. It *is* seductive because you don't have to be the one who makes the choices in your life. Having a *choice* is the essence of freedom, and when you hand over choice, you hand over control and become powerless. We do this when we remain in victimhood; thus, we are not free. Therefore, it is the power inherent in responsibility and choice that will free us. In the final chapter of this book, "Above All Else," we will be revisiting these two topics, going in-depth on how to "escape" from the victim trap and overcome the victim mentality.

If you choose to let the world decide your life, then so be it—that is your choice. Do not dare be a victim to your own choice to remain a victim! You must accept these consequences. If you want your life to stand for something more than victimhood, that is a choice you must also make. Your virtues will not happen on their own.

It is a radical pivot to start deciding *for* yourself, rather than *against* yourself. Facing all the aspects you've been avoiding for years takes immense courage and compassion. This work is the loving process of reclaiming everything you've been giving away. Begin by making the choices you don't want to make, playing a more active role in life, and participating in your fate rather than 'seeing what happens.' You may not be used to being the one who's in control. However, each step you take, each choice you make—no matter how small—will build your confidence and faith in yourself and the True righteousness of life. ✺

AVOIDANCE OF LIFE

"I went to the woods because I wished to live deliberately, to front only the essential facts of life, and see if I could not learn what it had to teach, and not, when I came to die, discover that I had not lived. I did not wish to live what was not life, living is so dear; nor did I wish to practice resignation, unless it was quite necessary. I wanted to live deep and suck out all the marrow of life, to live so sturdily and Spartan-like as to put to rout all that was not life, to cut a broad swath and shave close, to drive life into a corner, and reduce it to its lowest terms."
— HENRY DAVID THOREAU, *Walden*

hat we resist persists, what we fear owns us, what we desire escapes us, and what we avoid runs us. When we fight against something, it fights back. Consider Newton's third law of motion: every force encounters an equal but opposite force. When we are afraid, we are not able to act freely. When we desire something, we repel it because we are wanting it, not choosing it. When we are avoiding something, that thing becomes what orients us, not our true vision.

Notice how these all affect *direction*. These are subconscious strategies that direct our decisions. If we let all of these run us unconsciously, our life becomes about defending, fearing, longing, or avoiding. Look around you. How many people do you see who are defending or fighting against something, who are afraid to do what they want, who are always desiring and craving, or who are anxious and avoidant? It's probably a lot of people. How many of them seem consistently happy, fulfilled, at peace, and are enjoying life? How many of them are stuck?

It's not a coincidence.

You can't end what you don't want by defending against it. You can't get to where you want by fearing it and running from it. You can't get what you want by pushing it away. You can't live life by avoiding it.

We don't realize this is what we're doing, nor have we figured out that it isn't working to bring us closer to joy. The more we allow these behaviors to dominate our life, the less life we are left with. Everything becomes 'away' oriented. We are either moving away from what we don't want or what we want is moving away from us. We believe that if only we could do more of this (or better), we will finally escape it or catch it. We won't. We will only further the gap between what we want and who-we-really-are.

We will get there by going 'towards' or 'into' it, not away from or against. It is by surrender that we are victorious. It is by trusting in life, not avoiding it, that we will move forward towards healing and success. Many of us have lost faith in the process of life itself and remain stuck. We delay and postpone being fully alive until it's safe, but by then, it's too late. We fight for our limitations and discard invitations to adventure. We have given up the real thing for the plastic replica, trying hard to convince ourselves that it's what we've always wanted; everyone cheers for us, secretly in envy, while we're slowly dying on the inside with a mask on. I call all of this *the avoidant life*.

My friend, this is not how your life was meant to be lived.

> "People are strange: They are constantly angered
> by trivial things, but on a major matter like totally
> wasting their lives, they hardly seem to notice."
> — *Charles Bukowski*

A DISTRUST IN LIFE

What makes us want to avoid life so strongly? When we can't trust something, we don't feel safe. When we don't feel safe with something, we can't surrender to it. If we can't surrender to it, we try to control it. We think that by controlling something, we can protect ourselves from it. If we see uncertainty as dangerous, control grants us more predictability, which we equate to safety. The motto becomes: "The more we control, the safer we become." There is an argument to be made for this because, to an extent, it has real merit. We can see that law and order keep chaos and mayhem at bay. We can see the control provided by the structure of a house keeps the elements and potential intruders at bay. Being able to control our environment has lead to greater safety for humanity.

However, the futility of this flawed premise becomes clear when we reach our limits of control, when what we're trying to control can't be controlled, or when we no longer have the bandwidth to control any more things. When we mistrust, we simply cannot exert enough control to feel safe. We cannot control everything, everyone, everywhere, all of the time. This is an unquestionable fact. Yet, we try so hard to control what little slice of life we can.

If we can only feel safe when we are in control, and we can never be fully in control of everything, we always feel unsafe. This mythology dictates that only more and more control is the solution. It zealously preaches to us that more rules, more laws, more power, more regulation, more management is the way to be safe. Freedom is a threat. It seeks to add so many constraints and rules to keep us safe that it winds up suffocating us to death. This myth operates on arrogance, fear, distrust, and control. It feeds on acquiring and exerting power, but there is never enough it can obtain or force to be at peace. We see this mythology show up in archetypes of indignant victims, dictators, and the tyrannical father and devouring mother. We also see it in germophobia and in dystopian themes.

People who do not trust themselves or their judgments don't trust others. People who trust themselves and their discernment easily trust others. People who distrust require trust to be earned. People who trust do so in good faith until given reason otherwise, be it a gut feeling or evidence. People who do not trust need to be in control of, monitoring, and micromanaging others, or do it themselves. People who trust can let go and let others tend to themselves and their duties.

People who *do not* trust are afraid that something disastrous will happen if they let their guard down. If they do let their guard down and get deceived, they use it to validate their story and further close off. They do not trust themselves, and they do not trust that they will be okay.

People who *do* trust know that letting their guard down is the only way to have intimacy and connection. They know bad things can happen as well, but they trust their discernment. Even if they do get duped, they will recover gracefully and learn from it. They trust themselves and that they will be okay no matter what.

This fear and inability to surrender stems from a lack of trust in others, ourselves, and life itself. But where does this come from?

ORIGINS OF MISTRUST

The following are a few of the many stories we have about why we can't trust:

This mistrust often begins with the **mother** and **father**. Parents are our doorway into this world, and as such, they have dominion over us for a significant length of our early development. They are our primary images of the masculine and feminine archetypes, which determine to a great extent our default way of relating to men and women, and our own internal masculine and feminine aspects. If there are circumstances such as abuse, lack of security, needs that aren't met, violence, or abandonment, our trust is tarnished. Even less extreme dysfunction, such as prolonged manipulation, head games, teasing, judging, or not following through, can damage trust. If we can't depend on our parents for love, providing, and security as a child—who *can* we depend on?

Mistrust continues with **ourselves**. Our bodies are clumsy and failable. We make choices and discover we can be wrong often. We attempt and fail and then experience humiliation. We go to make a new friend and get rejected. We believe somebody who was lying, and then we feel stupid and foolish. We give our choices meaning and stop trusting ourselves. We ourselves lie, deceit, and steal from others. We ourselves break our promises and let others down. If we can't trust ourselves, it sets the stage for systemic distrust.

Mistrust also occurs with **our body**. We could be abused or touched inappropriately and then get blamed because of our body, or come to that conclusion on our own. We get bullied and teased because we look different. We get treated poorly because of our gender, age, ethnicity, or weight. We could have a sickness or disease that limits us, or we could have been taught our immune system is not enough. We learn to discriminate against our body, not trusting it is perfect for us.

We have experiences in life interacting with **other people** that give us reasons not to trust others. We get abused, hurt, bullied, or violated. We get lied to, deceived, and manipulated. People abandon us or disappoint us. We see the deception in the media and the corruption in government and business. We learn that we can't rely on other people, from showing up on time to being the source of our happiness.

We could have also learned to mistrust **nature**. We judge and distort the cycles of life, such as death and birth, and hunting and growing. We fear the animals of the wild that can 'get us.' We see the instability of weather patterns and their destruction. We may have been taught about germs, diseases, plagues, and the 'dirty' world. We may see the brilliance of man and civilization and see it as superior to the archaic ways of the wild. We could have been told that only technology will save us from the natural courses of life; that how nature works is wrong or lacking something.

Our experiences or dogmas could lead us to a mistrust against **God or spirit**. Perhaps we see the corruption and superstition of religions and decide science has all the answers. We could have lost someone we love and feel anger towards a higher power. We judge others for their ignorance and reject their belief system. We may have had something terrible happen to us and think, "Why did you do this to me?" We could have prayed for years without our pleas for help being answered. We could have grown up and been force-fed ideologies that we are now rebelling against. We may have felt like we were abandoned and deserted by God. We may not have any connection with or awareness of something greater than the material and simply don't know any different.

Finally, we can have a lack of trust in **life** itself. We could have had a rough time, experiencing challenges and let-downs. We may have failed and been rejected over and over again. We can look out at the world and see despair, suffering, and hopelessness. We could have had our dreams "stolen" from us by a soul-crushing job or a tragedy. We may feel like we were given a bad hand at life. Perhaps we've seen the hard, miserable lives of those around us. Maybe we've seen the lack of justice and fairness in the world's system and have given up. Life itself cannot be trusted.

All of what you read are *justifications* for our lack of trust. If any of this was your experience, I acknowledge that they are valid, real, and did happen. You have every reason not to trust. Pain and hurt have happened, and there's nothing I could write to take that from you. You may have a chest full of reasons why you can't or shouldn't trust yourself, others, or life. Your justifications for not being able to trust are understandable.

I have no interest in convincing you to stop being afraid and to start trusting in life more. If you are all set and perfectly happy being closed-off, skeptical, and protected, then it's not my place to tell you what's better for you. It's a perfectly valid choice that is somehow still serving you.

However, if you have a feeling your lack of trust is causing you to suffer more than it's helping, then I invite you to begin *surrendering*. If you can start to surrender more, rather than control or avoid, you will by necessity be trusting more. This requires you to let go of control and go *into* what you're avoiding, rather than running away or defending against it. Facing it is the only way through it. Surrender is how you begin to get unstuck.

*"You must understand the whole of life, not just one
little part of it. That is why you must read, that is
why you must look at the skies, that is why you
must sing, and dance, and write poems, and suffer,
and understand, for all that is life."*
— J. Krishnamurti

WHY THIS CAUSES US TO AVOID LIFE

A lack of trust in life leads us to avoid it. The *avoidant life* is inherently also the *untrusting life*. We stay away from what makes us uncomfortable or what is perceived as dangerous. This is the biological purpose of fear—to keep us from harm. The problem is that most of these perceptions are not relevant to our modern culture and lifestyle. Perhaps you're still stuck because you're avoiding something like rejection (or any number of things), not because you think something will literally kill you and eat you for dinner.

We are no longer avoiding what we don't trust because we're staying away from life-threatening danger, but because we are *out of relationship with it*. Our lack of trust comes from our lack of properly relating. When we avoid an aspect of life due to this, we lose access to its associated resources. For example, if we avoid exploration, we lose courage; if we avoid vulnerability, we lose intimacy; if we avoid feeling, we lose intuition. The more we avoid in life, the fewer resources we have access to. They're still there, but we can't make use of them. There is still love here even if we close off to intimacy, we just don't have direct access to it. By facing and reengaging in a healthy relationship with what we fear, mistrust, and avoid—we can regain access to any resource we may have abandoned.

Everything in the following section is something that, if you stopped avoiding and came into proper relationship with, your life would become richer and work better.

You may have all sorts of justifications and rationalizations on why you disagree. You may insist that your life is better by avoiding things such as intimacy, feeling, surrender, and responsibility. Of course you might: this is why you're avoiding it! These defenses are not based on Truth but on trauma, hurt, mistrust, fear, and distortion. From the perspective of pain, avoidance looks like safety—but this is an illusion that can never lead to peace. Yes, avoidance is a normal pain response—and now, at this point in your journey, it is what's keeping you stuck and oriented in opposition to healing.

This work is about choosing to be fully alive, not to live in a fantasy without pain, discomfort, or the need to be courageous. It's not about eliminating everything that makes you human to live a sterile, controlled, harmless life. This "utopian" ideal of life does not exist, and the quest for it only leads to more suffering.

THE AVOIDANCE KEEPING YOU STUCK

The *avoidant life* is one of repression, the grandest being of *feeling*. The **avoidance of feeling** is at the root of every avoidance. We avoid because we don't want to feel uncomfortable—whether it's something too painful or something too loving. For example, we can avoid people because we don't want to feel rejected or embarrassed, or because we are unwilling to allow ourselves to be loved and appreciated. We can avoid releasing our art because we don't want to feel criticized or because we can't accept the praise of our gifts. We avoid the 'good' as much as we avoid the 'bad'!

This avoidance is also the cause of much of our **anxiety**. An avoidance of *feeling* is the major source of anxiety arising in the body. An avoidance of *the now* is the major source of mental anxiety. This is why people feel anxious thinking about the future. Every time I see a client feeling anxious in their body, they are avoiding feeling. Every time I see anxiety in the mind, they are avoiding their body in the present moment—which is still related to feeling. When they stop avoiding, they are forced to be in their bodies, in the present moment, which results in feeling. This act of feeling is something the client is running away from because they think that what they feel is going to be painful or annihilating. When they start to feel, it can indeed feel that way. It can also feel compassionate and liberating. As they continue to feel more and more, and avoid less and less, the client's anxiety around that story goes away for good. This happens when they penetrate the story and stop using it to justify their avoidance.

This reveals that the epidemic of anxiety is not the *cause* of an avoidance of life, but the *symptom* of it. It's not that our anxiety causes us to avoid; it's that our avoidance causes us to become anxious.

WHAT WE AVOID

The following is a list of the top ways we avoid life, which I've found keep my clients stuck. While there is a nearly limitless supply of things to avoid in life, I've distilled them down to the essential concepts. Use this list as a starting point to expand upon even more specific variations. As you read, see if you can sense what lies below the concept and notice which 'feeling' each 'avoidance' is moving away from.

1. When you *avoid being in your body*, you are cut off from one of your most powerful resources and are stuck in your head, missing out on being *in* life.
2. When you *avoid the pain and discomfort* you feel within you, you are also *avoiding growth and self-love*.
3. If you lack the courage to try something without certainty, you *avoid risks*—which reduces your opportunities in life to nil, keeping you small and unheroic.
4. Using a failure as justification to give up rather than as a lesson will not move you forward towards success—you will use it to prove your story of limitation correct and further *avoid failure*.
5. You think the greater responsibility you take on, the harder life will be, but by *avoiding responsibility*, you lose all the freedom and support it brings.

6. *Avoiding accountability* strips you of your power and peace, creating a trail of chaos, injustice, and suffering in your wake.

7. If you're *avoiding structure*, you're rejecting the support and safety that will help you get to where you want to flow.

8. Without knowing yourself, you can't fully express or actualize yourself, and without letting others in, you will forever be alone—both require you to be vulnerable and stop *avoiding intimacy*.

9. Your *avoidance of spirit*, God, universe, or whatever you refer to it as, disconnects you from life itself and the most extraordinary intimacy there is.

10. By *avoiding the silence*, you lose access to your inner voice and cannot focus on the useful data or connect to Truth.

11. There is no end to what needs to be done, so by *avoiding the stillness*, you will always be rushing around busy and stressed without ever knowing the peace that permeates our universe.

12. By *avoiding humor*, you get caught up in taking everything personally and thus are attached and suffering.

13. There is no virtue in *avoiding joy* and being miserable— nobody joyous wants to be around that, including the best lovers, clients, and employees.

14. Everything is continually changing and evolving. If you resist or *avoid change*, you will stay where you're at and go extinct one way or another.

15. Your unwillingness to let go of power, control, or certainty keeps you a servant to those things and pushes away support when you *avoid surrendering*.

16. If you *avoid the shadow*, censor yourself, judge, reject the impure and dark, or only ingest sanitized ideas—you live in a tiny bubble cut off from your best resources.

17. A distortion or *avoidance of beauty* can create a bleak life and much suffering, whether by envy, judgment, suppression, or absence.

18. When you *avoid the masculine*, yang aspects, you are out of relationship with these qualities within you—the same for *avoiding your feminine*, yin aspects. You *avoid the polarities* within yourself, not trusting your own male and female aspects, preventing you from self-actualization and the full expression of your gifts.

19. Your *avoidance of people*, or rejection of men or women, comes from pain and fear. You are afraid of being betrayed, abused, heartbroken, oppressed, manipulated, used, rejected, teased, abandoned, or hurt—but you also don't want to be alone. This inner conflict creates much suffering in your intimate relationships and community, and also hampers your business.

20. *Avoiding your greatness* prevents you from moving forward and achieving your dreams. Thoughts of "I'm too much" or "I have to play small so that others can shine" are not true and are counter-intuitively narcissistic and arrogant. You unknowingly hold others back by not showing them what's possible.

21. When you *avoid weakness*, you are trapped in superiority and cut yourself off from your greatest gifts and resources, unable to appreciate their value in others and self. This leads to an inflated ego in compensation mode.

All of these things we avoid in life make it clear we don't like to feel vulnerable, uncomfortable, or uncertain. Anything that pushes us up against our shadow is something we want to push away. What we don't realize is that an avoidance of one is an avoidance of the other. This is why avoidance makes life duller and duller: we are removing everything that gives contrast! When we avoid death, we are also avoiding life. When we avoid risks, we are avoiding the reward. When we avoid feeling pain, we are also avoiding pleasure. Our fixation of filtering out our flaws results in the filtering out of our beauty and depth—yet millions go around thinking the opposite and wonder why they're depressed. An *avoidant life* doesn't allow for True Beauty because the intimacy, vulnerability, and rapture it brings, threatens the ego. Combine this with a narcissistic image, and you have a recipe for ugliness and great suffering.

The insane part of this strategy is that many of the things we avoid are actually things we *desire!* It's almost always the case that we avoid what will help us. I will repeat it because this is the key to the chapter: **we tend to avoid the very thing that would move us forward.**

Think about how many times you were stalling and delaying, and when you finally did the thing, everything started working. Interesting, isn't it? This tells us something vital: **we are conning ourselves.**

We know the answer already; it's a game we're playing with ourselves. We know *exactly* what would move us forward... or else how could we avoid it?! At some level, we know it will move us forward, which is precisely why we avoid it. This is proof that *we* are the one who is holding us back. We already have the answer. How powerful fear and discomfort are! We know exactly what we need to do, but we will hold ourselves back, play dumb, and pretend like we're a clueless victim.

We can spend years or decades playing this game. It's not bad or wrong—but what a waste of time and potential! We go about our lives without any urgency to live, until one day, we face our mortality. But by then, it's too late.

I urge you to start living as if your life depends on it—because it does.

> "To live is the rarest thing in the world.
> Most people exist, that is all."
> — Oscar Wilde

Don't wait until finishing this book before deciding to take action. If you want to get unstuck, see what you're avoiding and go into it *now*. Stop avoiding it and face it *now*. Feel and integrate what it's there to teach you *now*. Move in different ways in the body *now*. Make new choices *now*. Respond differently to your fears, triggers, and stories *now*. Confront things rather than run away from them *now*. Who cares about the rest of the chapter—stop and face something you've been avoiding *now*. Now is the only time you can do anything about it. You know enough now to stop avoiding something and face your fears... what are you waiting for? If not *now*, when?

There's no magic technique, energy method, or shaman needed to trust and stop avoiding—only courage. There is no way around it; you cannot outsource facing life. **This book only works if you work it,** by way of your initiative. This is not 'my' book; it is *your* book—take ownership of each idea and figure it out. You will learn much more this way, and your results will last.

As a final note, if you're interested in going deeper into how we avoid, deny, and distrust life and how to start allowing who we are, you'll enjoy my forthcoming book, *Reclamation of Allowing*.

LIVING IN A FANTASY

You've seen what we avoid in life and why, but how can we get away with this and still live? In order to live an *avoidant life* while still being alive, we have to somehow deny reality and create our own pseudo-world with its own set of rules. We must somehow separate ourselves from reality and the accountability of our actions in it. Here we begin to think "the rules don't apply to us" and "we're the exception." We must also give everything a new meaning in our head in order for everything 'out there' to make sense in our 'new world.' We must continue to redefine words and events to make them fit the narrative.

This pseudo-world we create is called a *fantasy*—and it's as delusional as it sounds.

Why does it require all this convoluted mental effort? The "solution" for avoiding life and remaining functional is to dissociate from the world by going into our head and living in the fantasy we've created there. This is a "magical" place where we can rule and live a perfect life. It is here where we can usurp reality. Up can be down, wrong can become right, and our fears, responsibilities, and consequences don't have to be faced. Here in the fantasy we are in control and omnipotent, which implies we are safe and not uncomfortable. We can exist in the world without having to be a part of it; we can live without having to deal with life.

As enticing as this fantasy world may sound when you're in pain, it is not real. No resolution is found here, only escape. Even if you manage to construct your projections in the world, they would be unsustainable and disempowering. We see this pathology play out in society and government to great detriment. Avoidance, denial, and escapism always catch up to us, just like debt.

Let's look at the qualities of a fantasy:

- It is based on escaping, avoiding, or not feeling
- It has to redefine words and give new meanings
- It is constantly defending itself against Truth
- It must justify and rationalize everything it does
- It distorts reality and deletes what doesn't serve it
- It is separate and dissociated from the rest of the world
- It must maintain the illusion and belief it is real at all costs
- It abhors vulnerability, accountability, and limitation
- It sees itself as the solution to suffering
- It alternates between inflated and deflated states
- It is not accessible, even if someone agrees with the illusion
- It is not real and has little effect on reality
- It never comes true because there is no choice

Can you see why fantasies lead to more suffering in the longterm? How they can never get you what you want? All of these qualities of a fantasy are the reason why they keep you stuck. These qualities are also why fantasies are challenging to identify when you're inside of them.

We create these fantasies out of the seeds of great trauma down to the everyday struggles of life. Sometimes we feel we need to escape; our circumstances are so traumatic that we need a place to find solace and refuge. Our imagination and fantasy can become this safe place. There is nothing wrong with doing whatever it takes to survive. There is nothing wrong with separating ourselves from horror. The problem occurs when we are no longer in danger and we keep the coping mechanisms running. Escapism and fantasy keep us in a state of disempowerment, where we feel we must cope because we have no power or control over our situation. This may help you cope in traumatic situations, but it will not help you to get unstuck now.

However, things don't have to be life or death to propel us into fantasy. Narcissism, megalomania, consistent disappointment or failure, or pain and suffering can all lead us to fantasy. Growing up in an environment that was fantastical would also naturally land us here. Our Western media encourages fantasy because suffering is profitable; many industries would collapse without society's endless suffering. The acting arts, spirituality, and politics are fertile grounds for fantasists.

THE FANTASY OF DESIRE

Another form of fantasy is when we are desiring. When we imagine our future, we can either have a vision based on choice and action, or a non-vision, such as a hope, wish, or fantasy. What's the difference? There is a weighted sense of realness to our vision, but our fantasies lack any 'weight.' They are all talk, all desire, but no choice or action taken in reality. You've felt the difference between someone who says they're going to do something and there's no doubt that it will happen—and someone you pat on the back and say, "Well, I wish you luck!" and expect to see them in a few years and nothing has materialized.

> *"All desire leads away from the truth* ⚹
> *of who you are and to suffering."*
> *— Karl Wolfe*

Those with a fantasy put tremendous effort into them, but the effort goes nowhere because it doesn't *affect* anything real. It's as if the person was living in a parallel reality next to us. We can communicate and see they are doing all of this work, but because it's not *here in reality,* nothing real manifests here. The only place where physical manifestations can occur is in physical reality, not our minds. When something doesn't manifest, we know for certain that it's still a fantasy because if a real choice was made, it would become real.

This is why it took me so long to become 'successful.' No matter what I tried to build my business or advance my life, it didn't have much effect. I struggled to affect reality, despite knowing all the "right" things. Why was it so hard for me? I had been doing everything isolated in my own fantasy world and had no idea. I was "living in between the walls"—I was somewhere doing something, but I wasn't really *here*.

Fantasies are something we make up to avoid reality. They can be about any time, past or future, but never about the present because 'now' is real and fantasies are not. The past and future are home to fantasy because all three don't exist. 'Now' is the only time that is real, and if we are fantasizing, we are not present in the moment. The two cannot coexist. Our fantasies can't exist because they are in opposition to 'the now.' This is why it's an avoidance.

Like all attachments, fantasies *must* lead to suffering because they're based on separation and illusion. We cannot access what we want, and what we want can't access us from this place. A fantasy operates from reality, but reality cannot operate from a fantasy. You can have nothing from something, but you cannot make something from nothing. This is why the fantasist struggles so much: he desires what is real but attempts to get it from an unreal place.

"Wait, are you saying that all thinking and daydreaming is bad? What about imagination or visualization? Does it mean I'm trapped in a fantasy?"

No, not at all. I've outlined this in the extreme so you can see the pathology easily. There is indeed a difference between proper and improper use of the mind. Fantasizing is the use of imagination for escaping, denial, and suffering. It generates minimal results, preferring to build a mental labyrinth of counterbalances to rationalize the denial it sits upon. There is a constant need to "make the numbers work" to ensure it doesn't crumble against new data. It uses the creative/sexual energy to create and uphold a fake world that's dissociated from, and in competition with, reality. It does this instead of bringing forth new ideas and creations into the world. Fantasy rejects what's true with a 'better true' in an isolated mind, rather than using the creative force to benefit all of reality. In this way, we can see how it is narcissistic.

Imagination, mindset, and visualization are all powerful resources on the way to creating your vision, but they are not everything. I've witnessed masses of people use these in vain because they're trying to avoid doing the work or are avoiding facing the fear, rejection, failure, and uncertainty that real-life creation necessitates. Our minds and metaphysical aspects are truly magnificent and should undoubtedly be cultivated. They give us access to perspectives beyond the material realm of *physical* reality. They are not, however, designed to be used to *avoid or bypass* the human experience or our physicality. These are a gift, not a weakness. Spirituality, self-help, and your mind will always disappoint you if you're using them to avoid life.

ARE YOU IN A FANTASY?

How do you know if you're living in a fantasy or not? It's tricky. The nature of fantasy is denial, so it can be a stubborn feat to be honest with yourself while defending against the truth. This is what makes the ego so diabolical! Despite the challenge of self-assessing, you may still find great value in reflecting upon it.

Here are some questions for self-inquiry. Think about a specific area in life, a behavior, goal, or desire that you have, and ask the following:

- Do you have trouble manifesting tangible proof no matter how hard you try?
- Do you struggle to explain it to "outsiders"?
- Do you do this to avoid anything? Is there something you don't want to feel?
- Do you use it to escape from anything? Your body, circumstance, pain?

- Do you those you trust find your life is getting worse by doing this?
- Do you find yourself dismissing or denying information that threatens its validity?
- Do you find yourself constantly having to justify it and resolve your cognitive dissonance?
- Do you feel protected by it and defend it if people "threaten" it?
- Do you have to consistently "feed it" with daydreams, affirmations, convincing, energy, rationalization, and hype to maintain its believability?
- Do you feel like it's your own little world? That nobody else can ever understand it but you?
- Do other people have difficulties seeing your vision or getting behind you to support it?
- Do you go up and down emotionally? Get excited and depressed, oscillate between grandeur and meekness?
- Do you see this as something that will save you, as a path out of your suffering?
- Do you notice yourself struggling and suffering still afterward?
- Do you feel even more isolated and lonely the longer you maintain this?

The more "yeses" that you answer, the greater likelihood of a fantasy. Take a look at what you're avoiding in your life from the prior section. Become aware of what correlations they have with what your life looks like now, and notice which qualities relate to those of a fantasy. You will quickly see what's a fantasy and what's not. You must be honest if you wish to know the truth. This book requires you to be more honest with yourself than you've ever been before—that's the only way it can help you get unstuck.

Living in a fantasy is not reserved for the crazy prophets on the street or those in insane asylums—we can do versions of this and still remain functional in society. We can live in a fantasy where everyone hates us, or everyone loves us. We can live in a fantasy where we are destined to be billionaires, or one where there's not enough money to go around. We can live in a fantasy where we are perfect and everyone should desire us, or one where we are broken and life is a struggle to fix ourselves. We can live in a fantasy where facts don't matter, or one where authorities are the final word on truth. None of these are real, but they are stable enough to distort our perceptions while staying alive.

The desires and goals we fuel our fantasies with are not reserved for the megalomaniacs and dreamers. We all have hopes and wishes we never really choose. We can want to have a business and fantasize about it, telling everyone and building up a lot of hype, but unless we *choose* to have a business and build one, it's a fantasy. We can hope to be a famous football star, buy all the gear and plaster posters on our walls, but unless we practice and put in the years of work and get signed, we are in a fantasy—no matter how much we visualize it or pray.

This lack of action and choice is because we're avoiding.

We cannot handle the cognitive dissonance between our self-image and our avoidance, so we build a fantasy to escape it. We live out our fantasy in our heads, which the world remains oblivious to. We think we're hiding out there to avoid suffering, but it's in our fantasies where we suffer the most. Our fantasies are fuel for our narcissistic image and are a rejection of life. These fantasies—along with our stories and images—are the very things that prevent us from having a real life.

We think that by doing all of this, we are avoiding suffering. We're not. An avoidance of life *is* suffering. An avoidance of our True Self *is* suffering. But living life fully and experiencing all its joys and sorrows? *That* is not suffering.

THE HEROIC LIFE

The *avoidant life* doesn't have to be your destiny. Your life offers the opportunity—as it does everyone else—to be *heroic*. Consciousness beckons us to express the archetypal story of humanity through our own lives. This "Hero's Journey" calls us all to adventure and is the same fundamental story expressed in all the great myths. It is 'heroic' because it tells the story of humanity: we heed the call, leave home, stumble and fall, learn, transform, face our demons, lose hope, die and resurrect, triumph over adversity, save the village, get the treasure, and become hope itself. That *is* the essential human story. This is such a terrifying yet rewarding path for us to take because it thrusts us unapologetically into one of many flavors of *the* eternal story. We take a leading role in the cosmic play—leading not because we are better than, but because we lead humanity courageously to the Truth.

This process—*life*—works when it connects us to our humanity. All of it. Not only the pleasant, fun, abundant, light parts—but the horrific, dangerous, chaotic, and shadowy parts too. But we don't like those dark, humany things, and so we reject them. We would rather have our comforts and fantasies than live a life that includes *everything*. Instead, we avoid the shadow and thus avoid life. We choose to sanitize, dilute, give up, and refuse the call. We choose the plastic replica, mask, and artificial apple treat instead of the genuine article. We filter out all the shadows and are left with a flat, two-dimensional life.

We may not realize it, but what we genuinely want is a *full*, not filtered, life. We think we want everything to be comfortable, and easy, and sanitized... yet why is it that when we live this way, we are miserable deep inside? The escaping, censoring, distracting, and filtering does not work—each based on a judgment, rejection, and avoidance of reality. The comfort-oriented, offenceless, "perfect" life that we've been peddled isn't the same life that lights us up, brings forth our potential, or gives us a meaningful existence. Far too many people never realize that they're not obliged to the mediocre requests of society. We do not have to take what's offered—we can claim our own vibrant life. At any moment, we can say "no" and choose something different.

You have two paths ahead of you: one is the path to a *heroic life*, and the other leads to an *avoidant life*.

The **heroic life** moves us from the realm where "all life is suffering" to a realm where we become a vehicle that brings consciousness forth into the world. Like Hermes, we become a messenger for the gods, and like the Philosopher's Stone, we "transmute lead into gold." In practical terms: we move humanity forward because of our journey. We begin to make our lives stand for something greater than our suffering. We do something about our situation or another's, rather than sitting around dwelling in misery. We move from the confines of our culture and upbringing, and begin to wake up to something outside of the mundane. Something inside of us stirs. We get a nudge... we hear a whisper. We are called to leave our ordinary way of being, with the attachments and comforts of everyday life, and begin to show up more fully in the world.

The **avoidant life** is a life of repression, and what is repressed is the fear of being who-we-really-are and everything that requires of us. It is the constant denial of the call. We simultaneously yearn for the fullest expression of our True Self and resent the quest to realize it. We look towards what we want, seeing the wasteland and dangers that lie ahead, and judge them. It appears hard, treacherous, impossible, and so we deem our truth not worth the risk. We turn away not only because of a lie, but towards a lie. A lie of ease, safety, and comfort. But how easy is a mundane, mediocre life full of suffering? How safe are avoidance and denial really? How comfortable is the lack of peace and fulfillment, or the boredom, depression, and emptiness? The avoidant life seems like the easier path, and it may be—on the surface. You don't have to face the fears, put yourself out there to be rejected, endure the failures, tell the truth, take responsibility, make hard choices, or risk your life. The costs of what is lost, regretted, betrayed, abandoned, denied, and shunned by taking this path are not as obvious, yet are perhaps even greater in their price.

Both are valid, and both will be a life that's exactly what you need... but only one is worthy of your divinity. Only one of these paths will lead to the treasures of this book. You cannot fully express or actualize yourself if you're avoiding life. You cannot awaken to your True Self if you're avoiding life. You cannot get unstuck by avoiding life. These are not effortless things to actualize. You can't become enlightened or become a hero by getting a certificate. You must accept the call and make the choice. You must throw yourself into life and let it forge you.

You must feel everything you're terrified to feel. You must face your mortality and take claim to each breath. Yes, it will ask of you more than anything else will—it will also offer more than anything else can. It's this path that enables us to share our gifts with the world and live fully expressed.

If you choose to have a heroic life, you must stop preferring fantasy over reality, you must stop avoiding the twenty-one things listed, and you must stop fixing and start living. 🐾

Stop Fixing and
Start Living

"We cannot change anything until we accept it.
Condemnation does not liberate, it oppresses. The
most terrifying thing is to accept oneself completely."
— Carl Gustav Jung

n this first part of the book, I have alluded to some of the
dangers and traps of traditional self-help and spiritual
development work. I've shared about victimhood, avoidance, trying to escape the human experience, narcissism,
and being stuck in our heads. There's a reason I know about them. All
the concepts I'm sharing in this book are all things that I've had to go
through and learn myself. I did not learn this in some course or get a
degree—it was through my journey of self-help addiction, seeking to
ascend my suffering, and overcoming a lifetime of victimhood that
brought me here.

In this chapter, I will share part of that journey.

As a child, I had warts on my fingers and was routinely teased
for them. In my mind, the bullying was horrific. At the time, I hated
the warts... but only because I thought they were why the other kids
didn't like me. All I knew was that nobody else had them, and I wanted
the awful feelings of rejection to end. I was confused and terrified. A

six-year-old bundle of love that nobody at school wanted to be around because of these bumps (at least that's how I felt). The kids were afraid of what they didn't understand and wanted to destroy it, and so was I. I didn't care what it took; these warts were a cause of agonizing turmoil and had to be annihilated. I thought that if only I didn't have them, then I would be accepted.

At the time, I saw the warts as something wrong about me that I must control, remove, and destroy. Whatever I could do to make the rejection stop. I had no idea that there are countless other children with warts that didn't face the problems I had—that it probably had little to do with my fingers. I didn't know any better. I didn't care about who I was. I was in emotional agony. From my six-year-old perspective, the environment was telling me that there was something wrong and unlovable about me. I thought it was the warts because that's what all the teasing was about. I didn't want to be teased; I wanted to have friends. The 'cause' of suffering had to go.

After a few failed attempts, they were eventually lasered and burned off by age eight.

Yes!

I was so happy, so relieved, so thrilled that I was normal now. That now people would like me. I was proud of going through the pain and effort to get rid of what people thought was bad. I wanted to be *good*. To be *lovable*, like them. To come back and say, "Look! You can touch me now! We can play together, there's nothing to be afraid of, the bad things are gone. You can sit next to me, it's okay, I'm normal like you!"

Finally—peace, acceptance.

...until they found something else to make fun of next year—and for the next ten years.

In retrospect, I see that it had little to do with my warts. What I felt arose from how I rejected my True Self in an attempt to be accepted by another. I let the pain of social rejection supersede the betrayal of myself. I wanted so much to be loved and accepted that I abandoned myself. Of course, as a child, I didn't know any better. Sad as it is, that's what we do at any age: **destroy ourselves because we believe** **we are unlovable, in order to be loved by somebody who doesn't**

love themselves. We might not think that's what we're doing, but on some level, we can feel when we're selling out. This form of self-betrayal often leads to denial—and always to suffering.

I HAD TO FIX EVERYTHING

This is not merely a tale about a little kid not wanting warts. The betrayal continues! By the time I was a teenager in high school, the teasing and bullying had been happening for years, and my self-esteem had been decimated. I struggled with girls now, too—as if regular social rejection wasn't enough. There were countless nights of crying myself to sleep because I felt like everyone else was out having fun except me. There were a few years of suicidal and even homicidal thoughts. I wanted revenge and to hurt a lot of folks that hurt me—and even innocent people. This was because I despised the innocence in myself that was rejected, and thus a source of my suffering. I was filled with hate, anger, sadness, despair, confusion, jealousy, hopelessness... it was a dark place for many years. The loneliness and ostracization were devastating for me; I took them personally and gave them a lot of meaning.

During this time, I was trying to figure out the 'why'—why was being happy so hard, and what was so wrong about me to be this disliked? In the beginning, like the warts, it was fairly superficial. I was grasping at straws, relying on the passing comments of my peers. At some point, a classmate suggested doing something different with my hair. He said it would look a lot better longer. I thought, "Okay, maybe it's my hair. Let's try it." I grew my hair out, and to my surprise, girls started paying more attention to me. "That's interesting," I thought, "I can actually get people to treat me differently by changing my appearance? What else can I change about myself to improve?" As you can imagine, many of the things I tried were surface-level fixes that only got me so far.

In my senior year of high school, I discovered much more that could be shifted besides my appearance. I found some basic self-help books that offered various things to say or how to approach situations with different attitudes—and they worked. After twelve years at school—feeling hopelessness, despair, confusion, and apathy—I finally had *hope*. It was the realization that **there were things that I could do to change my situation in life.** I didn't have to "just deal with it." This saved me from suicide by showing me I could save myself—the power of *true* hope. Nobody else was going to do it for me.

I realized that true hope is the recognition that you can save yourself. That you can bring yourself out of your own suffering.

From here, I went all-in.

There was more improvement in my early twenties, which also led to more destroying of my unwanted. All the qualities, traits, beliefs, and emotions I deemed "unlovable" I wanted to change, fix, upgrade, or hack. That icky shadowy stuff needed to be dealt with, and as a young adult, I decided to do whatever it took to transform. Now I knew that it was possible and had the tools to do it. I made a choice to do something about what I didn't like, rather than stay a victim as I had the first part of my life.

It seems elementary in hindsight and almost silly to say now. Yet, for me at the time, it was revolutionary. The idea that I could improve myself and it could lead me to a completely different life was nothing I had a context for. I thought you just dealt with whatever life threw at you—I didn't realize you could throw things that *you* wanted at life! Before this, I did not understand that I could also be part of what caused my future. That's how steeped in victimhood I was. My mindset was, "I can pick my food and maybe my job—but all the big stuff? Doesn't that happen if it's meant to?" It was one of the most significant wake-up calls of my life. It was the incredible power of personal development and healing that changed everything for me.

I continued this path, learning everything I could about self-help. I wound up going through professional practitioner training in various modalities at twenty-one years old. I went in thinking I was going to learn all sorts of cool tricks. I imagined I'd come out a wizard of sorts, but I emerged on the other side more of a cleric, a healer. Not anything I ever dreamed of, but I couldn't deny the benefits of the therapy and healing I had experienced. I began a deep-dive into alternative healing work, spending years (and a lot of money) trying even harder to fix myself. I most definitely became identified with my problems. I healed a lot and transformed myself over many iterations of identity.

However, something was off. Despite my breakthroughs, healing, and a much better attitude about life, I was still suffering.

Unbeknownst to me, my motivation through much of this was not wholly pure. I sought illumination, not for light and warmth, but to burn. Not to illuminate the shadow, but to annihilate it. It was not creative libido, but destrudo. I finally realized this when, after ten years of work—and despite incredible results—there was no end in sight. At some point, I began "doing the work" to avoid life. I saw my future down this path: always worried about being 'fixed enough,' continuing to burn off the unwanted for eternity, and forever pushing away peace. I was getting by, chugging along, plugging more and more data into the 'equation for suffering.' I was in my own personal (development) hell.

I knew I had to stop. I knew that if I didn't, I'd be stuck for the rest of my life trying to fix myself. And so I made a new choice. I decided it was time to stop trying to fix everything that was wrong with me and start actually living my life fully-alive.

STARTING TO LIVE

I still don't have it all figured out, I haven't fully accepted every single thing about myself, and I'm still in the process of what is unfolding next—but I'm no longer willing to put my life on hold until I'm perfect or perfectly ready. This is permission I've always had but never allowed for myself. It's something we all have, even if we don't accept it. You have permission to not be "perfect." You have permission to be who-you-really-are beyond all the judgments, problems, and fixing. You have permission to stop the compulsive 'persona development.' These permissions are built-in—I'm not giving them to you.

This addiction to fixing is another response to feeling broken or not enough. Or layered on top of that, a judgment that it's not okay to be or feel like that. We take away our permission to be flawed or feel less-than to protect ourselves against the pain those stories cause us. We do this because we know they're not true and we want to stop believing them. The problem is, we still do feel that way and are still buying into the stories—but we don't want that to be the case. If you won't allow or accept what you feel or think to be true, you are fighting against what-is and will always lose. We must be allowed to feel, be, and consider these are okay—even if it's not true, or else we become neurotic. We must surrender and move past the fear of "If I allow myself to feel this way, it's going to validate what I don't want to be true about me." Trying to con yourself to avoid facing a lie you're already convinced of isn't going to work. It's going to drive you crazy.

The secret is in the allowing. Once you allow yourself to be broken, not enough, or unlovable, you stop fighting against yourself. Once you stop resisting and fighting to protect yourself from your own distorted beliefs, you can begin to see the truth beyond them. We think that by stopping the fixing and accepting ourselves as-is, we are buying into a victim story or are destined to stay broken and suffer. This is the ego's scam and is the illusion keeping you stuck in 'fixing addiction.'

What would happen if you stopped all the fixing right now and started to do everything you've been waiting to do?

No more techniques and methods for releasing, clearing, fixing, or removing what doesn't feel good. No more hiding behind reading a book a day and applying none of it. No more bouncing from one healer to the next coach to the next therapist to the next shaman to the next modality. No more studying endlessly until you're perfect before ever attempting something new. No more using people to grow instead of having a real relationship with them.

No more waiting, delaying, or stalling. No more avoiding your current life until it becomes a future fantasy. No more putting off until tomorrow. No more deprivation to save for special occasions. No more plan-b's or giving up to get it right next life.

More meeting people that don't share the same perspectives as you. More going on adventures out in the world and exploring places you'd never imagine yourself going. More publishing, creating, selling, releasing, and speaking of things you haven't reached perfection in. More peace, more silence, more stillness, more awareness. More vulnerability, more transparency, more honesty. More touch, more intimacy, more surrender.

More letting yourself feel everything that's real without judgment. More direct experience of the now without being in your head. More presence without an agenda. More unknowns and uncertainties without expectation. More mistakes without guilt.

What would a life like *that* look like for you?

This all requires great surrender and self-compassion.

In my life, I see this as a daily practice, not a one-and-done. I'm not waiting to write this book until I have all the answers. I'm not afraid to get into a relationship while I'm still figuring things out. I'm not waiting to have the business and life I want until I finish all my learning and have it 100% embodied. I'm not waiting around gathering data until I'm sixty with a gray beard just so people may take me more seriously. New things arise as I move forward. Stories want to come back for a visit. When I get caught up in any of it, there is no drama. I respond more often with humor. I know it's okay because now I'm aware of it and can make a new choice. I no longer beat myself up or take myself out. I stop, have compassion for myself, and make a new choice. I encourage you to take a similar approach rather than beating yourself up even more.

Stopping the fixing can be the start of the rest of your life.

A CROSSROADS

You are now at a crossroads. You can continue being stuck, doing things the same way, and getting the same results. You can keep struggling and beating yourself up for doing it. You can set this book down and spend another few years trying to overcome it in an "easier" way.

Or... you can do something totally different. **You can stop fixing and start living.**

"Stop fixing" does not mean you stop moving, growing, learning, or healing. It doesn't mean you won't have disease, need to make a shift, make better choices, or have to exercise. It doesn't mean you are excused from cruel behavior because now you think you can do no wrong. It doesn't mean that everything you've been doing thus far was a waste and is now invalid.

It means:

- You stop the story that you're broken and stop addictively and neurotically looking for your next "fix."
- You approach your process from a place of wholeness rather than incompleteness.
- You abandon the quest for peace outside of yourself and enjoy the heaven resting inside.
- That everything you've been doing was necessary for you to get to this point.
- You will let yourself have fun, mess it all up, do it wrong, be a rascal, and fail a whole bunch without making it into another reason to suffer.
- That whatever you choose is okay.
- That there's nothing wrong with you because you no longer need to "fix yourself."
- You retire the "Equation for Suffering" and stop using it to justify your stucky story.

It will take some time. It's a *process*. You don't have to do it all at once in one grand flash. Have patience and compassion with yourself. It's only the ego that rushes or needs to be somewhere else. Some of the best advice I've received has been to give myself a decade. This takes all the pressure off of having to be there instantly (wherever *there* is). If I get there in four years, that would still be fantastic. By putting ourselves through all the stress and anxiety of "needing to have the end-all-be-all as soon as possible," it only gunks up the works. It's not about the length of time, but the pressure we put on ourselves. You'll get there faster by slowing down.

Don't only take my word for it—claim this and experience the divine serenity for yourself. These concepts are meaningless until you have a direct experience of them. The inconvenient reality is that this is not something anyone can give you. As I wrote in "Where Change Happens," the concept or belief of "being enough" is not the same as the *experience of knowing* you are enough and embodying it. This is the "level of change" beyond the persona-identity. It's the stopping that lets you connect with the silence and stillness, allowing "change" to occur as Truth incarnate.

People are always asking, "Yeah, but *how*? How do you stop doing all of this stuff? What's the *secret*?"

Here's the secret: you just *stop fixing*. There is no magical technique around it. It's really that simple. You stop fixing yourself by stopping everything you're doing to avoid being human. None of it is real. All the fixing does is validate the belief that you're broken and not enough, which is the cardinal Equation for Suffering. Stop it. If you claim that you "don't know how to stop," I will be teaching you how to genuinely stop in a later chapter.

Take the following to heart and live from this knowing:

You are enough. You are lovable. You are not broken. There is nothing to fix. The only thing to do is stop; stop all the searching for fixes that sustain your illusion of being broken.

PART I SUMMARY

Part I has been about getting to know the many ways you've arrived to being stuck. Getting uncompromisingly honest with yourself about how you've been showing up in the world. Getting shaken out of your rigidity and holding patterns of perception.

In summary, in each chapter you have discovered potential reasons for why you're still stuck, including:

1. You are holding on to stories that are not True or that no longer serve you.
2. You are focusing on the wrong level of change, you're out of relationship with your True Self, or are avoiding being vulnerable.
3. You are creating the struggle by searching for the solution, you're hoodwinked by secondary gains, or are too identified with your problem.
4. You are relying too much on your intellect and not trusting your intelligence due to a judgment of feeling.
5. You are caught up in your "self" and have built a narcissistic image, attempting to get your needs met yourself.
6. You are suffering and on a path of seeking or are rejecting what makes you human.
7. You are trapped in blame and victimhood, refusing to take responsibility and accountability.
8. You are avoiding life itself and not allowing what is true to inform you, having yet to answer the call of the *heroic life*.
9. You are making your life about being broken or are addicted to fixing.

What you've read so far has leaned more towards 'why.' The next half of the book will be more explicit on the 'how.' If you still haven't had a breakthrough on 'why,' do not fret: there is plenty more explanation on why you're still stuck to come. In Part II, I'll be showing you how to break through and continue this process.

PART II

MOVING FORWARD

A Universal
Approach

> "As above, so below;
> as within, so without;
> as the universe, so the soul."
> — Hermes Trismegistus

 n the beginning, it is proposed there was a singularity that propelled an inconceivable amount of energy from its origin. This continued expanding at extreme densities, heat, and speed. Everything in the universe in *chaos*— rushing from a single point, all at once, in all directions while it was still nothing material. It was so hot and dense with energy that it took about 380,000 years for the initial burst of light to shine through.

This was the "Big Bang," and it is believed by physicists to be the conception of our universe. Everything we see and know came from this singularity.

Fast-forward about 13.7 billion years, and there is *order*. Physical laws, matter, radiation, gravity, electromagnetism, and so on govern the known universe. There are now potentially trillions of galaxies, more stars than grains of sand on Earth, and many of those stars with dozens of planets orbiting them. There are countless black holes, supernovas, nebulae, asteroids, subatomic particles, and other cosmic stuff not yet discovered. It is incomprehensibly enormous.

If the Big Bang theory is accurate, it means this enormity came from a single source. If energy and matter are considered the same, and energy cannot be created or destroyed, then the potential for everything that is and will ever be must have been condensed within that single point. What exists today has not been added in from another universe but found within the potential energy of that original singularity.

The bang hasn't stopped banging either. It is still expanding and still evolving from all that light and energy-matter. The manifestation of what we see today is not a separate result of a cosmic explosion billions of years ago—it *is* the bang itself. The Big Bang is not only our atomic ancestor, but we are literally *it!* We look quite different than we did 13.7 billion years ago, but you and I are the same bang.

> ✵ *"A blade of grass is the journeywork of the stars."*
> — *Walt Whitman, Leaves of Grass*

PATTERN RECOGNITION

We've established there was a 'bang' of energy and light at the conception of our universe... but did you know there is also a 'bang' of light that occurs at the time of fertilization at the conception of a human? Zinc is released in a flash of light when the egg is successfully activated by the sperm. This finding wasn't only measured but observed. Scientists have been able to photograph this burst of light as it happens. I've seen photos of this myself, and beholding an egg emitting light at the time of conception is astonishingly beautiful.

Isn't it curious how what happened at the beginning of the universe also occurs at the beginning of life?

Let's stay with this idea and connect some more dots:

There was a Big Bang, which science believes created our universe. It was undoubtedly the brightest event that has ever occurred. There is a burst of light at the time of conception between egg and sperm.

The speed of light squared is the bridge between matter and energy. In our modern technology, what always indicates power or electric 'life'? A light.

The first words of God in Genesis are, "Let there be light." Eastern mystical traditions teach aspirants to 'wake up' or be 'reborn'; this is always described with terms such as 'illumination' or 'en*light*enment.' Native traditions associated day and night with the sun dying or sleeping at nightfall, and its rebirth or awakening in the morning.

What is the pattern here?

The examples of 'light' illustrate that beyond culture or belief systems, that between scientific reasoning and myth—there is a common thread that runs through them. We see this archetype emerge universally throughout civilization. It points to a symbolic Truth—*whatever that may be*—revealing a primordial property of consciousness.

Whether you think there's a correlation between the Big Bang and enlightenment, the conception of a child and Genesis, or science and mysticism is irrelevant. What matters is your willingness to accept the underlining *pattern*.

If you can see that what's going on 'down here' mirrors what's going on 'up there,' and if you can recognize that 'in here' somehow mirrors what's going on 'out there'—you possess one of the most empowering perspectives for relating to the universe that has ever been taught. Your recognition of this sacred pattern will change the very nature of how you see reality.

It has been shared in many ways before:

- Einstein demonstrated with E=mc2 that matter and energy are one and the same; that the potential of one is contained in the other
- Eastern traditions teach that duality is an illusion and that we are all one
- Christ said, "The father and I are one"
- Pythagoras saw the cosmos and the body as a harmonious unity; Plato and Leonardo da Vinci later shared this view as well

- In Hermeticism, there is "as above, so below" and "macro-cosm and microcosm"

This is a diversity of fingers pointing towards the same eternal Truth. Do not look at the words. Do not get caught up in judgments of the finger, or you will miss it. Look beyond and see what they are all pointing at. Likewise, the words in this book are not *it*—they're merely fingers pointing you towards the actual thing.

> *"Everything in the universe is within you.*
> *Ask all from yourself."*
> — *Rumi*

As the Heavens, So the Earth

In ancient days, the high cultures of the world had a sophisticated grasp of the heavens. Pyramids, temples, and holy sites often aligned with astrologically significant events or constellations. The sun was worshiped, and solstices were deemed holy. Planets were exalted and even played roles as gods in western mythological pantheons. Medieval royal courts were designed to mimic the patterns of the heavens. Our calendar and the names of days are based largely on the celestial bodies of our solar system.

I have seen firsthand the importance of astronomy to early Christianity. When I was visiting Florence, Italy, I went with a great teacher to explore one of the medieval basilicas. We noticed that there were celestial markers centrally designed into the original floors. A grand groove ran the length of the church that marked various planets at specific intervals. From the lack of any information about it and the chairs that covered it, it was apparent that whatever this was once used for was no longer of importance. The relics of our ancient ways remain elusive unless you know what to look for. The cycles of the heavens were of supreme importance and curiosity, far beyond seasons and crops.

The ancient mystery schools, alchemists, mystics, and great spiritual teachers also knew of this connection. They experienced the relationship between what's 'up there' and what's 'down here.' They saw past the individual as some isolated, self-contained, irrelevant, separate, extra part that was accidentally dropped into an environment from which it did not belong. They were tuned-in to a greater awareness of our place in the cosmos—one that many of us in the modern world have lost touch with.

But we do not have to rely on mystical wisdom alone to understand this principle. A scientific, mathematical way to demonstrate the ancient Hermetic maxim of "as above, so below" is through holography and fractals.

A hologram is a three-dimensional image created from an interference pattern of light. One of its defining properties is that every part of the image contains the whole. If you were to cut the hologram into pieces, you'd still be able to see the entire original image in each cut piece. If you were to do that with a standard two-dimensional image, you'd only have the part you cut per piece, like a jigsaw puzzle.

Fractals are patterns that reoccur at scale. Each part has the same quality as the whole. We can see this in the formation of galaxies, crystals, and the unfurling of ferns. Each one can be defined with a mathematical formula and repeated indefinitely, smaller or larger.

We can sum up these two ideas as: **The parts or lower levels (below) contain or mirror the whole or higher levels (above), and the whole, the parts.**

There are many empirical examples of this in our world:

- The Fibonacci sequence, golden mean, and other sacred math is found throughout nature and art
- The blueprint for a whole life form is found in the DNA of each individual cell
- The expansion of a star is birth, and its collapse is death, just as all life expands to live and contracts when it dies

- As mentioned, mathematically provable in fractals and holograms
- The branches of a tree in the sky mirror its roots underground
- The exact same atomic elements that make up the celestial objects make up us
- The functions of our cities mirror that of ourselves—waste management and intestines, plumbing and our veins, communication networks and our nervous system, government and our brain, hospitals and our immune system, entertainment and our pleasure senses
- The orbit and rotation of electrons around a nucleus in an atom is the same as planets around a sun

This list illustrates concrete ways we can see the holographic, fractal nature of reality manifest in our physical universe.

As we move beyond what is easily measurable, it is reasonable to assume there are other ways this manifests in life. While more subjective, they are far more practical and applicable. The most helpful of these is the inside-outside connection of our consciousness.

What does any of this talk about holograms, space, and mystics have to do with getting unstuck? In order for us to establish the universality of an idea, we must see how it applies, well, universally. Like all good tales, we unravel the tapestry of relevance as we go.

Now that the stage has been set, and you can rationally see how what's 'above' somehow corresponds with what's 'below,' we shall begin to explore the practicality of this paradigm-shifting premise regarding our stucky story and awakening.

AS WITHIN, SO WITHOUT

Suppose we look out into the world and evidently see that what's above and below mirror each other. The next step is to look inside and see the same thing. 'Inside and outside' is synonymous with 'above and below.'

Here are some ways we can see this manifest in us:

- What we feel in our emotions reflects in our body language
- What sickens our psyche can sicken our body
- How we see the world mirrors how we see ourselves
- What we judge about others we judge about ourselves
- The archetypes of humanity as a whole play out in the individual
- Our seemingly unique struggles are the most universal
- What's going on for the individual reflects in the society

The macrocosm and microcosm reflect each other. We are not occurring in isolation—we are a part of the whole. The whole is visible within each of us, as the hologram.

What you struggle with is what humanity struggles with. The conflicts of a culture are the conflicts found within its individuals. What you want to fix within yourself is what you see broken in the world. How you treat others is how you feel you deserve to be treated. The cycles of nature are our own cycles.

THE OUTER REFLECTS WHAT'S WITHIN

How we see the world is a reflection of our mental worldview. We interpret our experiences through individualized filters that distort, delete, generalize, and give meaning. We project our stories, beliefs, judgments, and limitations onto everything around us. This is why ten people can be at the same event, and how they each recount it can sound like ten totally different events. We are living in our own somewhat inaccurate versions of a shared world—one that we each think is real.

This illustrates the inner-world outer-world principle of 'as above, so below.' The perception of what we see around us reflects what's going on within us. The biblical way to see this is that God created man in his image, and so we create in ours. The world we see around us is our creation, and it is in our image. It is our projection that we perceive in the world around us.

For example: If we hate people and think they're looking to screw us over, this is what we will filter our experiences through. We will see a world full of hate and betrayal through our projection, and that's the world we will live in. Or perhaps we have had positive experiences early in life and decided that people are quite lovely, and that's how we see the world. We will have a starkly different life based on the choices we make and perceptions we choose.

What if what we see around us isn't what we want? Are we stuck with this perspective? Of course not. Just as we created this distortion, we can uncreate it. It is the same power we abandon when we choose victimhood. We have to ability to transmute what doesn't serve us into something more useful and empowering.

ALCHEMY

Here is where we shift from *understanding* our perception to *changing* it. We know "as above, so below"—but it's also "as below, so above." Changing how you feel changes your body language, and changing your body language can shift how you feel. You can create shifts in your external world by shifting internally, and you can also create change within by showing up differently in your outer world.

How do you do it?

Inside-out: If you want to change something in your life, change it within yourself first. If you want to have more things to be grateful for, you need to start being the person who's grateful. If you want more money, you need to find that wealth within you. If you want more beauty and joy in your life, start allowing yourself to feel more beautiful and joyous. If you want more passion and connection in your relationships, indulge in your own sensuality and inner-intimacy.

Outside-in: If you want to change something inside, change it in your life. If you want to feel more grateful, be generous to others. If you want to feel more abundant, see the abundance in everything around you. If you want to feel more beauty and joy, observe yourself in the beauty of nature and the playfulness of its creations everywhere you go. If you want to feel more sensual, start using more of your senses to explore the melodies, textures, colors, scents, and flavors in your everyday life.

The key here is understanding that both of these come from your own choice and action. None of these examples depend on circumstance or another to change you. If you wait around for the world to change to feel differently, you are disempowering yourself. You are saying, "I am not powerful enough to determine how I feel. Someone or something else has the power over me to make me feel different." If you go through life this way, you are at the effect of the world and will remain a victim to it. Many people in our modern society move through relationships in this codependent way, oblivious to the cages they put themselves and each other in.

To be empowered demands responsibility and accountability. It is to say, "I cannot control or force anyone else to change, nor can they me. If I am to change, it is up to me. If someone is to change, it must be their choice and their actions to change. We can inspire and we can love, we can teach and we can empathize—and at the end of the day, what we each feel is up to us." People whine that it's not fair, but personal responsibility is the only thing that could ever be fair.

THE PHILOSOPHER'S STONE

As you've learned in Part I, when we cease being victims and take responsibility, we become free. This freedom allows us to no longer be stuck with our default perception of the world. This sovereignty is not only one of will, but of reality. We are free to create our own life, rather than go along with the consensus trance.

The secret is that we have the ability to change the way we see the world.

This is alchemy. It is the right use of mind. We are transmuting from one level of consciousness to a higher one. As we shed our ignorance and become enlightened, we see what was once lead now as gold. It's not the matter that changed our mind, but our mind that changed the matter, and the only thing that matters is that our mind has changed.

181

Once we make our unconscious interpretations conscious, they no longer operate as "that's just the way things are" beliefs. Once we illuminate what is dark, we see things differently. We are then no longer at the effect of our stories and can willfully choose how we see the world. We can stay unconscious or become lucid. We can distort our perceptions (positively or negatively). We can suffer or be in joy. We can be abundant, or we can be scarce. Reality will keep being real, and we can see it accurately or keep distorting it.

A DIRECT EXPERIENCE

When people realize they can change their perception, it's usually through positive psychology, self-improvement, or new age practices. They want to make everything 'better.' Positive, exciting, sparkling, more and more. The booby trap is that those are our *ego's* definition of better. Often, people end up getting what they thought was 'better' and were similarly as miserable. Getting plastic surgery or putting a better coat of paint on your view of the world is not what I'm referring to. That is still an avoidance of life.

We will keep interpreting and giving what we see meaning until we are ready to accept accountability. Only once we want to see ourselves honestly and completely—to look in the mirror and perceive accurately—will we see the Truth. This Truth with a capital 'T' is not a personal truth, but a reality beyond ego or interpretation.

We've all experienced this Truth, whether we realize it or not. There is *something* that keeps the planets orbiting and spinning that we call gravity. There is *something* that produces what we call life. There is *something* we feel when we are in what we call love. There is *something* that creates what we consider physical reality. There is *something* that occupies our body while we live, and no longer does when we die.

These are all True. They don't require any personal interpretation or scientific or religious understanding to happen. All of these happen with or without our meanings, math, or ego. They are self-evident. What that *something* actually is, has been open for debate since humans could reason. Yet, the ability to reason was not the cause or source of that *something*. Reasoning only allows us to understand and explain what is *already* real.

The more we can sit in the silence and stillness of that *something*, and the less we spend in the naming, labeling, and proving of it—the more accurate our experience of reality will be. Dropping the proving, deleting the need to understand, stopping the compulsion to figure it out, quieting the neurotic stories and judgments, and surrendering the defenses will open you to the divine around you.

This practice moves us towards 'symbolic awareness,' which means that we experience directly without interpretation, language, or thought. This is the realm of the mystics and shamans. This is the world of myth and archetypes. There is more Truth and reality here than any word I could write or facts you could learn—just as there are more nutrients and flavor in a bite of steak than the word "steak."

How do we get there?

PURIFICATION

The more we get out of our own way and stop the analyzing and interpreting—the more of life we allow in and can truly experience. The more we are *in* life and the less we are *watching* life. The more 'above' and 'below' come into lucid relationship, and the less we are tricked by illusion. This all leads us into greater resonance with our True Self and the Tao.

Ultimately, what we need to do is drop *all* filters. We don't want to distort positively *or* negatively—we want what's pure and accurate. We want to be able to see the beauty and love *and* the horrors and evils within the same thing. We want to see what's happening around us without taking it personally, giving it meaning, or judging it. We want to have a direct, symbolic experience of reality, not an interpretation or analysis through our heads.

This is what 'purification' means. Purification is not some twisted punishment or repressive puritanical dogma—it's quintessential healing. Healing doesn't mean it's always rainbows and unicorns. This healing is indeed the fire of facing what we've distorted, denied, and suppressed. This is the flame mystics refer to. It's the burning-off of impurities—the fire of purification. We are making our windshield crystal-clear again. We are removing the contaminants from the water. We are taking the filters off our camera lens and ensuring what appears on the photograph is what matches what everyone sees. We are aligning with the Tao; making the father and son one; we are Buddha in the immovable spot. We are aware of the illusions of our world and still pierce through it into reality.

This is the heart of this work. It is more than merely getting 'unstuck.' **This book is about waking up to the lies and illusions that got you stuck in the first place—not layering even more on to get by.**

As all revelations of Truth end, purification ends with illumination, bliss, and peace.

How You Do One Thing...

This chapter thus far has been mostly conceptual. We have laid the groundwork for understanding the nature of our universe in order to know how we move through our own lives. By understanding that which mirrors us, we can see ourselves from a new perspective.

We have established:

- How our universe is holographic and fractal
- How what is within and without us mirrors each other
- How we distort our perceptions and project onto the world
- How valuable it is to drop our filters and see our world accurately
- How we can experience life directly by dropping our judgments

Now that we have a grasp on these principles, the question then becomes: "how does this metaphysical wisdom help me stop struggling in physical life?" None of this theory means anything unless we can apply it to our own daily life—but without the doors of perception open, the application lying ahead is easily dismissed.

Moving forward, we may sum up this chapter into a single, practical phrase: **"How you do one thing is how you do anything."**

This phrase will become your new mantra. Say it every day until it becomes a part of who you are: "How I do one thing is how I do anything."

The more you presuppose it to be true, the more you will see it everywhere, and the more benefits you will reap. Do not be lenient with it; it works better when you apply it strictly, not as a vague, half-baked ideal. It is universal, and as such, applies universally (which you know to be true from the last many pages we've spent demonstrating the principle).

Hence we can assert some way, at some level, the following is true:

- How you approach making your bed is how you approach your marketing
- How you see the world is how you communicate
- How you draw is how you eat your meals
- How you go to work out is how you go to business meetings
- How you focus on your household is how you are in bed
- How you hug reflects how you relate to people
- How you treat the janitor and CEO is how you treat yourself

Let's explore a few of these and see how they correlate. It's in this correlation you will see *the divine pattern* in its most practical, yet non-rational, way. The following sections present questions for self-inquiry into the relationship between each approach. Keep the phrase "how you do one thing..." in mind as you read.

Bed & Marketing

Do you make your bed every morning or let it go until whenever? Are the sheets kept clean, fresh, and tidy—or dingy, old, and messy? Do you have fine linens or cheap synthetics? Are you militant about how everything is made each time, or do you make it look good enough?

Do you have a schedule or system in place for marketing, or is it whenever you have an idea? Are all your websites current and updated, or does the year in the footer refer to three years ago? Are you using the free and cheapest versions of everything, or do you pay for professional services? Do you obsess over your professional image, or do you let people see how you usually are?

Worldview & Communication

Do you see the world in order or chaos? Do you feel bitter about 'them'? Is everything a drama? Do you never feel certain?

Do you write in long-winded run-on sentences without proper punctuation, or do you write grammatically correct? Is there bitterness in your voice and a scowl on your brow? Do you use eight extra exclamation points? Do you end your speech in an upwards intonation?

Drawing & Meals

Where do you place your pens, pencils, and paper, and how are they organized? What is your focus and attention like? How do you feel about the time you're spending? Do you have professional-grade or cheap tools?

Do you set the table or grab flatware and napkins whenever? Do you watch TV while eating? Are you guilty and in a rush, or relaxed and present? Are you dining with silverware or plastic?

Janitor & CEO

Are you treating them the same or different because of their role? Are you taking their position into account before you even deal with them? Do you elevate one above the other? Do you look at what they can do for you or how you can help them?

Do you expect to be treated differently because of your position? Do you feel entitled or oppressed? Do you put others on a pedestal above you; do you put yourself above others? Do you feel taken advantage of, or are you generous?

You get the idea.

Did you compare and see how this was valid or invalid with previous experience? Are you going to nitpick and find flaws as if this was an argument you had to invalidate, or are you going to get the point I'm making and see how you can apply it to your life?

How you're approaching this idea is how you approach other things in your life. How you're judging and thinking about this is what you do to yourself. How you're approaching this book is how you approach other things in your life.

This is not a book-reading—this is your life. How you read this book is in some way how you live your life.

USING THIS TO GET UNSTUCK

When we're stuck, we're often focused on one thing: where we're stuck. This can put us into a bias where we are misperceiving the situation and leaving out all sorts of data. We're so used to it, we delete and generalize information that's right there that could be useful in moving forward. It's the proverbial "forest through the trees."

I have good news and bad news:

The bad news is that what you're doing there is probably holding you back in other areas too.

The good news is that what you're doing there is probably holding you back in other areas too.

It's bad news because you're probably stuck in other areas in the same way without realizing it. It's good news because if you can make a shift in those other areas, it'll make one here too. Once you can see why you're still stuck, you have an opportunity to change it. Not make

187

it wrong, not make it right—but to try something different to get a different result and see how that works. This openness to experiment and explore with different perceptions and approaches—rather than judging and making a story out of it—is a highly functional way of moving through life. This offers us an unlimited potential of outcomes because the range of possibility is limited only by your ability (and willingness) to see things from a different perspective.

Many times our 'stuck spots' get magnified the more we focus on them. We try to rub a stain out of our shirt but end up only wearing the fabric down. We can put so much pressure on getting that stain out that we eventually rub a hole into it.

If you're still caught up in one area, and nothing's changing, you can stop putting so much pressure on it and look at something less 'charged' to regain vision. You can focus on a similar aspect in an unrelated area that doesn't have the same triggers, charges, or stories attached to it. Let's look at an example of how you could go about it.

A PRACTICAL EXAMPLE

Bob has been trying many things to get clients in his business and is still stuck. For the past three months, he's been obsessing over it, and despite learning a lot, he doesn't feel any closer to his vision. The more he tries to get clients, the more he pushes them away.

So he stops focusing so much on that area and takes a pause. He picks an unrelated area of life and assesses how his intimate relationships are working. By assuming "how he does one thing is how he does anything," Bob may find out that there's something glaringly obvious that's hanging him up there too—a shift that would directly apply to his business situation.

Our dear friend Bob assesses his love life. And to nobody's surprise, he hasn't had any partners for years. Moreover, in his social life, he sees he doesn't have many friends. Not a big problem for Bob because he's so busy anyway. A professional doesn't have time to mess around... right? But he does begin to wonder why there hasn't been anyone in his life... It turns out it's because he hasn't been out meeting anyone new. This makes sense.

Bob isn't naive; he knows there's something else to it.

He meditates on it and digs deeper.

Ah-ha, there it is. He drops into it. Already it doesn't feel good. He sees a few memories of his mother getting upset at him with chores. He sees another memory of a high school girlfriend that cheated on him with a rich jock. He feels inadequate.

What is this really about? He feels that no matter what he does, he's never enough. He sees how he has never felt quite good enough to be with anyone as a serious partner. Bob has been waiting to be wealthy, in-shape, fully healed, and good in bed before he's ready to meet anyone. He's attached so much of his self-worth to finding a great mate.

Bob looks at his business and sees the parallel. He's not out where his potential clients would hang out, so of course he's not getting new clients. Bob notices that he secretly doesn't feel quite experienced enough to charge as much as he's been asking. He sees that he doesn't feel confident in the value he's providing, even though nobody has told him otherwise. He sees that he is making 'having clients' mean something about himself and was unknowingly using them for self-validation.

Bob can see that even though his business and love life are entirely different parts of his life, he's approaching them in the same way at an unconscious level. Now that he is aware of what's really going on, when Bob makes the right shift in his relationships, he will affect the same shift in his work. Or, if Bob shifts the way he relates with clients by letting go of his story, he will also open that same space for a partner.

This is because **how Bob does one thing is how he does anything**.

I've been Bob, and so have many of my clients. We all do this in our own ways. Applying this *universal approach* to every place I've been stuck has helped me see past my blind spots and uncover how I self-sabotage and hold myself back.

By assuming this maxim to be true, you can rapidly begin to make new choices in the 'easy' areas of your life that will transfer over to the more challenging ones. This takes all the pressure and focus of what you're obsessing about changing and allows some new perspective to seep in. This cascading effect shows up in your thoughts, feelings, body, relationships, bank account, behaviors, clothing, health, and literally everything else.

For example, if you:

- Shift how you move physically; it will change how you move through the world ideologically
- Shift how you give to your customers; it will change how you give to yourself
- Shift how you treat people you don't like; it will change how compassionate you are towards yourself
- Shift how you create space in your home; it will change how you hold space for clients
- Shift how you pick up a fork, take food from your plate, take a bite and chew; it will shift how you take in new information
- Shift how you embody an archetype; it will change how you do it in life
- Shift how you love yourself; it will change how you love others
- Shift how you see abundance in nature; it will change how you see it in your house
- Shift how you pick up a guitar; it will change how you touch your lover

It's all the same thing.

When you apply this principle, take care of not comparing apples-to-apples directly. You may find that the behaviors and mindset you have between different things are entirely different, and then say "hogwash." But with further introspection, you may find the timbre, the feeling, the meta approach, the worldview, the qualities, or the results to be the same. It may not be in a physical way, but rather in your mental approach. It may not be what you believe, but your process of relating. Think symbolically and metaphorically, rather than only literally and rationally—even though in many instances it *is* literal.

CONCLUSION

Let's bring it all together. If you can recognize that what's above mirrors what's below; that everything you see around you is a projection of your mind; that healing is not about putting on better or more positive filters, but dropping distortions altogether; and that how you do one thing is how you do anything—then you are able to heal yourself by aligning with the Truth.

The more you clearly and accurately see the world around you, the more you accurately see who-you-really-are inside you—the more real and accurate your life becomes. The closer your life aligns with reality, the less suffering you have.

The people that suffer the most are the ones with the greatest distortion in their perceptions. The one who distorts by living in a fantasy world of rainbows and unicorns suffers similarly as the one in a fantasy of demons and monsters. The one who sees the world only as evil people suffers similarly as the one who only sees kind people. They both suffer because they are living in a world that isn't real, and only what is real and true can heal and bring peace. The positive filter removes real threats and dangers that can harm or kill us, and the negative removes real kindness and abundance that supports us.

Only a fully-expressed and a fully-experienced life can ever truly satisfy and fulfill us. A life where we discern and choose wisely, but not judge and select based upon a faulty assessment of what is positive or negative.

We struggle due to a distorted perception of ourselves, which mirrors the world. Accuracy of perception is only possible without judgment. Only Truth ends suffering.

This chapter can be a turning point for how you move through life. Apply this *universal approach* with earnest effort, and you will experience for yourself that when you change one thing, you change everything. 🐙

WHEN WRONG
WORKS

"Forget safety. Live where you fear to live.
Destroy your reputation. Be notorious."

— RUMI

 umans love to be right. We also love to *do* it right. Whether that's morally right or functionally right, we are wired to align with correctness. That's why you've been doing all this work: because you think something's wrong and you want to make it right. You want your life to work correctly, or at the extreme, you need everything to be perfect. This all goes well if what you think is right *is* actually correct. If your results match your intentions, and you know when enough is enough, then you're probably fine.

...but what happens when your results don't match? What happens if, somewhere along the road, what you think is correct gets mixed up and you don't even realize it? What does it look like when what you "think is correct" is actually incorrect in reality?

You start to say or think things like: "I've been doing everything right yet nothing works!" or "That wasn't my intention!" or "The more I do this, the worse things get!" or "It needs to be perfect" or "It's not fair, I don't get back what I put out."

It can be maddening! It can feel like you're going crazy when you do what you were taught is 'good' and it makes your life worse. To spend all the time, money, energy doing something that has worked for everyone else and still fail. To be trapped in between doing the 'right thing' and suffer, or doing the 'wrong thing' and being bad.

This dynamic has kept me stuck more than anything else. For so long, my results didn't match my effort. In my head, I thought I was doing all the right things and knew all the right stuff, but the results I was getting told a different story. I knew something was off, but I went into denial because it didn't make any sense. I insisted that I was doing it the right way because it made sense to me. I assumed I needed to do more to get the results I wanted, thinking I wasn't doing enough. Well, it didn't help—it got me more of what I was already getting, which I didn't want.

This pattern showed up anywhere from business to my relationships, because as you know, *how you do one thing...* The most fascinating place I saw this was in my body.

I remember early on in my martial arts training, I would be moving how I thought the sifu instructed... and then I looked at myself in the mirror and saw something entirely different. When I thought I was relaxing, I was tightening. When I felt like I was standing forward, I was actually leaning back—all sorts of wacky stuff. In my mind, I was sure I was doing it right, but physical reality showed me my mind was incorrect. I could not deny what I saw in the mirror or the feedback I was given. I knew that what was revealing itself in my body was a reflection of distortions in another part of my life. (You will have a chance to experience this for yourself later in the chapter, "A New Way to Move.")

What was going on, and why did I have things so wrong? How did others get it but not me? Was this a specific psychological condition?

This phenomenon was not something I had ever heard of despite a decade of transformational work. Nobody had ever mentioned anything about this in fitness or psychology, yet it was clear that this was a real thing that had eluded me in understanding why my life wasn't working. Once I learned the reason for this frustration and how to identify and correct it—areas of my life that never worked before started to become functional. I realized that this was a new psychological theory that nobody else in traditional or alternative medicine was discussing or able to address.

STUCK IN REVERSE

Have you ever had the baffling experience where you saw someone who you thought was "not doing it how they're supposed to," ended up solving it faster or were treated better than you? Have you ever had the frustrating experience where the more you did what was "right" or "good" or what you "should" do, the worse things got?

It is a curious thing to do something that feels correct and have it fail miserably. Sometimes it makes us angry and resentful, wanting to be mean, or bad, or not care anymore. Sometimes it makes us confused, depressed, and bitter, wondering why it works for everyone else but not us. Sometimes it feels like no matter what we do, we're always wrong, even if we try and do everything perfectly. It is another curious thing to do something that feels totally wrong and have it work well. Sometimes we think we did an awful job, or we felt selfish, or we were mean, but everyone else says they thought highly of us. Sometimes when we hardly try, don't care at all, or are unattached, we do better than when we really care and try hard.

I've witnessed many instances in my life and with clients of how we think we're doing 'good,' but it ends up hurting us or another—and when doing it 'wrong' ends up being helpful.

Here are a few examples:

- We think that we're being good parents by doing everything for our kids, but we are actually codependent and end up hobbling them later in life. Or we think we're being protective and keeping them safe from getting hurt, but they grow up afraid of failing or taking risks, not knowing how to learn from their mistakes or figure it out themselves.

- We think we're being 'so nice' and 'so giving,' but sometimes it's a manipulation. We have an agenda or are acting in a way that's attached to an outcome. It's not true generosity and kindness because we're trying to get something and end up being resentful when it's not returned.
- We think we're protecting people by imposing new restrictions or helping by giving handouts, but we're actually being victims who end up taking away people's liberties, power, and sense of self-reliance.
- We think we're being not-selfish or not-arrogant by rejecting compliments or gifts, but we're actually being selfish because we deny the other person their joy of giving and don't have to feel our discomfort receiving, and we're arrogant because we think we don't need it or them.
- We think we're comforting someone who is "feeling bad," but we are actually acting superior, thinking they aren't strong enough to do it themselves. We're rescuing the person from their own self-love and take away their healing process. This is called 'rescuing,' and it is done primarily because we're not comfortable watching them feel something we don't want to feel ourselves, and then we try to stop it in them to stop it in us.
- We think we're trying to find an easier or quicker way but are avoiding what works. We end up making it harder for ourselves than if we did the "hard" thing to begin with.
- We think we're being narcissistic by talking about our story, but we're actually being generous and showing up.
- We think that hiding out and playing it safe will keep us alive, but it only keeps us from living life.
- We think that by being generous we will have less, but we actually have more the more we give—consider hugs, laughter, joy, gratitude, and smiles.
- We think that letting the other person decide is generous. We think that we are giving them the option to pick what they want, but we are afraid to lead. We are actually

unwilling to take the risk of making the wrong choice ourselves and place the burden on them.

- We think that our 'negative emotions' are there to hurt us. To feel better, we need to stop feeling them. When in actuality, they are there to teach and heal us, and the resistance, repression, and avoidance of feeling is what actually hurts us.

These are some of the countless ways we think we're doing the 'right thing,' but the reality is the opposite.

These opposite outcomes are called **reversed-results**. When these occur, it means that what we have labeled or identified as 'good' or 'right' or 'correct' is inaccurate. We have it *backward*, which gives us the unexpected opposite outcome. What we think is 'wrong' is actually correct, and what we think is 'right' is actually not.

It's as if the kitchen faucet had the hot and cold water pipes installed backward, and the more you turn the knob to get cold water, the more you get burned with hotter and hotter water. You can see the label says "cold," so you truly believe you're doing the right thing and following instructions. Unbeknownst to you, the pipes are switched under the sink without the labels being changed. How were you supposed to know? You had no idea; you did it 'right' and still got burned.

This is exactly what happens in that list of examples.

Like electrical wiring, our internal 'wires' are switched and left with reversed labels. We might know the words and what they mean, but embodying it and living it shows we have our definitions incorrect. This 'wiring' usually gets set in our nervous and energetic systems as we grow up, so we have no idea it's backward because it's just how things seem.

We are blind to it because it's within our *chain of perception*.

This *chain* includes our previous experiences, beliefs, stories, meanings, judgments, and other things that new data is parsed through as we experience it. It's like an effect rack for guitars, where each effect takes the prior sound and modifies it one-by-one until it's out of the speaker. As new data comes in through our own 'chain of perception,' it passes through all those filters which taint the information—one of these being our 'crossed wires.' Since this crossing is part of how we perceive everything, we don't typically see it—just as we don't see our retina or optical nerves. Because of this 'blindness,' in order to become aware of this reversal, we usually need some sort of feedback or a new level of awareness to recognize it.

What we're doing in this work is removing as many of these 'guitar effects' as possible so we can have the purest input and output in our body and mind. We want a clean signal, not one with distortion and noise applied. This is similar to how we 'collapse the stack' of our *perceptual stack* of filters, as discussed in the chapter, "An Equation for Suffering." This stack of filters is only one aspect of distortion that lies within the chain of perception.

The embodiment of this 'wire crossing' is what I call ***reverse-wiring***. This is when we move through the world in a way that we *assume* will generate one result, but in reality, it creates the opposite. We assume it will because we've been 'wired' to see hot as cold and cold as hot. This wiring occurs when we give the wrong meaning to a distorted interpretation of reality, often subconsciously, and it becomes the new 'reality.' This condition can arise top-down from the mind to the body through beliefs, or from the bottom-up through physical trauma or energetic imbalances of polarity in the body.

However, this effect isn't isolated to your own life experience. We may be born into a family living in a distorted reality for generations and know no different.

For example, five generations ago, an ancestor may have had a trauma and gotten reverse-wired. This distortion was passed on to their children, all the way down to one of your parents. Your great grandparents would have attracted partners and friends, or even a career and city that resonated with the distorted perception. By the time you were born, many people around you were wired that way, and it was "just how things are" for your family. From there, it becomes the same for you. You were then raised, often with the best of intentions, with a way of operating in the world that doesn't work for the life you want to live now.

This reverse-wiring is one of the top reasons we get stuck because what doesn't work feels right, and what would work feels bad. It creates decades of neural pathways set up in the 'wrong direction,' misaligned chemical reward systems, and stories that justify the struggle. The harder we try, the worse things get. The alarming part? We're nearly all oblivious to it.

SUPPRESSING MY SMILE

One of the most illuminating reverse-wirings for me was around my smile. For many years I'd start to smile really big and then unconsciously force my smile into a frowny-smile. I still looked happy, but I was suppressing the sides of my mouth and cheeks from rising. It's the kind of smile you see on someone who is ashamed or embarrassed that they are smiling. After noticing this for a few months, I came to understand I did this whenever I felt too feminine. If I was smiling and it brought up feelings that felt feminine, I subconsciously got scared and nervous because it felt 'gay.' I had all this judgment around that feeling and didn't want to feel that way when I smiled, so I did the frowny-smile to avoid the feeling.

It was terrifying and confusing, and it made no sense that my sexuality was correlated with my smiling. I eventually got to the point where I no longer wanted to avoid and deny. I had to know what this was really about—I couldn't keep censoring myself. Whenever I noticed myself do this, I stopped, and let myself feel the uncomfortable femininity. I had to be willing to feel gay, and even *be* gay, in order to stop suppressing myself. I had to get to the point where I was willing to do and be whatever it took to be true to myself—even if it meant a total collapse of my sexual identity.

"People will do anything, no matter how absurd,
to avoid facing their own souls."
— Carl Gustav Jung

As I let myself finally 'feel gay,' I realized it had nothing to do with a desire for men. This was not a homosexual feeling but repressed feminine energy that I misidentified. Allowing myself to feel this, I further realized what the whole complex was about: *beauty*. I was avoiding feeling my beauty because, at some unconscious level, I distorted and gave an incorrect meaning to what I felt while smiling. This feeling was not about sexuality, but I had to be willing for that to be the case in order to go into it and find out. For so long, I thought people would think I looked gay or girly when smiling (a threat to my then western male ego) because that's what it felt like to me, and so I avoided it.

I could not have been more wrong.

As I started to let myself feel this beauty that wanted to come through my smile, I felt uncomfortable and self-conscious. All the stories and judgments rushed in on red-alert, trying to protect me from danger. But I faced these stories and surrendered to the feeling more and more each time. I thought I was going to get beat-up or something; my body was going berserk. No wonder I avoided feeling it!

And yet... the response from those around me left me dumbfounded.

People gave me sweet compliments on my smile, and women said how I looked more masculine and confident and sexy when I allowed my full smile. Nobody had ever complimented my smile before then. I looked more masculine by letting myself feel more feminine! I was in disbelief. For decades I had it backward—I thought by feeling less feminine it would make me appear more masculine, but there I was, allowing myself to feel beauty and femininity, and it had the complete opposite effect.

It was a pivotal awakening. I saw how backward I was for so many things. It was as if I was living in an upside-down reality compared to what was True and functional. No wonder I had such a hard time in life—I was wrong about everything. I had all the right labels and definitions, and I knew all the right things—but they were the mirror image in reality, and I had no idea.

What I thought was freedom lead to restriction. What I thought was being nice was actually manipulative. What I thought would make me money only brought poverty. What I went for to seek pleasure never brought me joy. What was truly beautiful I found disgusting or deemed it boring. What was real seemed limiting, and what was a fantasy I was drawn to. What I thought would lead me to success made me homeless, sleeping in my car. I avoided color and contrast, thinking I'd stand out too much, which led to a dull wardrobe (and life). I rejected the natural order and cycles of life and food, thinking I was being healthy, but I became malnourished instead.

The more I did things that made me feel like a fraud or not ready, the more I did things that forced me to show up bigger in the world. What I thought were things I had to hide from others to seem cool, wound up being the commonality that brought us together. The times that I felt vulnerable or shared something 'negative' about myself, the closer people felt, and the more they connected and supported me. The more I allowed myself to show up in my shadow and be honest about it, the more the right people could love me. The times that I allowed myself to feel what I didn't want to feel, the better I would come out feeling.

My life was one reversed-result after another. It was all reverse-wiring. Everything in my life started to work the more I did things 'wrong.' What you learn from this chapter may very well save your life, as it has mine.

Let's look at a couple of common examples that further detail how reverse-wiring can practically manifest in our life.

EXAMPLE: TRADING LOVE FOR ABUSE

We could be a few years old and see our brother get all the attention from misbehaving. He's getting spanked and hit, and then hugged and coddled, with our parents spending all day talking with him—while we feel neglected and alone in our room. We are so young we have no idea what that's really about, but we see attention as love and hitting as physical affection, and we know that we're not getting any of that, but he is. We crave our parents' love and approval as children, no matter what it looks like.

So we misbehave and get hit and scolded, and that seems like love to us. We act out to get attention like our parents and siblings also do. We see our mom do the same yelling-hitting with dad, fighting every day because that looks like a relationship to them at some level. They don't know any different. They are playing out the myth they grew up with, simply matching up with what feels 'right'—AKA what they feel and know to be 'normal.' How could we ever know it's dysfunctional if everyone around us does the same?

Continuing this throughout childhood, we see it 'works' and conclude that this is how we must manipulate and act in order to get our needs met. So we play the dynamic out for another twenty years and end up in an abusive relationship ourselves. We are unconsciously drawn to argue and get hit because that's what feels like love and home to us, even if we conceptually 'get' that it's abuse. Many people don't escape this because it doesn't matter what the conscious explanation is; it's the *unconscious* wiring that needs correction.

We know this is reverse-wiring because the abuse feels like love, and kindness feels repulsive. Respectful affection is boring and unsatisfying, despite saying that's what we want. Instead, we seem to attract relationship after relationship with abuse and drama, despite saying we hate it. All of this validates our stories.

Again, this is not 'victim blaming'—it is understanding the hidden reasons why we do destructive things and how it plays out in our life. This is about taking responsibility for how we create our life, and it's about taking accountability for our part in our own abuse—so we can stop, heal, and have a healthy life without blame or excuse.

Nobody wants to think they want to be abused, but if we are willing to see the truth, we can see how we switch love with abuse, affection with drama, and passion with destruction at the subconscious level. Without realizing that we have this reverse-wiring, we will never be able to escape the self-destruction. We will keep pointing the finger at the bad guy and stay in victimhood, perpetuating the cycle. It's not fun to talk about, it's not politically correct, and it can be hard to surrender enough to see how we play our role. Yes, they are responsible for what they did, and so are we. Seeing our role is an integral part of overcoming these patterns and cycles, and it must be addressed if you want to truly get unstuck.

EXAMPLE: SETTING BOUNDARIES

We have been taught to be nice to other people, be giving, and not be selfish. As children, our parents tell us to hug and kiss family members, perform and entertain, and do things to make them happy and proud. If we don't want to do it, family members may coerce, demand, bully, tease, embarrass, or ridicule us into doing what they want. They pass it off as 'parental rights,' 'custom,' 'showing them you love them,' and 'just having fun.' Phrases like "If you loved me, you'd do this for me." or "You love your mother, don't you? You don't want her to be sad or upset, right? Go give her a hug and do what she wants." or "I'm the adult what you want doesn't count, you must do what I say, you don't have any say." or "I don't care if you don't like uncle Jack, you're being rude, go give him a kiss."

This is abuse.

There is a difference between a child's obedience to their parents and a parent who violates a child's sense of trust and safety with manipulations of shame and guilt. These behaviors train us to feel like we don't have a say in what we are allowed to feel or want to do, which carries into adulthood. They condition us to let other people's will or desire supersede our own sovereignty. These mythologies tell us we should feel bad, wrong, or guilty for not wanting to do something that makes us uncomfortable. To feel like we're the bad guy or are responsible for another person's happiness. To feel helpless and powerless. To abandon ourselves for the love and acceptance of authority.

At the extreme of this behavior, I hear countless horror stories of this dynamic leading to sexual, physical, and emotional abuse as children grow up. These families almost always have distorted or confusing boundaries and are ran by shame and guilt.

Even without abuse, these experiences of distorted boundaries present us with challenges later in life. We end up being martyrs or over-give of ourselves. We let other people walk all over us like a doormat.

We emotionally prostitute ourselves to gain acceptance and approval in our relationships. We engage in codependent activities and dramas. We allow disrespect because we're afraid of conflict.

We know this is reverse-wiring because the disrespect feels normal, and standing up for ourselves is terrifying. When we go to set and enforce boundaries, we feel like we're being selfish, mean, or strict. We feel scared, undeserving, unworthy, or anxious when we go to stand up for ourselves. It's backward because boundaries are healthy and necessary. They are respectful of self and other, and are nothing to feel guilty about.

Living a Backward Life

When we are reverse-wired, it may seem that "backward" is more functional. To go fast, we slow down. To get bigger, we must get smaller. To feel more beautiful, we allow ourselves to feel ugly. To understand others, we must understand ourselves. To get, we must give. To see the truth, we must look at the lies. To feel good, we need to go into all the "bad" feelings.

It appears that if we want to go forward, we must go backward. This is what things look like when we are reverse-wired.

From this place, we must move in the opposite direction to go in the correct direction. When we are reversed like this, it seems counter-intuitive to do things the "wrong" way. But this is when wrong works. Now that you understand what reverse-wiring looks like and how it works, let's apply it to your life.

DETERMINING IF YOU'RE REVERSE-WIRED

How do we know if we are reverse-wired or simply doing something that doesn't work? The most direct method is to figure out what the opposite would be and try that.

What would the opposite be of what you're doing that isn't getting you a desirable result? Does the idea of that make you uncomfortable, defensive, or avoidant? That's probably the "wrong" way that in reality is correct, or at least would work a lot better for you from where you're at. If it feels like the "wrong" or "hard" thing to do from a stucky story pathology, you're probably on the right track. Whatever this is, that is what you want to try for a while instead. Don't do it once and give up; you have to give it some time to see what the stories, addictions, and avoidance is about so you can penetrate them.

If you end up doing it "wrong" and get worse results, it may be something other than reverse-wiring. If doing the opposite gets you better results and it's something that feels odd or unusual compared to normal, then that's a good sign you were reversed. Outside of professional feedback or Cinesomatics®, testing things like this is the best way to find out for yourself.

There is no avoiding it: you have to take the risk, be courageous, be willing to fail, and try it 'wrong' to know for certain.

> *"Avoiding danger is no safer in the long*
> *run than outright exposure. The fearful*
> *are caught as often as the bold."*
> — *Helen Keller*

Here are examples of how to 'do the opposite' of a reverse-wiring:

- If you feel like saying "no" is scary and rude, start saying "no."
  You may see that people respect you more, rather than take advantage of you or see you as a pushover.
- If you think that taking what you want first will displace others or make you look selfish, start doing things that feel selfish and put yourself first.
  You may see that your needs get met quicker, and other people see you as someone who is assertive with initiative.
- If you think that being 'salesy' is wrong and gross and yet you aren't getting any new clients, try being more 'salesy' and see if you get more sales.
  You may see that your definition of selling is distorted, and

205

*when you sell people your valuable service, they are happy you
have helped them.*

- If you think having your girlfriend pick all the restaurants
  is generous and a way to make her happy, try being more
  selfish and pick them for the both of you.
  *You may see that what you thought was selfish was actually
  leading, and she's happier that way.*
- If you think being skeptical is keeping you safe from the
  dangers of the world, try being open-minded.
  *You may see that your fear was keeping you from exploring
  life, and with more options and experimentation, you are able
  to select safer ideas you would never have known about or an
  activity you enjoy.*
- If you feel like structure takes away your freedom and not
  scheduling anything is more flowing, try to schedule everything.
  *You may see that a schedule provides for more freedom because
  you know exactly what is when and where, you can coordinate
  your availability with others, and you remove non-productive
  time, which creates efficiency and more free time.*

These are a few out of hundreds of possible examples. You must
spend the time to go in and discover what these are yourself. These
resolutions are less about what mentally or conceptually would be
considered incorrect and more about what *feels* wrong. Go to the
place you're avoiding, the direction that feels outside your comfort
zone. The approach that's in the opposite direction of what you usually do (the one that keeps you stuck). This is the solution to what we
discussed in the chapter, "An Avoidance of Life." Can you see how
we get reversed-results from living an avoidant life? It's the *opposite*
of the heroic life!

It will usually feel awkward and 'wrong' if you're doing it correctly—that's the entire point. When we're so used to doing it one
way and then do the opposite, it can feel awful at first.

SELF-LOVE FEELS AWFUL

I remember quite a few times living with roommates, where I felt like I wasn't being respected and wanted to say something but was afraid to cause conflict or attack. I waited and waited over multiple occasions until I had enough of feeling like a prisoner in my own home. When I got up the courage to enforce my boundaries, it felt terrible. My insides felt all twisted, and I felt like I was coming face to face with destruction. It was as if my primal brain was concerned they'd attack me, or I'd be rejected, or have to fight to the death. It did not feel good to me at all to speak up for myself.

It is no wonder so many people struggle with this—the agony and anxiety we put ourselves through doesn't seem worth it.

But it is. What we don't realize is **that horrible feeling is actually self-love.**

What we *think* we're doing is avoiding conflict, but what we're really doing is running away from self-love. When we go so many years without respecting ourselves, without setting and enforcing boundaries, and without standing up for ourselves, we get reverse-wired. Each of those things is loving to self and other. Enforcing our boundaries is not rude, mean, bitchy, selfish, or entitled, despite what others (who benefit from you believing that) would like you to think. It doesn't matter who or what is disrespecting you; I don't care if it's the president or the king—you deserve to be treated respectfully. Genuinely standing for truth and love is never wrong.

But somewhere along the line, we have accepted a different story— one that makes self-love feel like acid and allowing ourselves to be mistreated a noble act. If you are not used to loving yourself, it will likely feel awful at first because you're reverse-wired. Self-love will feel bad, just as abuse feels normal. Being respected and treated well will feel uncomfortable, whereas codependency feels like home.

A prime example of this is the 'victim' from the chapter, "The Victim Trap." To the victim, freedom feels like danger, love feels like a threat, responsibility feels like blame, and accountability feels like guilt. This is why it's so hard to help someone in victimhood because, to them, many of the things that would actually empower them feel like the opposite.

This type of response eventually changes as our wiring gets corrected, where abuse truly feels dangerous and bad, and love truly feels safe and good, and we're no longer addicted to the self-loathing, self-destruction, and self-abuse. This process requires time, practice, and diligence to form new neural pathways and penetrate the stories that justify the lie.

As you 'flip' your approaches and behaviors to potential reverse-wirings, notice what your result is. If you **are reverse-wired** regarding something, you will likely be uncomfortable doing the opposite and may be surprised by how people treat you or the results you get. They will be more functional or 'positive' outcomes compared to the 'correct' or 'right' way you've done before. If you **weren't reverse-wired** around that particular approach, then you'll likely find it feels close to normal, and you'll get a lot more blowback and inferior results.

THE NEED FOR BETRAYAL

If you attempt these 'flips' with people that know you well who are used to the stories, dynamics, and manipulations, they may not respond with such welcoming arms. People expect us to act in a certain way and will try to keep us in our place—the place they have put us in their minds. Sometimes it's jealousy or meanness, and other times it's simply our minds keeping a stable orientation of reality where consistency and order feel secure. Usually, it's because we are playing into each other's myths and stories, and when we change and they don't, there's now a gap. This is a dissonance that makes them uncomfortable.

They may say "crabs in a bucket" phrases like:

- "Who do you think you are?"
- "That's not like you."
- "Don't be so sensitive!"
- "That's not the Sally I know and love."

- "I liked you better before you read that 'still stuck' book."
- "Are you going to leave me?"
- "You've changed. We're concerned about the new you."
- "Do you think you're too cool for us now?"

If you know for certain your life is working better, that you are more functional, and are happier, **these phrases are a good thing to hear.**

These phrases are meant to keep you down as you rise up and change. People don't usually want to change, which means that they don't want *you* to change, and so these are favorable indicators that you are. And that's what we want—we want people that used to disrespect us, ignore us, mistreat us, not appreciate us, and judge us to now treat us differently. The functional, healthy, and supportive people will get it and give you positive reinforcement that it's better being around you. The people who aren't will likely say these kinds of phrases in a way that doesn't sit well.

There are many people we love—family, friends, lovers, clients, employees, customers—that are not willing to move forward in their life and so will subconsciously, or even overtly, want to hold us back. We are entangled in codependency, manipulative games, abuse, habits, responsibilities, and cultures that glue us to limiting or even destructive relationships. If we wake up from this, take responsibility and accountability, heal, and make new choices, we can reach a point where we grow apart. This is normal and okay.

As you do this, be aware there is a certain 'gravity' that keeps us attached to these mythologies and people. There can be years or decades of momentum built up. Similarly to how it takes tremendous initial energy for a rocket to reach escape velocity, it may take some initial effort to 'escape' the pull of our family, culture, and stories. It may feel like betrayal or abandonment to you or them. If you or they take it personally, you may feel guilt, or they may try to guilt you as you try to break the codependency and existing relationship dynamic.

This is, again, normal. If you are sure that what you're moving towards is self-love and growth, then you must proceed through this 'stucky web,' or you will get sucked back in.

Yes—what I'm suggesting is *betrayal*. Not because that's what it really is, but because that's what it often feels like. It feels like stopping these stories betrays our family, culture, and years of work. It can feel like we are abandoning those that seem to care about us for some selfish gain. It's not. If anything, it's a betrayal of the abuse, codependency, manipulation, and mythology, which are themselves the true betrayal. But we must be *willing* to betray them in order to break through, even though that's not what is really happening. **It is a betrayal of the story and suffering, not the people.** If we feel bad about doing something loving for ourselves and others, it exposes another reverse-wiring on the way out of suffering.

And that's what this is—*loving*. It is *loving* to stop abusing despite the other person not wanting you to. It is *loving* to leave a dysfunctional relationship (for both people) even if they don't like that you're leaving. It is *loving* to do what you are inspired to do with your life, even if your controlling parents are disappointed. It is *loving* to take away junk food from a child even if they throw a fit and hate you for feeding them healthier meals.

We cannot let the superficial reactions of those who are ignorant deter us from what we know is right for us.

In this context of reverse-wiring, when we allow ourselves to do what feels like betrayal, we are demonstrating an act of courage and love. This form of betrayal doesn't mean we do things to disregard or harm others. It's not revenge or distrust. It's not about neglecting others or isolating and being greedy. It's not even about anyone else. It is about your sovereignty, maturity, health, healing, growth, and accountability that allows you to be an example of self-love for others. You may look like the 'bad guy' to those who are stuck in abuse and codependency, but you are also a leader who can show others that it is possible to break free and live a life of respect, love, joy, beauty, peace, functionality, and service.

Our dreams require us to betray who we 'should' be for who we are to become. It's self-betrayal to acquiesce to the demands of a dysfunctional relationship. It's self-betrayal when we abandon ourselves for a lie.

Our loyalty must be with truth, not suffering. We can only give when our cup is full. We can only offer to others what we allow for ourselves. We can only truly love others if we have self-love. We can only truly respect others if we have self-respect. We can only truly be generous if we are generous with ourselves.

PERFECTIONISM: THE OTHER WRONG

Sometimes the reason we're stuck is not due to a full-blown reverse-wiring. We can come from a place of trying so hard to do it right that we end up getting reversed results. We try to be perfect or do everything right, but instead we get in the way of everything we want.

We get so transfixed on doing a good job, being a good person, doing it correctly, following the rules, doing it perfectly... that it ends up awful. The fun, joy, spontaneity, juice, breath, and life all get sucked out of it. It's like a painting turned gray from over-correcting. Or a house that has rules for everything to keep the kids safe, but then they're afraid of doing something wrong and don't feel safe.

We're afraid of failure, making a mistake, and looking like a fool. Afraid of disappointing our parents, losing our friends, being attacked, burning in hell, being a bad person. We're afraid of dying, of messing our life up. We're unwilling to be ourselves, in the glory of all our gifts and flaws.

We don't feel safe in being *human*. So we filter, censor, fix, and do everything we can to erase our flaws and weakness so that we are no longer vulnerable. We want to look perfect, act perfect, create perfection, and be perfect in order to feel safe or be lovable—but it can only ever lead to the opposite result. **Our attempt at perfection is the antithesis of our lovability.**

> ✄ *"In heaven, all the interesting people are missing."*
> — *Friedrich Nietzsche*

This need to be perfect comes from our core wounds of not feeling like we're enough or that there's something wrong with us. We grow up feeling like we were never enough, that our work wasn't good enough, that we could never be right no matter what we did or said; there was always something to nitpick or disapprove or judge about us. As children, this creates massive neurosis because the main thing a child wants is love and approval from their parents, and they will adapt and abandon themselves in any possible way to obtain it.

You are now not allowed to be wrong, fail, make mistakes, or express yourself honestly because:

- You will be seen as weak or a failure
- You will disappoint your parents
- You will embarrass your parents, tribe, or self
- You will die or get hurt
- You will be a bad little boy or a bad little girl
- You will be fired, lose clients, or become destitute
- You will be rejected or ridiculed
- You will lose, lose respect, or lose status
- You will let everyone down who depends on you
- You will no longer be desirable or lovable
- You will be punished, disciplined cruelly, or go to hell
- You will do something that ruins all your hard work

We are frozen—afraid to try new things we may be bad at, afraid to fail and make mistakes, afraid to take risks that we will probably end up doing wrong, afraid to look like a fool or bad person—and so we don't do anything. We don't move forward. We don't experiment, attempt, explore, or try... and so we learn, grow, innovate, and evolve as fast as a sloth. The need to be perfect and do everything right paralyzes us.

The way out of this trap is to start doing things wrong. Mess it all up. Make mistakes. Fail on purpose. Get rejected on purpose. Try to do it bad or poorly. Let go of any attachment to outcome. Do the opposite of what you would normally do—go in reverse, do it backward, change the order. Be a bad boy or bad girl if you're always 'good.' Try foods, games, genres, and hobbies you've never tried. Give yourself permission to do it all wrong and be okay with the consequences. See what you learn. Notice what it feels like. Observe the results, internally and externally. You have to be committed and let go. Surrender and indulge in it. Own your experience of doing it wrong; don't do it half-assed.

My clients often experience a release and an opening. More freedom. More ease. Less pressure. Less constraints. More playfulness and humor. More creativity and intuition. Less dogma and rules. Less control and more surrender.

Applying this to your own life, you might notice:

- The painting might have more freedom and breath and creativity in it
- The date may be a lot more relaxed and fun because you don't have an agenda
- You are able to brainstorm a lot of potential new ideas for products
- You actually really enjoy something you once judged and rejected
- Things that used to be hard seem a lot easier and even fun
- You are much more flexible and adaptive
- People find you more charismatic, funny, authentic, and confident
- You are a lot less stressed, anxious, or compulsive

As you do these and figure out when wrong works, you will realize that whatever meanings or judgments you had about "the wrong way" were inaccurate. When we give ourselves permission to do it wrong and mess it all up, we discover that the consequences are nothing like we expect.

It's a beautiful thing.

If you're stuck or have realized that you've been a stick in the mud, I invite you to become the fool. Do the opposite of what you've been 'doing right' if that hasn't brought you the results you want. It may not be what you're expecting, and it may have consequences, but it's going to be different. Anything different is the right direction when you're stuck, because it leads to new insights through feedback. 🐾

THE ESSENTIAL
EXTERNAL

"The truth will set you free,
but first it will piss you off."
— Joe Klaas

ou can get a lot from a book, but not everything. You can do a lot of your healing work by yourself, but not all of it. You can go fast alone, but you can't go as far as possible. You can gain a lot of knowledge from reading, but not embodied wisdom. It is right and well to be self-reliant, self-studied, and independent. However, it is not everything.

If you are stuck, chances are it's not because you haven't learned enough on your own. You're likely still stuck because you're too close to yourself: you have biases, blindspots, filters, and self-deception. There are things you're doing, thinking, or perceiving that are so natural, familiar, and habitual they don't seem like anything. You simply don't know what you don't know.

Dwelling on old data in the same ol' way ain't gonna reveal anything new.

Similarly to how you can't see your own face without it being reflected back to you, there are some things about your internal reality that can only be revealed through the external world. We learn who we are through our experiences with one another. It is not due to a failure on our part that we must rely on others—it's by design. The external is equally as essential as the internal. As within, so without.

We won't get far if we are locked away in our own little world, trying to do everything ourselves without any help from others. We need fresh perspectives from another person, an experience in the world, or new feedback. A closed system goes stale quickly—think a small pond versus an ocean. Without new input into our lives, we spin our wheels trying the same things in different ways, while thinking it's something new. It's like trying thirty different kinds of pasta thinking you're exploring all these exotic foods, getting out of your comfort zone... but it's all the same thing—wheat.

This is one of the biggest cons I see people do in this work. They read more and more of the same kind of books, attend the same types of seminars, work with the same teachers—and nothing changes except for the names and faces. They stay busy, spend money, and studiously learn fresh takes on the same ideas for years—all while in denial. They pretend like they're trying new things, that they're dedicated to changing, that they are doing the work—but what they're *really* doing is avoiding the very thing that would move them forward.

It's using 'healing' to not heal and self-help to hide out. It's a big scam—a game to play to avoid having to do the uncomfortable, foreign, scary, confronting things that would force them to show up in their lives. They want to feel and appear like they're making progress, but they aren't willing to stop struggling and make new choices.

On rare occasion, when someone like this comes through our workshops and are attending year after year without making any new choices, we ask them to stop coming. They are only invited back once they stop using me, the participants, and the healing energy to hide-out and hold themselves and the group back. It's a wake-up call for folks—as it was for me when I was told the same thing. We offer great patience and deep compassion for people's shadow in my trainings. This work is not for those who want to use learning and spirituality to avoid real change. There are people who are simply not ready, which is fine, but it's a disservice to them and those who show up sincerely to enable the behavior in our groups.

This is an extreme example, but many independent and self-motivated people are hiding out in healing work. We need to see the truth of how we are showing up in the external world to see the truth of how we are inside. We try to do it all ourselves 'at home,' but we cannot do it all, alone, forever. We can do a lot for a while, but eventually, we reach an upper limit of what we can do by ourselves.

The real question we want to ask ourselves is, "why do we *want* to do it all alone?"

FEEDBACK IS THE KEY

The biggest challenge we face when learning the truth and knowing if what we're doing works is that we are "in our own box." Inside our boxes of reality, we hardly question what we think is true because of the very fact that we believe it's true! Inside our minds, we live in our own little world where we think what we do works—and sometimes it does, but not always for what we ultimately want in life.

To escape this conundrum, we need *feedback*. This feedback comes in two forms from the external environment to help us track the reality of what's going on:

1. Feedback as input from others
2. Feedback as manifested results

Combined, these two forms of feedback allow us to 'triangulate on the truth' by connecting the dots from numerous reference points. Like GPS, which uses three satellites to pinpoint your precise location through triangulation, multiple forms of feedback help you discard the extraneous input and hone in on the common denominator. For example, if your bank account, employer, homestead, lifestyle, health, friends, and family are all reflecting the same thing—chances are there's some truth to it. If a random guy off the street judges you, that's a lot less reliable reference point.

The more reference points we get of what works and what doesn't, what's true and what's false, what it looks like to be in our head or in our body, the more we can begin to observe and adjust ourselves accurately. When it comes to getting unstuck or discovering our reverse-wiring, external feedback is an essential piece we can't get from our own head.

Feedback as Input

Feedback in the form of input is having someone else report back to you what they see. The person acts as a mirror to reflect back to you how you're showing up to them. Only the facts of observation and impact. This is what we typically consider 'giving feedback.'

Feedback Does Not Have:

- Value judgments
- Advice, meanings, opinions, or interpretations
- Stories or projections
- Likes or dislikes
- Mollycoddling or hand-holding
- Rescuing, excusing, or enabling
- Fixing or coaching
- Attack, defensiveness, or blame
- Agendas or hidden motives
- Motivation or cheerleading
- Exaggeration or dilution
- Superiority or other 'levels'

If any of these are present, it is not feedback. It may be something else useful, but it is not considered feedback.

Apparent by what it is *not,* giving and receiving clean feedback can be a challenge. We hardly experience it in our daily lives. People don't want to hurt our feelings or offend us. They may be jealous, and want to attack us, make us wrong, project, or hold us back. Or they may want to 'help' and give opinions, advice, coaching, comfort, or inspiration—which are not *bad*; they're just not *feedback*.

You need to have someone that can set all that aside and only report the details of what they see. Receiving feedback is best done through someone you trust to give it to you straight: a coach, therapist, mentor, mastermind partner, teacher, or business adviser. Your friends and family tend to be unreliable sources, as they'll likely be stuck in the same stories as you. The challenge is finding someone who's not afraid to offend you and who doesn't project their distortions onto you. If you don't have a few people you trust to give you feedback, make it a priority to find some. A great place to start is with others who have read this book. The foundation it provides for sharing feedback offers fertile ground for exploration, whether you create a formal study group or discuss casually over cocktails.

Having a group of people to tell me the truth when I'm lying to myself or disconnected has saved me. This has been so instrumental in my life and business that I now facilitate group trainings to cultivate and share feedback at the highest levels. We see people who have been stuck for years move forward quickly because they finally get told the truth—feedback that nobody else was able or willing to say.

These group feedback sessions are invaluable because you get to see if you're:

- Lying to yourself and others or telling the truth
- Disconnected or connected to yourself and the space
- Being vulnerable or pretending to "do vulnerability"
- Having the impact you want compared to your intention
- Full of it or actually being genuine
- How you're leading and following, and how others respond
- If you're bypassing, defending, justifying, or letting the feedback in
- Feeling what you're really feeling or if it's merely a show
- Present and in your body, or off somewhere in your head

219

It's impossible to see ourselves accurately through our filters, so we must look to the outside world to see the effect we're having. You may think you're being one way, but you may be doing something completely different in actuality. Without feedback, you're trapped. Having someone give you feedback is a direct and straightforward way to find out how you are actually showing up in the world.

WHAT DOES GIVING FEEDBACK LOOK LIKE?

Remember what you learned in the first chapter about stopping the stories and only reporting what's real? It's the same thing for giving feedback. We simply reflect back what we see and feel about how the other person is showing up. Again, no judgments, interpretations, or meanings. If we offer ideas or suggestions, they may be helpful, but they're not technically *feedback*. We want to stay away from those when sharing feedback.

When we **give feedback**, we only give observations—not interpretations, assessments, or instructions. Feedback should only be given as a reflection; it is not coaching, therapy, solving, rescuing, judging, suggesting, or advising. Feedback is when we mirror the other through us; it is not our projection. When we give feedback, we report the details of what we see and feel.

To **receive feedback**, the person listens. No explanations, no justifications. There is no need to respond or judge the feedback. Simply open, let it in, and feel. That is often enough to induce a shift in awareness. The receiver may ask for clarification or respond with further information, but generally, the more people talk when receiving their feedback, the more they tend to not be listening. (We will explore this deeper at the end of the chapter.) Concluding with a "thank you" or "I see that" is enough.

The upcoming examples are within the context of therapy, but the same principles apply everywhere in life. If you are in a **leadership** position, you need to know how to give feedback to, and be able to receive it from, your followers. If you are a **parent**, you need to know how to give your child feedback lovingly and accurately, without abuse, codependency, or manipulation. If you are a **manager or executive** in a business, you need to be able to give and receive feedback from your employees in a productive, open, empowering channel. If you are an **artist** of any kind, you must be able to ask for and receive feedback about your work in a constructive way to grow and improve. If you are in any **relationship**, communication is everything, and being able to give and receive appropriate feedback without blaming, attack, or arguing will transform your relationships. If you want to become a **good listener or speaker**, understanding the communication principles of feedback will make you world-class. Everyone will benefit from the concepts of feedback, even if you don't use feedback as a formal method.

Let's say someone was at one of my workshops watching a fellow participant demonstrate an embodied archetype. Below are a few examples comparing proper feedback with what *not* to say:

- "It looks like you are out in a field digging" *instead of* "Wow, that's bad. I think that's wrong. You should stop doing this one. You look like a stupid ditch digger."
- "It feels like there's a lot of sadness" *instead of* "What's wrong, are you okay, why are you crying? You can skip this part. Andrew is mean anyway."
- "This movement looks different than the last. There's more joy in your face" *instead of* "I like that better than Bob's version, try moving your arms like this."

Do you notice the difference?

The first phrase is reporting the details (proper feedback), and the second is filled with projections (not feedback).

What usually happens is that people get caught up in their own stories, manipulations, codependency, projections, or judgments and end up holding others back thinking they're helping. People want to protect each other's feelings or rescue, or they get jealous and withhold feedback. They introduce *their own* stories and shadow into the other's process, and now the other has to consider both person's shadow material. It can become a mess.

Unfortunately, this is the norm. Most people don't get or give real feedback. What they usually share is a morsel of data encompassed by noise. It's not to say this 'noise' isn't valuable in the right context, as all of the projections and agendas get revealed and addressed in our workshops. We not only give feedback about behaviors but also about the feedback given. This ultimately leads to lessons and breakthroughs for everyone. Our professional feedback training is considered by many clients, the most hardcore feedback process in the world for a reason. When people's lives and businesses are on the line, we do not mess around. People need to know the whole truth, fast, without distortion—and that takes practice.

The more you share, the better you get. Once you understand what real feedback is and what it looks like, you can give and receive feedback without all the extras. You are able to tell the truth effectively, and that becomes a great service to the world.

The other thing about giving feedback to others is that we often tell them exactly what *we* need to hear ourselves. There is nobody else out there. We are the same. When you give others feedback, you're giving yourself the feedback as well. When you're generous with telling others the truth so they can move forward in their lives, you experience that same generosity for yourself. What you see that might help someone else get unstuck may hold something in your stuckness, too.

You may still be stuck because you've only had advice, opinion, coaching, and not much real feedback. If you become better at giving feedback, it can help you get better at asking for it and receiving it. You will know what to look for in someone giving it, what is helpful, and what is unhelpful. You will start to be able to tell when someone is manipulating you, lying to you, withholding, jealous, and everything else in the "feedback does not have" list. Even more importantly, when *you* are doing these. Giving feedback shows you how you're showing up for others, and we know that how you do one thing is how you do anything. How you do it for others is how you do it for yourself.

Learning how to give feedback and discern what's useful or not is more than a therapeutic practice. Mastering the underlying principles can potentially save you years and millions of dollars when it comes to know who to hire for guidance, who to trust, and who to employ. It can be the difference between finding a mentor who holds you back or one who lifts you to the stars. It can be the difference between the therapist who saves your marriage or who facilitates its demise. It can be the difference between a friend group that loves and supports you or one that's jealous and gossips about you.

WHAT DOES AND DOESN'T WORK

Far too many people bring others down than lift each other up. If we are gifted and nobody tells us, or worse, puts us down our whole life for it—how will we ever know our beauty and strength? We can go our entire life not knowing our beauty, gifts, and functionality if we're surrounded by people who are jealous or unable to see it in us.

I've had many clients come in thinking there was something wrong with them and how they saw things. I quickly saw these people were actually incredibly functional and gifted, but the people around them didn't recognize it. These were bright lights that adopted the dim mindset of the jealous or ignorant around them. In little time, we helped them see the truth, and their lives took off. They weren't doing anything wrong. They simply never had anyone outside of the bounds of their restrictive cultural mythology tell them how functional they were.

Imagine if Bach were to come to you for help, feeling stuck because he couldn't make his bakery business profitable. He feels pretty bad about himself, like a failure compared to the rest of his baker family. You wouldn't say, "Poor Bach, maybe you should try the latest baking tactics or clear your negative emotions." No. You'd say, "Get this man a piano!" and only then would you start to see him thrive. Sometimes we don't grow up in a culture that can see our functionality because it doesn't compute with its values. Far too many of us end up as bakers instead of composers, simply because the people around us don't have any context for our gifts, and so they are deemed useless. We then live our lives without ever questioning it, oblivious to the stories that we adopted as fact.

"Mr. Anderson thinks everything inside him is
worthless and embarrassing. Isn't that right, Todd,
and that's your worst fear? I think you have
something inside you worth a great deal."
— Tom Schulman, Dead Poets Society

The feedback is there to show us our distortions *and* accuracies in the space. It shows us our stories, mythologies, and archetypes that run us. We see what is possible for others and ourselves. We require reference points for what does *and* doesn't work in reality, outside of reverse-wiring, fantasies, and other distortions. It's easy to focus on the 'negative' and what we need to do better. What's as important—perhaps even more—is knowing when we are shining. We can easily grow up reverse-wired and think that our gifts are our curses, just as much as we can believe our dysfunction is normal. Feedback is the only way to know which is which.

For example, the feedback "you are playing small" and "your presence fills up the space" are equally loving. It is likely, however, that we don't feel both the same. It is common to say one is negative and one is positive. However, this is not accurate. Both are loving because both are telling the Truth.

We may look at these two and determine that one is more or less functional than the other. We might desire the results one produces over another. One outcome may be in more alignment with the natural order, or *Tao*, than the other. But neither feedback is good or bad, right or wrong, positive or negative. The feedback reflects *what is*, not what "should be." It is up to each of us to determine what we do with that data.

APPLYING FEEDBACK IN DAILY LIFE

As you can imagine, most people aren't accustomed to knowing what to do with genuine feedback, let alone give it cleanly. It can quickly become messy outside of the proper containers, boundaries, and expertise. When you are out with your friends or are having dinner with family, it's not the appropriate time to give feedback as you would in a workshop. That's not to say discussing with friends and family is never helpful; they know us the best! They may have a lot to offer us in getting unstuck, and if you both agree you want to give each other feedback, ensure they've read this book and understand what feedback truly is. It's beautiful being able to help others, and knowing how to give feedback will allow you to be of great service to them, too. However, please remember to ask for permission, set appropriate boundaries, and establish expectations for giving feedback if you're going to do this formally. I will also repeat: feedback is reporting the data. It is not advice or opinion.

Recall that feedback does not have (identical to prior list): value judgments; advice, meanings, opinions, or interpretations; stories or projections; likes or dislikes; mollycoddling or hand-holding; rescuing, excusing, or enabling; fixing or coaching; attack, defensiveness, or blame; agendas or hidden motives; motivation or cheerleading; exaggeration or dilution; superiority or other 'levels.'

The right input doesn't usually fall in your lap every day: you must choose to get feedback. Actively ask for it. Do not be shy! Insist on asking for feedback and do it often. "Do you have any feedback for me?" It's that simple. Not "What do you think?" or "Can you give me advice?". Request feedback specifically, not compliments or criticisms. Permit the other person to speak truthfully. Assure them that you will not be offended, take their feedback personally, get defensive, or lash back. You will get more useful data when people feel safe enough not to censor themselves. Of absolute importance is that you honor your word to do so. Show that you can receive their feedback gracefully, or they may be more likely to withhold in the future.

When someone gives you feedback, receive it. Find the truth in it and take action upon it or make the shift by letting it in. People will be happy to give feedback if you use it to help yourself, but they will find it a waste of time if you don't use it. Many people want to help and share, but most won't volunteer their feedback because of social politeness. Demonstrate you are open to honest feedback, make it easy for them, and people will tend to give it to you if you ask sincerely.

Here are some examples of formal feedback:

- "When you spend your day playing games, you often seem dissociated the rest of the night."
- "I noticed that you don't receive compliments well from other women."
- "I don't feel safe when you disrespect my boundaries."
- "You are more open and connected to me when you're present. Being on your phone pulls you away from the space."
- "I don't feel like I can trust you when you gossip about others to me."
- "It excites me when you touch my neck that way."
- "I feel respected when you say that. It also feels like you're respecting yourself."
- "It is not trustworthy behavior when you lie to customers in order get a sale."
- "The song you wrote has a lot of passion and emotion in it."
- "I've noticed you do a lot of other people's work and then complain. It feels like you're martyring yourself."

Just report the details of what you see and feel.

If you're not interested in formal feedback, you can still begin to put these ideas into practical use. One of the easiest ways to start practicing this in daily life is by reporting the details in everything you do. You don't have to turn this into therapy or coaching. Simply start reporting the details of what you see and feel, rather than inflating it, turning it into a drama or story, or any of the other things in the list of "Feedback Does Not Have." Do this when observing what you do, what you see others do, and the world around you. This approach aligns with the idea of 'collapsing the *perceptual stack*' as discussed in the chapter, "An Equation for Suffering," where we want to see reality and the data of what-is, not 'what-is with layers of distortion on top.' Feedback is the same.

Another easy way to apply this is when giving compliments or criticism. When you give compliments, report the details of what you see and feel. Here are some examples: "There is a lot of beauty coming through you right now."; "You feel lighthearted and joyous."; "That shirt brings out your eyes."; "I really enjoyed your performance, I laughed a lot!" No attachment to response, no agenda, no manipulation, no hype and exaggeration, no rescuing, no envy—no nothin'! It's like feedback, but more sociable and casual. Instead of criticizing or even 'constructive criticism,' replace it with feedback (if it's necessary to say anything at all). Check in with where your need to criticize is coming from first.

Remember, feedback is not about being a robot devoid of feeling. Reporting genuine feeling is true and valid. It's not only about criticism either; we need to know what we're doing well and the beauty of how we show up, too. It is loving to know and tell both what is and isn't working for us and others. We don't need to make anything 'positive' or 'negative'—we can tell the truth without any spin.

There is no "good" or "bad" feedback—it's just information. All feedback is love.

Feedback as Manifestation

The physical world lets us see how we're managing the internal world. We know this to be true from the chapter, "A Universal Approach." As above, so below. Natural laws dictate that we must be doing *something* functional if we can affect change or get results in the physical world. Effort, investment, energy, money, time, and resources are required to get anything done. It's a reason why we assume people with big houses and luxury cars are successful or beautiful people are healthy. Since material results require physical labor, resources, and other people, the social and tangible proof reflect the person who achieved them. We know there's *some* correlation between a person and their results, so we fill in the blanks.

The characteristics and qualities of a person are revealed through the years of showing up in the world *doing things*. Thoughts are essential, but alone they are not enough. We must also take action and make choices consistently. This delayed track record over time—which is visible for all to see—makes our manifested results in the world an essential type of feedback. It gives us time to see the cumulative result, not only our sporadic thoughts or actions. These indicators include our health, body, possessions, achievements, influence, relationships, other people's opinion of us, money, art, products, children (to a degree), environment, and impact on others.

If we had to pick one, the single most contentious material indicator would be *money*.

A lot of people have hang-ups around it, but it's a useful measuring tool. The great thing about money is that it's countable, and numbers don't lie. If your bank account has $30 in it and you're going around talking about how rich you are, you're lying or delusional. It's not a perfect indicator by any stretch, but there's a reason people say "show me the money" when they want to see proof.

This is not superficial or materialistic. It's not the things themselves that are so important, but what they *reveal* about us. The importance I'm placing on the material is not really about the material: it's about the intangible qualities they point to. Our manifested results are used as mirrors; they are not the goal in and of themselves. This is where a lot of people lose themselves in the pursuit of riches. The riches are not in the riches—they are in who you had to become to get them.

We need this external form of feedback because it's easy to con ourselves or stay in denial. Getting feedback from manifested results help break our spells of delusion. For example, if you talk about how great of a music producer you are but don't have any tracks to show, you're fooling yourself. If you call yourself a bestselling author, but only because you had a few pages published in someone else's book, you're full of it. If you talk about how healthy you are and yet you're obese, refuse to exercise, and are on five drugs—you're in denial. Far too many people use 'positive thinking' to bypass accountability. It's a great way to get out of pessimism and negative thinking, but it can also be a great way to live with our heads in the sand.

The proof is right there for us to see for a reason. We have this physical reflection to start warning or to encourage us before it gets bigger. We have material and temporal stability, plus natural laws that keep us oriented towards reality. All these dissociated pseudo-spiritual folks think physical reality is bad—it's a blessing! How else would we experience anything? They get it all wrong: the outer world reflects back to us so we can see inside—the place where everything comes from.

Our manifested results ultimately show us the consequences of our choices—and thus, the *actual* choices we made. They let us know not what our hopes and wants were, but our choices and actions. We will dive deeper into this idea in the last chapter, "Above All Else."

ESCAPING OUR PERSONAL HELL

But what if you don't want to look at the facts or do anything about it? What if you want to live in denial? You're not going to stop, and you can't directly argue with the data, so you'd have to change the rules and live in some alternate world in your mind to handle the cognitive dissonance. A parallel world rife with distortion, reverse-wiring, and justifications for everything. Story after story, exactly as a liar has to keep telling more and more lies to uphold the first. It's a virtual reality of suffering, void of responsibility and accountability—and anyone else. Your own Prison of Eden. It's insane.

Again, ask me how I know this one. I've lived in this world a good portion of my life until I started getting feedback. It's a horrifying feeling when you find out you've been living a lie—at least it was for me. A small, lonely world between the walls, with excuses and reasons for every defense—smashed open like a snow globe. My little backward reality, gone. All that hard work, energy, and effort to sustain distortion and fantasy invalidated. It was disorienting, confusing, frustrating, and boy did I fight and cling to it. I had invested so much into that reality, and I didn't want it all to be in vain. But I could no longer go back to what I knew, now that I saw it was false. I didn't find my newfound freedom fun at first. I felt like I was starting over again from scratch, but at least I could start on a path that I was sure was *real*.

We all do this in our own way, to varying degrees. No one is immune—we all have our unique strategies of denial. This is okay, as long as you are willing to hear the truth about it—or else your life will stay the same. The great thing about feedback from others and through the physical world is that it gives you an opportunity to *see*. You are no longer ignorant and must make a choice between sleeping or awakening.

> *"A great man knows when and in what*
> *way he is a little man. A little man does*
> *not know he is little and is afraid to know."*
> — *Wilhelm Reich, Listen, Little Man!*

Start to ask for feedback, join a group committed to telling the truth, or hire someone you trust to do it (see the Postscript). Be open to growing, learning, and improving when you most don't want to. You will get feedback you don't want to hear and some uncomfortable truths that bother you. Sometimes you'll get repetitive feedback about something you think you already know. These are some of the most important because we want to dismiss and not take a good look at them. When we avoid feedback, it's usually because we're trying to get away with something. I only recommend this process because I do it myself. I've added group programs in my own business because I have experienced firsthand how instrumental learning to give and receive feedback is for getting unstuck.

Stay vigilant and receptive, especially when it's hard to accept it.

DEFENDING AGAINST THE TRUTH

Many times we get feedback, but we do not receive it. We hear it, but we do not listen. The feedback does not go in. Perhaps we understand the feedback intellectually, but we stay in our heads without letting ourselves feel it. Maybe we disagree outright and keep the data at bay. Neither of these allow the feedback inside. As I have stated in the preceding section, all feedback is love; thus, we know this also means we are not allowing love in.

Remember: when I say "feedback," I mean *feedback*—not judgment, advice, projection, attack, opinion, or stories. These are not real forms of feedback, and they are not interchangeable! As you read, you may hear a voice that comes in and says, "But what if they're wrong? What if they're projecting? What if they don't understand?" These are valid questions from voices that are trying to protect you, and in this context, they become obstacles. There is no 'wrong' feedback. There is no understanding involved. Feedback is not projecting. If there is any of that going on, it ain't *feedback*.

Receiving (or giving) feedback is not about liking it or disliking it, agreeing or disagreeing with it. It's about *listening*. When we receive feedback, we listen, feel, and let the truth penetrate us.

When we are defending, we are not listening. When we are liking or agreeing with the feedback, we are being just as defensive as when we are disliking or disagreeing with it. All are judgments. When we are judging, we are comparing the incoming data with what we already know to determine if we will accept it or not. This may be appropriate out in an insane world, but it is detrimental when receiving feedback. If we are assessing, we are not listening: we are parsing and analyzing. We are comparing the feedback with an existing model in our head to see if the new information fits.

Can you see the problem with this?

Nothing new gets in! It's a way for our ego to stay in control while we appear to be receptive. It's a con. We won't let any new data in that would help us change and make a new choice. We only get more of what we know, with little trickles of 'approved' insight. Liking what we hear feels good and affirming, so we try to construct a fantasy world where we only focus on hearing what we like.

We do this to prevent unfiltered data from coming in. Unfiltered *anything*—in or out—is a threat to the ego. We do not trust that what is real will stick, and what is false will fall away. We do not trust that we will get what we need to get, so we must find, grasp, and process in order to get it. This is because we do not trust others, which means we do not trust ourselves and our discernment of who we're listening to. We do not trust our intuition, subconscious, or higher self to know what is true and what is false. This is because we are in our heads, not in our body, feeling.

It is an arrogant, distrustful, and defensive posture. We are not listening. From this place we seek to control.

If we would let ourselves feel complete, become still and quiet, and listen to our inner voice, we could hear Truth—the Truth without that resonates with the Truth within. We would know what is real and what is not, and no longer fear listening to feedback.

WHY WE DON'T LISTEN

I've watched participants doing this with feedback for *years*. They *think* they're listening, but they are not. They're in their head thinking, not feeling or listening. We can't hear while we're thinking. These are the same folks who keep showing up and wonder why they are not getting the 'big breakthrough.' They are judging, comparing, and competing with the others, wishing they would move forward too. Yet, *they* are the ones not letting themselves move forward because they are unwilling to surrender and let the feedback destroy them.

Being destroyed is what receiving some feedback can feel like. When feedback comes in that strikes a chord with a loaded story, it feels extremely threatening. To surrender to that can feel like death. Why is that? True feedback reflects back only what is real. What is real invalidates illusion, which is what our stories are and what our narcissistic image is. We feel like the feedback will annihilate us because we identify with our stories and our persona rather than our True Self. If we were to truly listen, we would let the truth in, which we're afraid would invalidate all that we've built-up. And it would.

What we've built up, no matter how precious, is a false idol. It has been built to shield us from our unconscious fear of annihilation. We don't logically think we'll die, but the subconscious response is the same fear. This fear comes from the ego, and we must have faith that we will not die if we let the feedback in. We know we are safe because the Truth destroys what is false, and so what is left must be real—and who-you-really-are is real, for the True Self is the only thing that can be.

We don't usually consciously realize this is what's going on, but when we distill it down to the deepest archetypal levels, some variation of this gets revealed.

If you've already been getting feedback, but to no avail, this may be why it hasn't helped. Assuming it's truly feedback, perhaps you're not actually *listening* to it. You may be discarding everything that would help you move forward. You discard this data because you think you know it already, it's irrelevant, or it goes against your beliefs. Perhaps you're power-tripping your coach or therapist.

You are in total control, only letting in what you're looking for: what validates your stories. You're (secretly) looking for another way to hide out: to not have to change or make a new choice.

What you fail to realize is there's a good chance that all that discarded data is precisely what you need. In your liberal habit of "take what you like and discard the rest," you've left the best parts of yourself. Your judgmental defenses have betrayed you. You've abandoned yourself for comfort and protection. Your disregard for feedback is a discard of love. When we refuse to open up and listen, what we are really doing is defending ourselves against love. We can't see the feedback as being love because of our distortions. Defending is an act of protection, and this comes from fear. Thus, a judgment and discard of feedback ultimately comes from the fear of being loved. **Our avoidance of feedback reveals how much we resist being loved.**

DEFENDING A LIE

The Truth requires no defense. This is why we feel defensive about our persona—because it's not True. The narcissistic image is unsubstantiated and made of nothing real. The Truth of who-we-really-are can stand on its own; it is transcendent. It is indestructible because it is unattackable. When we feel defensive towards criticism, accusation, or projection—we know that whatever we want to protect isn't real. If we need to defend it, it's not something worth defending. Since nothing

True can be attacked, why would we want to keep our allegiance with something untrue?

When we get defensive, we know that somewhere there lies a lie.

This is the lie we tell ourselves about not being enough, being broken, or not having enough. The lie is the persona, mask, or image. The lie is our story. The lie is our unworthiness and unforgivableness. The lie is our guilt and shame that fears retribution and punishment. The lie is what we feel about ourselves that isn't true.

Why would we defend such things? This is a question only you can answer. Think about it. Feel into it. Why do you continually choose to defend your lies instead of surrendering to the truth?

There are other reasons we may get defensive when receiving feedback.

It could be that what they're saying is not truly feedback. In which case, it isn't applicable, so why bother defending against something that isn't true? Something in it is hitting a nerve, which can be explored as soon as the defenses lower and the other stops projecting. It could also be that we distort the feedback on the way in and turn it into an attack. This is self-directed because we took the love and 'turned it' into an attack. We are using the other person to abuse ourselves with their words. We are using the healing energy to make ourselves sick. Yet, what we directed at ourselves cannot be their love, or any form of it, because Love can never be used to attack, even ourselves.

We have instead perverted our interpretation of their feedback and created a weapon in our own image. It's our own self-hatred that we project upon the feedback. The love within the original feedback cannot be used to hurt, so we must create *a distorted image of the feedback* in order to attack ourselves. We then use that illusion to beat ourselves up, or we use it as justification to retaliate against the person who gave the feedback. None of this has anything to do with them or the data they reflected. This insanity is only about our rage against a distorted image of love.

When we are defending a lie, not listening, and pushing away love—it makes it incredibly difficult for anyone to give us feedback. Ergo, we stay stuck.

The feedback is there to free us from our own bondage. Seldom do we verily choose freedom. We want to cling to our security blanket, even if we're drowning and it's pulling us under. We identify so much with our suffering that we think our story is our treasure, and love is a robber coming to steal it from us. When in actuality, the suffering is a shackle, and feedback is the key to freedom. Talk about reverse-wired!

WHY THE TRUTH CAN HURT

Why is it hard to hear the truth? Why does it hurt so bad when we get feedback and see something about ourselves that we don't want to admit?

Truth, like love, isn't itself painful. The illusions are causing the suffering, and the meeting of the two reveals the obscured pain. It appears as if the truth is hurtful, but it is the truth that illuminates preexisting suffering, not what inflicted it.

It's as if you were in the dark woods and shined your flashlight upon the bushes and saw a wolf. You seemed 'fine' beforehand when you were ignorant, but "now" you are in danger because you see the wolf in the spotlight. What we do is mistake the flashlight as the source of danger instead of the wolf. The wolf was tracking you the entire time. You were *already* in danger; the light simply brought it to your attention. Likewise, we can perceive feedback—truth—as something that causes us more pain. It's not the feedback that's painful, nor was it the flashlight that caused danger.

People like to think that things were so much easier, more comfortable, and less painful before waking up to the truth. As they say, "ignorance is bliss," but we can see here that purposeful ignorance is merely another way to suffer, achieved by avoiding the awareness of our suffering.

It is dangerous and insane. It can only eventually lead to suffering down the road. The only way out of any of this is to stop and surrender. We must be willing to tell and hear the truth—and accept all of its consequences—or else nothing in our lives will change. 🐝

YOUR LIFE IS
NOT ABOUT YOU

"Non nobis solum nati sumus.
(Not for ourselves alone are we born.)"
— MARCUS TULLIUS CICERO

here was panic. She was two weeks late. *"Was it too late to get her period? Was she pregnant?"* I sure hoped not. We had only been seeing each other for a couple of months. We had no interest in having a baby at that time. I was starting a new business, financially unstable, and hyper-focused on myself and my career. It was not the ideal time for me.

It wasn't a certain pregnancy, but it was possible. I had to get serious and come to terms with a potentially significant life change. I felt panic and apprehension. I would be a father with this woman that I recently met and raise a family that I wasn't asking for. And so I turned inwards and thought about it. At first, it was about me: my life, my work, what I'd have to do and give up, how it would completely derail my plans and take me out. How could I provide? What did this mean about my choices in life thus far?

I, I, I.

I saw how completely self-absorbed and narcissistic it was. There could be a beautiful new human life, and all I could think of was myself.

237

Was this the kind of person I'd become? Have I only imagined a life that was about me?

I wanted to defend and justify because, boy, did I have a whole slew of reasons why I should be thinking about myself first. But I didn't—I surrendered. I started to feel deeper into it. I imagined what it would be like to have a child and life partner, which I had never spent much time doing before because it seemed so far off.

What would we do, where would we live, how would we parent?

Movies flashed through my mind.

I came to terms with what that life would look like. I accepted the idea my life would no longer be only about me and what I wanted, but about her, the child, us—this family. I saw how my selfishness and immaturity had pushed real love away for years, terrified of being stuck and miserable.

I let go of all the stories. I found peace. And you know what the weirdest thing was? The idea was quite wonderful.

I had started to imagine a life where I shared my joy, love, shadow, light, insecurities, wisdom, failures, and humor. It was a life that didn't turn out anything like I was imagining—and oh, what a relief! There was no grand fantasy or striving, nor was there any perfection in sight—but it was real, and full of life and love. The manifestation of this vision required a lot of work. It had its challenges, but it was a lot of fun too—fun I could never have alone. It was still not something I wanted right then, but I had surrendered to the possibility.

Before this moment, I never had an interest in family life. I always imagined that was down the road. I had been living isolated and independent. I was so consumed with 'making it' so that I could be happy that I missed such an obvious path to it.

As we eventually found out, this was not the time for that path. While she ended up not being pregnant, the experience allowed me to mature and see a life that was not only about me. I had a glimpse into the responsibility and joy that comes with that life, rather than a 'burden' and 'loss of freedom' I saw it as when I was a younger man.

It was a wake-up call about the limitations of my self-centeredness and isolation.

A lot of what was discussed on narcissism in the chapter "The Most Important Person" is directly applicable here. Keep in mind the ideas of *narcissistic supply*, *objectification*, *narcissistic image*, and *meeting our own needs* as you read.

WHEN IT'S ALL ABOUT YOU

One of the predominant reasons we stay stuck is because we don't realize how often we are 'making it about us.' There are so many subtleties and layers of our backward rationalizations that it can take some effort to pinpoint our narcissistic tendencies. We must train ourselves to recognize the self-absorbed behavior in ourselves and others. If we can become aware of these without judgment or giving them meaning, we can reorient our behavior and prevent ourselves from being manipulated.

Here are some common ways in which we make things about ourselves:

- Taking what others do or say personally
- Letting our insecurities dominate our behavior
- Turning everything into a drama or joke
- Being loud or always the center of attention
- Acting awkward, uncomfortable, nervous
- Making our struggle or suffering the dominant topic
- Going to events where we are wrapped up in our fears and anxieties
- Making a scene about paying or our altruism
- Causing problems, confusion, or chaos
- Doing it all ourself so we can take credit or martyr
- Being withdrawn so that people are forced to come in and get us
- Manipulating or misbehaving for attention
- Being unwell with a secondary gain of having people take care of us

- Conversations are about us or about our help
- Getting defensive and 'stealing the suffering' from another
- Feeling guilty or making a scene because we refuse to receive something
- Rescuing someone because we don't want to feel what they feel
- Not wanting to sell our art or product that could help someone because of fear
- Staying in poverty where all our focus is on survival
- Withholding our creativity, gifts, ideas, love, forgiveness, help from insecurity

All of these are subtle (or not so subtle) ways to make it all about ourselves! Notice how common these are. They happen so much that we don't even realize they're not honest behaviors.

How do you fall into these narcissistic traps? What is it about these behaviors that "make it all about you"?

The reasons are:

- Your focus or the group's focus is on *your* thoughts, feelings, needs, or problem
- Your focus is inwards or removed from others
- The focus becomes about your mistake, insecurity, or drama
- It can create positive or negative attention towards you
- It can hold other people hostage to your stories, drama, and suffering
- You may be helping someone, but there's a hidden agenda for you
- Even if your behavior isn't impacting anyone else, you are still in your head cut off from the space
- You don't let the other person decide for themselves if they want it or not
- You are so caught up in surviving and meeting your basic needs that there's no availability for others

At first, it may not seem obvious how these make it about you, but the deeper you look, the more you will find they are.

Let's take this to the extreme. Being sick is all about *you*. Being poor is all about *you*. Being insecure is all about *you*. Being afraid is all about *you*. It's not that these are wrong; it's that all the focus in your life becomes about fixing and solving your own issues, leaving no space or resources left for others. You need to spend time and money to get healthy and functional. You need to get money to survive day-to-day, week-to-week. You withhold from others until you're more confident. You don't solve that big problem or connect with someone who needs you because you're afraid. It's all about *you*.

It doesn't mean you're a greedy, selfish person. It's simply that the choices you've made force you into self-preservation. This place is a stuck place, and the more you move from here, the more you stay here.

Think about what can happen when you're not here. How much more can you give to those you love? When you're healthy and energized? When you have a surplus of time and money? When you're willing to be uncomfortable and make the hard choices? When you're able to do what others fear? Unquestionably more!

> "A hero is someone who has given his or her life to something bigger than oneself."

> "When we quit thinking primarily about ourselves and our own self-preservation, we undergo a truly heroic transformation of consciousness."
> — Joseph Campbell

"Okay, I see how these make it about me, but what's the problem with that?"

Let's look at the consequences of these for others and yourself.

How it negatively affects others: People have to wait for you. They are slowed or stopped by you. They have to put their own plans or needs on hold. They are being manipulated and used. They have no access or intimacy with you. They are now a part of your story and

AWAKEN TO YOUR TRUE SELF PART II

drama. Your suffering gets spilled onto them, and now they have to deal with what you won't. They leave interactions with you feeling drained or exhausted. You have no resources left over to contribute or help them. We are caught up in scarcity, taking to meet our needs.

How it negatively affects you: You don't get to heal; instead, you validate your problems. You become a "crap magnet," attracting people that do the same. You lose access to all the resources of the space when you're cut off from it. Your world gets smaller and smaller. You have to deal with the consequences of your chaos, which tend to lead to more problems. Mature people don't want to be around this kind of behavior, so you lack quality friends. You remain in scarcity mode, never being able to fill your cup.

Another concern is that many times these "me, me, me" behaviors tend to be dishonest. We have mimicked these behaviors and attitudes from those around us, thinking it's a normal way to get what we want, without realizing how manipulative it can be. Manipulating to get what we want never leads to fulfillment. It only validates the story that we cannot have what we want, let alone get it honestly. It's all a distorted attempt at getting our needs met.

Remember, we often aren't consciously aware of what we're doing. This is what 'awakening' is really about—waking up from our ignorance and illusions—not gaining magic powers or leaving our bodies.

If you still don't recognize the problems around making everything about you, you're likely being ran by this mythology. That is okay. We don't see these behaviors as selfish if we're caught up in them. We're not necessarily intending to be malicious or dishonest, yet that may be what's happening. This work is about illuminating the hidden underlayers of your consciousness; it's not about making you wrong. I invite you to explore how you may be doing these behaviors—for your own benefit—rather than trying to assess if this applies to you or not.

You would not believe how many times I thought to myself, "This doesn't apply to me at all," and it ended up being the exact thing I was doing to stay stuck. I was so engulfed in it that I was blind to it. We think focusing on our problems even more will get us out—it won't. It's the opposite. Our ego is great at conning us with superiority.

"The best way to find yourself is to
lose yourself in the service of others."
— *Mahatma Gandhi*

MEETING OUR NEEDS

Many of us are living out our adults lives attempting to fulfill our needs that weren't met as children. Rather than actualizing or creating from beauty or joy, we seek (and avoid) the relationships and careers we think will finally fulfill these needs. Until they are met, we are unconsciously driven to meet them, sometimes in unhealthy ways.

Our culture often mistakes suffering for entertainment. When I say entertainment, I don't mean having fun, joy, pleasure, play, or creativity. I don't mean things like spending time together, creating art, or inspiring others through media. These are not suffering. The 'entertainment' I'm referring to is the kind we seek when we feel bored, lonely, depressed, anxious, and empty. The kind we perform when we want approval, acceptance, ego-boosts, validation, and attention. It's not that entertainment *causes* suffering; it's that much of what we find entertaining *comes from* suffering. When we look to be entertained we are avoiding, and when we look to entertain others, we desire attention.

A few examples of this are the class clown, the trouble maker, the drama queen, and the show-off. We often don't see the underlying story because we are laughing or being entertained by the archetype, though eventually it "gets old," and we have enough. Compare this to real humor, joy, and play that never gets old. Some people don't feel this way and are attracted by the dysfunctional entertainment and 'hover' around the person (think groupies). Both the entertainer and the entertainee are ran by an underlying story that distorts and confuses this dynamic for actual joy, humor, or play. This can easily become codependent. Real joy, humor, and play aren't at the expense of anyone, including ourselves. When we prostitute ourselves for validation, attention, approval, or affection, we are abandoning ourselves.

Imagine a child who's parent makes them earn or compete for their love and affection. The child is told to sing, dance, perform, kiss, and say the right things to make mommy and daddy happy. Love, affection, and nurturing are withheld until the child performs. So the child performs, and the parents are happy, and there's love. What's so bad about that? Well, when the child *doesn't* want to entertain, or kiss, or say the thing—or if the child fails or doesn't do it perfectly—love is withheld. Their love becomes a bargaining chip, a weapon—which means it's not actually love at all. Do they see it as abuse? Probably not; it's what affection feels like to them.

In this example, we see a child who is entertaining because they are trying to get their needs met, and a parent who is using their child to avoid their own lack. Both aren't aware of their suffering. Both don't see their part in the codependent entertainment dynamic as manipulation. Both are trying to get their unmet needs somehow met.

This is not to say our relationships shouldn't be fun and full of great joy and laughter!

Indeed, there should be beauty, play, and artistic expression. The problem is when it becomes entertainment, manipulation, and abuse towards self and other. We can bring humor and joy into people's lives without having to entertain and generate drama or noise for attention. We can express ourselves artistically without selling-out for approval. We can add value without manipulating and making it the "Me, Me, Me Show." We can be accepted and loved without having to 'dance for our dinner.'

… **We are lovable without having to earn it.**

If that's true, then why do we do all of this? We manipulate when we believe we can't have what we want.

The irony is that if you truly let yourself ask for what you want and genuinely make it about meeting your needs—without manipulation, drama, or agendas—you no longer "make it all about you."

"Wait—so by purposefully making it about me... I'm no longer making it all about me?"

Often that can be the case, yes. It becomes a genuine request for help. You are being honest, not manipulating. This is more functional because it is no longer about suffering: it's about *nurturing*. You are saying something that is real, something that is true. You are no longer hiding, having an agenda, or trying to cover up a vulnerability. You are *allowing* yourself to be helped, not attacking others to get what you want. People who are mature adults *want* to support you. They *want* to respect your boundaries, treat you well, and help. They will be *glad* you told them your needs without having to decipher them. Adults do not need to be manipulated or compete for attention and love.

That we *don't* have to manipulate others in order to get what we want is unbelievable to many people.

"I can tell the truth and simply ask for what I want and get it?"

It doesn't seem possible for many of us. This is the reverse-wiring, which often gets set in at childhood. We may have learned how to meet our needs narcissistically, as detailed in the chapter, "The Most Important Person." We may have grown up in an environment where our needs weren't met, that we couldn't "just ask" safely, or that we had to lie, cheat, and steal to survive. We may have lived around people that were always taking because there was never enough; we had to fight over it and take what's ours or go without. We may have had parents who made us compete for love, attention, and affection. We may have grown up in an era or culture that was life-or-death-tough, and we never recalibrated to a safer, easier, more abundant time as adults.

I acknowledge this may have been your experience in the past— and if you are reading this book now, it is not how it has to be going forward.

Your future doesn't *have* to mimic your childhood, but if you don't make new choices, there's a good chance it will. You can decide on a different way. A way where it's safe to ask for what you need. A way of life where it's safe to tell the truth and report how you feel without ridicule or attack. It doesn't mean everyone will oblige, or you have a magic genie, or you can act entitled. However, if you're sincere, I bet you'll find people are willing to listen and help you more often than you think.

The solution to this behavior is to stop the stories and suffering. You simply ask without agendas or attachment to outcome, and in response, say "yes" or "no" without fear of repercussion. "This is my need. This is how I feel." No stories, games, or manipulations. No taking it personally or giving meaning.

This solution will require a whole new level of honesty, vulnerability, and communication with those around you. It may require surrounding yourself with different people. It may be uncomfortable at first, but this is how we can create shifts in the entire culture: one-by-one. Imagine the permission you give and the example you set to your community. How you lead by cutting through all the stories and drama, communicating with courage and trust. Your leadership gives true hope.

NOT LETTING IT BE ABOUT US

One of the most elusive yet manipulative ways we make things about ourselves—is by not letting it be about us. This is just a reaction to being out of relationship with true generosity and allowing ourselves to receive. We think we're being humble or gracious, but it's actually a game we're playing. This 'game' can be observed when we are being celebrated, but we dismiss it; when we are given a gift, but decline it; or when the attention is on us, and we act out and make a drama to push it away. We are not allowing.

A perfect example is the person who puts their hands up and goes hysterical with insecurity when a family member goes to take an everyday picture or video with them happening to be in the frame. All of this drama is created. Instead of being about the beauty and joy in sharing the moment, it becomes all about them. It's the same energy but polar opposite of the person that has to be in every photo and makes people retake it until they look perfect. Both extremes are making it about them. There are many graceful ways to respect boundaries, to decline, accept, or appear in the shot that doesn't make it all about us.

We also do this behavior when we are sharing something wonderful and then become self-conscious and shut down, forcing everyone to pull it out of us. We are uncomfortable with the attention, with receiving, and with being loved. We reject the celebration of our lovability and make a scene. This inadvertently makes it all about us and our avoidance. It's not 'being humble' when we reject love, appreciation, admiration, or attention. It's actually *arrogant* because we make it about us not wanting to be selfish or needing anything. That's, again, all about us. It's about our discomfort, ego, and appearance—not the joy, celebration, gratitude, wisdom that others are receiving by focusing upon us.

Perhaps we're injured, sick, or sad around other people, and they can sense it. We don't want to make it about ourselves, so we try to hide it or say "I'm fine" when someone offers to help. Since there is something wrong, we make it about our pride, independence, or fear of vulnerability—again making it about us. The other would get joy from helping, we'd let someone in and feel grateful, and both would be better for it. Letting it be about us works much better than rejecting, being prideful, struggling, and neither being uplifted by trying to not make it about us. This is an excellent example of trying to meet our own needs and the narcissism behind it.

Sometimes we do this because we have trouble receiving or we feel that we don't deserve it. The stories and reasons around this are endless.

Sometimes we do this because we are modulating our appearance to others or ourselves. We don't want to look or seem or be a certain way, so we change our behavior. Perhaps we don't want people to think we're selfish, so we don't accept the thing. Or, maybe we want people to believe we are gracious, and so we nominate someone else. Or, even more arrogantly, we want to appear mean, crusty, and selfish so people will want to leave us alone—even if we aren't. We make all these things mean something about us. Even the idea of not caring about what people think is about us!

It's all fake.

Why? It's inauthentic because it turns it all into a performance and manipulation, rather than a real expression. We start changing our behavior to be perceived differently by others and ourselves. We are aware of the space and how we are relating to it. We become self-conscious and begin modulating and censoring what we do and say. We go from unfiltered presence to a filtered, ego-approved script. We start defending against the space and those in it. When we're making it about us, it shifts how we are relating to the space. We shift from 'one thing as a whole' to 'some-other-thing separate from the space.' The only thing this behavior serves is our persona.

RELATING TO THE SPACE

I remember the three years I assisted my late mentor at his workshops; it was the most demanding job I've ever had. On the mornings of the first day of each workshop, I'd be anxious and nervous. I was afraid of getting yelled at, of messing up, of being called-out, of getting in trouble. It would usually come true.

I can still hear his voice echoing in my body, "You are holding the entire group back. You are being narcissistic and are trying to take the group out. You are withholding and making it all about you. You don't want to be here."

I'd feel like everything was closing in on me, nearly nauseous. I was confused and frustrated. I felt defensive and angry. I was panicking inside of myself, thinking:

What the hell does that mean? How am I taking the group out? I'm just sitting here! I'm not even talking; how can I be making it about me? I'm letting all these people talk! I'm not doing anything; stop what? I can't even 'not-do-anything' right. Everyone is staring at me like I'm ruining their lives. I feel like the biggest piece of trash, and I don't even know what I did. I want to run away and die. This feels awful. Please pretend like I'm invisible, don't hurt me.

It took me three years to stop all this behavior and understand what he was saying. *Three years.* It was a lifetime of stories, manipulations, narcissism, and self-destruction to penetrate and heal.

The key to the breakthrough came when I realized that **I arrived with those thoughts and feelings**. The responses I had were not *because* of him: his feedback was *referring* to what was already within me! I kept showing up to the workshops with these stories, addictions, and terror. My preexisting fears of being attacked led me to subconsciously invite, or 'ask,' to be attacked. My self-loathing was subconsciously draining the joy and ease from the space. My superiority and competitiveness were causing me to withhold and 'let' people talk rather than contribute. My wanting to hide and run made it seem like I didn't want to be there. My paranoia and anxiety caused me to make mistakes by trying to be perfect. It created all this tension for everyone in the room, and because I was so caught up in it all, I had no idea.

Why did I keep showing up if I seemed so miserable?

This was not about a workshop; it was my *life*. The things that got triggered within me at these events were all things that I was already carrying around with me. I was afraid I'd never break through and that I'd be stuck the rest of my life if I didn't figure this out as soon as possible. Talk about pressure! In my mind, I made every workshop mean I was either doomed or helpless. I was fixated on how broken I thought I was. I was desperate to get healed. I felt so messed up that all I was focusing on was getting my healing or learning the magic trick that would finally end my suffering. I felt so depleted in life that I was using everyone to 'recharge my batteries' before I was at a place to contribute.

The problems themselves *were* my problems, like I talk about in the chapter, "An Equation for Suffering."

It was hard to be of service when I was making it all about me and my suffering. I was so caught up in trying to get unstuck that I couldn't see anything—or anyone—past it. I needed *my* breakthrough; I needed *my* healing.

We would tell the participants doing similar behaviors: "You are trying to *get* something. What are you *bringing* to the space? You will get whatever you bring to this class."

It was difficult for me and many others to truly hear this. It's easy to listen to the words but to *really 'get it'*—that's something else entirely.

249

It has to 'sink in' to the body, to be absorbed, not fall upon deaf ears. The biggest obstacle we'd hear was: "But I'm paying for this, why should I have to give and teach and contribute? Of course I'm here because I want something. I want to be taught and healed! I don't want to do your job for you. *You* are supposed to be fixing *me*; that's what I paid for." I think a lot of people felt this kind of entitlement. I know I did.

However, I noticed that not *all* participants felt this way. There were some that shared fully. That gave a lot of feedback, offered a lot of ideas. They taught, provided wisdom, and held space. They spoke often and supported others when they spoke, even if it was unrelated to them. They also stayed quiet and truly listened. They showed up and stayed present for others. They were always punctual. They were gracious. They weren't competing or withholding, but generous.

And you know what? They tended to be the wealthiest, most successful, healthiest, and happiest participants. You could feel they were somehow leaders in their community. They had people around them. A lot flowed in, out, and through them. It was all visible in their body, in the way they moved and showed up in the space. They got what they needed, contributed what was needed, and got on with their life.

The ones struggling the most? Yep, they were the ones trying to 'get' the most. There was a "what's in it for me" attitude. They didn't listen or follow the instructions, but only thought they were. These were the intellectuals who thought they knew everything already, like from the chapter "When Intellect Slows You Down." Some had money, but they weren't *wealthy,* nor were they happy or pleasant to be around. Poor and rich alike were suffering, looking to be fixed, or looking for the 'secret powers.'

This struggle was my life for years. My epiphany came when I realized that I had it all backward. I believed that I need to be fixed, whole, complete *first*—then I could give of myself, show up present, and be generous. This was proven to be absolutely, irrefutably wrong. It was the generosity, gratitude, and graciousness that came first, not the other way around.

Scarcity and fear mentality is what runs all of this. The only way out of this is *faith*—not some victimy religious dogma, but true faith.

It is a trust in something greater than yourself. It requires you to let go of control, surrender, and know that who-you-really-are will be okay.

- The more you show up, participate, give, and contribute to the space, the more you get from it.
- The more you teach, the more you will learn. The more you share, the more that is shared with you.
- When you're comparing, you're competing. If you are doing things such as being jealous, withholding, judging, or acting superior, you are in competition.
- The more feedback you give and help others, the more you give that to yourself.
- If you can see and appreciate it another, you have it within yourself, too—you must, or you wouldn't even be able to recognize it.
- If you move the group forward, you move yourself forward. If you make it all about you, you hold everyone back, including yourself.
- When you come with an agenda, looking to take, you won't get much from it. You get what you give, first.

This isn't about workshops or classes—this about showing up in life. It is work, family, friends, strangers, sports, art—everything. The 'space' isn't a group of people or a room: it's what's around you wherever you are in the world. It's not only about other people, either: you affect *everything* in your life. Even if you can't see it, even if we don't yet have the instruments to measure it, you have an effect on it and it, you. *As within, so without.*

Focus on Others

When we are stuck, we can get caught up in our stuckness and make it all about ourselves. We can lose sight of those around us and what they are going through. We become obsessed with our own fixing, healing, overcoming, making it, and succeeding that we miss all the ways we can help others. When we are wrapped up in this head noise, we get consumed with what's going on inside and have nothing left for those outside.

We don't see that **being of service to others could be the very path of our own success**. Our struggle becomes what blinds us from potential salvation.

If you're stuck in your own life trying to figure it all out, perhaps taking a break from your attempts to stop struggling—and helping someone else instead—will be of better use. You never know who you'll meet, what you'll learn, or what impact you'll have engaging in someone else's life. Taking the focus off of what you're doing and being of service to someone else may be exactly what will help you. It's a shift in orientation and focus; it doesn't mean you have to abandon your own vision.

We think that in order to get what we want, we must focus on ourselves—but the reality is that if we can help others get what *they* want, we can also get what we want. It's the opposite of what we think. Yes, you guessed it—another reverse-wiring.

> "Don't aim at success. The more you aim at it and make it a target, the more you are going to miss it. For success, like happiness, cannot be pursued; it must ensue, and it only does so as the unintended side effect of one's personal dedication to a cause greater than oneself or as the by-product of one's surrender to a person other than oneself."
> — Viktor E. Frankl, Man's Search for Meaning

I'm not suggesting over-extending yourself, martyring yourself, being a guru for others to solve a problem you haven't solved. I mean genuinely being of service to others and providing them value, not a "value" *you* want to give them, but something *they* need and value themselves. It's about real generosity. Don't fall into the trap of starting a business to help others in order to get yourself unstuck or doing something nice to feel better about yourself—that's still making it about you!

Reflect on the following:

- What if you were to make your life about family or community?
- What if you were to make it about solving a problem for humanity?
- What if you dedicated your life and resources to something greater than yourself?
- What if you supported someone else's project, product, or purpose? What if you allowed others to come in and support you?
- What if there was no longer anything wrong with you and you had everything you needed—how much more generous and gracious could you be?

When we are stuck in our problems, we are making everything about us. We think being more in our heads to solve a problem (caused by being in our head) will resolve it, but it won't. We think that making it even *more* about ourselves will somehow get others to help us, but it won't. What *does* work is getting out from under our own problems and starting to be of service to others. What *does* work is seeing what we can bring to the table, rather than worrying about what everyone else is bringing us. Shifting the focus of our resources and energy to solve another's problem can be a rewarding change of direction. **I invite you to discover what happens when you start seeing how you can serve the space instead of how the space can serve you.**

THE MARTYR ARCHETYPE

What happens if you *have* been making your life about others, and you're still stuck? It could be that this doesn't pertain to you, or it could be that what you've been doing is not what you think.

Let's find out:

- Do you feel under-appreciated, worn-down, bitter, or resentful?
- Do you feel your efforts aren't fruitful or you don't get the recognition you should?
- Are you tired of being the only one who cares?
- Have you been putting other people first, but you never seem to be considered at all?

If so, you may be acting out a 'martyr' story.

This martyr archetype is someone who gives of themselves for others but does not receive. They give and give, or do and do, for others but abandon themselves in the process. This martyrdom works on the flawed premise that one must subtract from themselves in order to add to another. One must go without or with less in order for someone else to have. It is an act of great sacrifice. This is the key—it is a *sacrificial offering*. Since it is not based on genuine generosity, and the folks running this tend not to receive well, it inevitably leads to resentment or bitterness. This is because the giving-receiving cycle does not complete, and the martyr is left to meet their own needs. This ultimately validates their story and perpetuates the suffering.

Contrary to how it appears, this is not really about being generous and putting others' needs before one's own. There is an underlining dysfunction that motivates it. It could be scarcity, paranoia, a fear of letting go of control, righteousness, or arrogance. It could be a deep unworthiness, undeservedness, guilt, or a path of self-abuse and punishment. It could be a reaction-formation against selfishness, one's own or from another's. This can be seen as pride or self-righteousness over those that focus on themselves, often with comments or thoughts of judgment or superiority.

As odd as it may sound, *both* sides of the extremes—selfishness and martyrdom—are making it about themselves. One is making it about rejecting and martyring themselves and feeling undeserving—and the other is about selfishness and unmet needs. Both are coming from scarcity, and neither is truly generous. True generosity creates more for both people involved; it does not require one to lose. The self-centered will keep attempting to fill their void, taking from others—perhaps in hopes that one day they will be filled enough to give. The martyr will over-give and feel drained, justifying with duty, pride, or righteousness, inevitably carrying resentment as their void grows.

When we stop making it about ourselves, we are in abundance. **Generousness and gratitude are *feelings*, not mere acts; they aren't the result of wealth but the *cause* of it.**

We can both give *and* receive fully; there is no need to pick sides. This 'one or the other' game is a farce. There is no true giving without receiving, or receiving without giving. Both *must* occur together, for both parties. Think about a hug: when you hug, you are both giving and receiving. The best hugs are when we are both doing both. Even if one person is only receiving and can't hug back, they may still give playfulness, joy, and gratitude. The giving-receiving often isn't expressed in the exact same way, making it hard to account for an obvious exchange.

When this simultaneous give-receive does not occur, it breaks the natural cycle and doesn't feel so great. We struggle with things such as: making and spending money, giving and getting gifts, asking for what we want and knowing what others want without having to ask, and giving and receiving love and affection. This is what we discussed in the chapter about narcissism, "The Most Important Person."

We must be in relationship with both giving *and* receiving, ourselves *and* others, within *and* without. The either-or game always creates an imbalance and struggle. There is no reward for claiming "I'm good at giving" and "I'm bad at receiving."

Some folks are stuck because they are making it all about themselves thinking that will work. Some think they are making it about others but are actually making it about themselves. Some folks are stuck because they are martyring themselves and over-giving. Some think they are making it about themselves, but they won't allow or receive from others.

If you're used to abandoning yourself for others, taking care of yourself may feel selfish. If you're used to making it all about you, focusing on others may feel like you're losing something. You must be willing to feel these in order to find where the truth lies, or else you know you're ran by the avoidance. If you don't want to feel greedy or selfish and you've been martyring and abandoning yourself, perhaps it's time to let yourself be selfish and see how that works. If you've been self-centered and clinging on, afraid to lose yourself, perhaps you may want to let yourself surrender to something—or someone—else and see what happens.

What will free you is found in what you're fighting against. Your avoidance is your release.

CONCLUSION

As you make your life less about your problems, you begin to realize how much more to life there is than working on yourself. It absolutely has its place, but it's not a replacement for a life shared with others. The entire reason we want to be better is to lead more effectively, be better parents, be better lovers, be better employees, be better artists, and be better humans. All of these are for partaking and contributing to our communities in better ways so that we may live a happier, healthier, more meaningful life.

> *"Everybody can be great…because anybody can serve. You don't have to have a college degree to serve. You don't have to make your subject and verb agree to serve. You only need a heart full of grace. A soul generated by love."*
> *— Martin Luther King Jr.*

If you've been so focused on your own life, your own problems, your own learning, your own success, and you're still stuck—see what life brings when you start focusing on others. If you've been so focused on others and you're still stuck—see what life brings when you start taking care of yourself, asking for what you need, letting it be about you, and allowing yourself to be supported. You can take care of yourself without being narcissistic, and you can serve the world without martyring yourself—there's a middle path.

QUESTIONS TO LIVE BY

This is a series of questions you can ask yourself when making a choice to help orient yourself. This is not a technique to perform every time you need to decide something, but it will be beneficial to memorize and use for self-inquiry. It can also be worthwhile to write your answers down as a formal process if you're stuck.

Ask yourself the following questions:

- Do I stand for something greater than myself?
- Do I see others as separate from me?
- Am I giving first or trying to get first?
- Does my vision include others and being of service?
- Am I allowing support, or am I trying to do it all myself?
- Am I adding to the space or taking away from it?
- Am I collaborating or competing?
- Am I making this about me?

Beyond the answers, pay attention to what comes up around them: the stories, limitations, excuses, feelings, myths, and judgments. These may reveal more useful data than the straight answer alone.

These questions are a way to bring greater awareness to your intentions, not tell you what you should or shouldn't do. Use these questions as a compass to guide you towards a more fulfilling life. 🪷

Dragons &
Their Treasures

*"The cave you fear to enter
holds the treasure you seek."*
— Joseph Campbell

n the depths of a forbidden yet faintly familiar cavern, a treasure chest lies locked and rusted over. Surrounded by monsters and dragons, shrouded in foreboding darkness, its guardians keep it safe from those who dare to penetrate the cavern's depths. The stench of rotting flesh-of-failed-attempts gags the air. Nightmarish ghouls claw at the gatekeepers' bound feet, while belligerent swine chomp at the remains of pitiful attempts.

A desolate landscape of despair, alienation, terror, and humiliation scares off the trepid traveler. A thousand-leagues-deep of suffering, sadness, grief, and loss repel those who fear the shadows. A conniving landscape of traps, labyrinths, and funhouse mirrors distract and confuse. A treacherous isle of sirens, narcissists, and nymphs easily seduce those who sail towards the inner sanctum.

No, brave hero, this is not a hellish world in a galaxy far, far away—this is all inside of you. A world of your worst nightmares protecting your most secret treasure, locked in the depths of your subconscious. **This is your shadow—and it's not what you think.**

259

Enlightenment, Unfolding

If we are to wake up from our struggle, we must wake up from our illusions. The *shadow* plays a central role in our awakening. As you explore your dualistic nature, you pass through various levels of awareness on how humans relate to lightness and darkness.

First, you're told heaven and hell is a place you go when you die, depending on if you're good or bad. You are taught the duality of right and wrong, good and evil, reward and punishment. You are told it's serious. You must obey and not question it.

But at some point, you start to question it.

Then, you realize heaven and hell are happening right here, right now, and your own guilt and judgments place you where you feel you deserve in each moment.

> "All the gods, all the heavens,
> all the hells, are within you."
> — Joseph Campbell

Next, you realize it's all a projection—that the beauty and ugliness, the wonder and evils of the world, all come from within. That if you can see the good and beauty in others, you have that within you. If you can see the potential and greatness in another, you have it too. If you can see the evils and treacherousness in others, you have that too within you.

Then, you realize how much of that you've judged. You realize how you've suppressed and avoided what you don't like about yourself—shoving it down into your shadow, pretending like it doesn't exist. You notice that what you try to fix 'out there' is what you don't accept 'in here.' You see how your fears and anxiety manifest from unresolved shadow aspects.

Next, you realize everything you want, everything that you need to be happy, you have locked safely away in a chest that lies faintly beyond the inner guardians of complete annihilation.

Eventually, you realize this treasure is who you've been the entire time. You understand that all the demons, dragons, evils, and horrors are all also you—often the best parts of yourself misidentified, discarded, and sent to the Island of Misfit Toys.

Soon enough, you realize you set the whole thing up. You're the treasure, you're the chest, you're the depths of the inferno, you're the guardians, you're the darkness and the light, you're you, and you're the world. It's all you. *You're it.*

Finally, you realize the human story—the hero's journey, the cosmic joke and dance. That it's not about winning or finishing, but the process of discovering what has always been yet is ever-expanding. Experiencing yourself as what is always changing, but also eternally True.

> "Jesus Christ knew he was God. So wake up and find out eventually who you really are. In our culture, of course, they'll say you're crazy and you're blasphemous, and they'll either put you in jail or in a nut house (which is pretty much the same thing). However, if you wake up in India and tell your friends and relations, 'My goodness, I've just discovered that I'm God,' they'll laugh and say, 'Oh, congratulations, at last you found out.'"
> — Alan W. Watts

Knowing the story isn't enough—we must partake in it. These words do not take away your suffering, nor do they invalidate where you are. They do not by themselves change you. It's one thing to be enlightened while reading, and it's yet another to become self-luminous. One is as the moon, the other as the sun.

Your shadow is not what you think it is.

ILLUMINATION?

There is no illumination without Truth, and no form of truth can be found through denial. We attempt to deny the parts of reality we wish weren't so, like children that cover their eyes with a blanket hoping the monster will go away, saying, "If I can't see you, you can't see me." We are suffering and looking for a way out of it, not realizing that 'it' is life itself.

It is vanity to use spiritual insight for the purpose of avoiding life. The Mysteries reveal to us the Truth so we can live in harmony with the Tao, not to usurp it. Divine revelation is not a cosmic bypass. Understanding the secret order of the universe does not excuse us from it—au contraire, it binds us to Truth as its steward.

Truth is inclusive, not exclusive. It includes all of reality at the proper degree of order and accuracy. A solid clay cup sitting still on a table doesn't become a lie when we realize it's 99.9% empty space, made up of invisible spinning and vibrating atoms. Nor does it cease being mostly empty space and spinning particles when we can only observe it as a solid, stationary cup. We see things behaving in ways at the quantum level that we don't see happening at our classical level of physics, yet both are considered true within the same space. They do not invalidate each other—*both* are true at their appropriate degree.

> "One does not become enlightened
> by imagining figures of light, but by
> making the darkness conscious."
> — Carl Gustav Jung

Likewise, our shadow material doesn't stop being shadow material once we see 'oneness.' Harmful things don't stop being harmful to us because we know everything at the highest degree and order is ultimately love. We are still here in a physicality that necessitates duality; hence we must play by these constraints.

Yes, we can align ourselves with a higher order of truth. Yes, we can focus on what we want. Yes, we can overcome perceived constraints by discovering higher orders of physical laws. Yes, we can pierce past the dark behaviors of a person and see who-they-really-are beyond that. Yes, we can see through the lens of non-duality.

But if we pretend that what is happening is outright not occurring, we are judging and rejecting a part of reality, which is: a) extremely arrogant, b) untrue, and c) dangerous.

LOVE & LIGHT

I see many well-intentioned folks get hoodwinked by 'the spiritual path' and end up inadvertently abandoning themselves. We discussed this in the earlier chapter, "The Spiritual Path is Failing You." They set out on a path of only being 'love and light' and wind up being completely at the effect of their darkness. This *must* be so because whatever we are out of relationship with runs us. They are oblivious to the grave danger and risk they are to others and themselves from this kind of dissociation. Ask me how I know.

> *"Today we hear a lot of songs about love,*
> *and the mention of the big love thing on the way.*
> *You know what I would do? I would buy a gun and*
> *bar my door because I would know there is a*
> *storm of hypocrisy brewing."*
> *— Alan W. Watts*

This darkness is not to be taken lightly; these behaviors can be perilous. It's undeniable. Simply observe the horrors and atrocities in our communities. Our shadow material can represent the worst parts of humanity—and we let it run amok in our unconscious, not wanting to even acknowledge it exists. This is backward. It's much safer to expose and be honest about our shadow aspects than lie and cover them up. But it seems much easier to point the finger elsewhere than admit we have it in us as well. This is the danger: when we are acting ignorant to our own or another's shadow, that is when treacherous and horrific things happen.

There are many of us who, while not taking such an extreme path, still get lost. Those of us who want to bring genuine goodness to the world—to change things for the better and serve the world from our heart—get seduced by the ideals of the light and blindsided by the realities of the darkness.

I get the allure. I empathize with the ideals. I comprehend the reasoning. I've been there—I've done nearly every concept I write about in some form or another.

We want to be a good person who is doing the right things, and we want to feel good while doing it. It makes sense that we'd like to get rid of the parts of us that threaten our good persona, our good life, our good morals. We want to cut out the parts of us that yearn to do things such as seek revenge, kill, cower, hurt, sabotage, and violate. To leave behind feelings such as shame, guilt, fear, pain, insecurity, rejection, inadequacy, and weakness. We couldn't possibly admit that something lurks within us that desires to do any of those things; that we have some part of us that feels any of that. We're told we should be "evolved, conscious beings who are above all of that."

What would people think? How could we live with ourselves?

TYPICALLY HUMAN

So what do we do? We do what man tends to do when he doesn't understand something—we try to destroy it. We attempt to get rid of it in ourselves, and we try to remove it from others—or remove the people outright.

We grab our pitchforks and march to get rid of the people 'out there' that remind us of what we want to eliminate 'in here.' However, we can't seem to legislate, incarcerate, incinerate, or convert enough people to ever make it work. How could it? We miss the irony of expecting something to be removed from the world that still lives on inside of us. That doesn't work out too well, either. As hard as we try to get rid of the unwanted parts of ourselves, we can't seem to permanently remove them.

None of this works because all of these unwanted things *are part of you*. And, come to find out, you can't really get rid of *you*. We can get close, however. If we sincerely seek to annihilate what's inside of us, we take ourselves out in major ways—sometimes from life itself. This self-annihilation can also lead to illness, murder, or war.

We thus find ourselves in a conundrum: we can't get rid of ourselves, yet we still don't want these uncomfortable things around.

What do we do instead?

Historically, instead of destroying or facing them, we take the magic pill: "I don't care what you have to do, make it go away." We hide, suppress, deny, and avoid all of those "dark" things internally and externally. We offload them to the underworld. We put them in ghettos. We separate, segregate, discriminate. Anything we can do to not feel vulnerable. We do this as individuals and societies at large.

We shove these undesirable parts of ourselves in a chest, lock it tight, and toss it down into a deep, distant place where only monsters roam—hidden inside where nobody dares venture, even us. A well of avoidance so deep and obscured that you never hear or see anything hit bottom. Because we know that at the bottom of this deep, dark well, we will see something we don't want to: our reflection.

More than dragons, more than demons, more than infinite hell and darkness—what terrifies us the most about looking into our shadow—is *us*. The idea that what lies in our shadow is who we *really* are.

The shadow isn't what you think.

WITNESSING OUR SHADOW

The way we typically handle our shadow material doesn't work. As you can see below, none of the choices lead to a life you'd want:

- Destroying it is futile.
- Avoiding it makes us anxious.
- Dissociating from it numbs us.
- Indulging in it exasperates the suffering.
- Suppressing it gives it power over us.
- Dwelling on it feels awful.
- Blaming others disempowers us.

- Forcing others to change never works.

Well, of course they don't lead to a desirable life! When you act from fear, what results do you expect?

Now that you know this approach doesn't work, what the hell *do* we do about our shadow material? It's a curious question. What makes us feel so compelled to *do* something? I never hear anyone asking, "What do I do with all my light material?" The answer to both would simply be to *experience it*. This response is baffling only if your understanding of 'shadow material' is distorted.

Your shadow material represents the best parts of yourself that the ego misjudged, deemed undesirable, and regulated to the trash bin. Some parts present themselves as destructive behaviors, others as disempowering thoughts, and some as unpleasant feelings. They are aspects of yourself that you've misidentified and abandoned, which now run you unconsciously and cause havoc.

If we choose freedom, it requires us to know the truth. To know this, we must stop denying and take responsibility. If you want to overcome the control the underworld has over you, you must go into the place you're avoiding. That is what will set you free. Our choice calls us to face our dragons—after all, creators are responsible for their creations.

The only way out is *in*. But we try to come up with any other way *besides* going in, don't we? We hide it or hide from it. We deny having any part of it. We try all sorts of techniques, strategies, methods, and processes to fix without facing. We think seeing it makes it real. We believe that owning it will mean we are sinful. We feel like admission implies guilt, and that always leads to punishment. It's as if taking full accountability will bring us to our knees and strip our power. We are terrified that even acknowledging our shadow will instigate our fall from the Garden.

Yet, the reality couldn't be any more different.

The aspects of yourself you believe will harm, when in proper relationship and union, will protect. The facets of yourself that you think will cause others to reject you will be what allows people to cherish you and relate. The vulnerability which you strive to patch-up is the opening that lets love in. The flaws that you so wish to erase, paint the texture of your character. The limits of your abilities force you to get creative. The darkness you fear will engulf you, leading to your exaltation as a luminous human.

Not only do we have it backward, but as we learned in "When Wrong Works," the resolution can be found by doing the opposite.

SHADOW WORK

In this work, the way out of the darkness is *in*. Rather than avoiding our shadow and trying to become faeries of rainbow light, we go *into* it and let our shadow material inform—and transform—us. We want to get into relationship with our shadow, not try to destroy it or run from it. This is called *shadow work.*

It's a simple, albeit not necessarily easy, process. To begin your shadow work, simply start doing the opposite of the previous list of what doesn't work:

- Stop trying to fight it, and allow it to be what it really is
- Start feeling what you're avoiding feeling
- Go into the root of the story instead of trying to escape
- Let it be seen, heard, and acknowledged in the light
- Make a choice and move forward in a new way
- Own it and accept responsibility for the consequences
- Stop trying to get the world to change to accommodate you

Notice there's nothing about fixing or judging here. It's a completely different approach from how most of us are used to handling the "worst parts of ourselves." These can be extrapolated beyond shadow work to serve as sage principles for life.

The reason we'd even want to go through all this to face our shadow is to regain access to all the resources we've abandoned. This is the treasure that we have unknowingly locked away. All treasures have a map, and your most guarded gifts are no different. Yes, *gifts.*

Your ego has deceived you—your shadow is not what you think it is. You've stopped adventuring for your gifts because they're no longer treasured. You have been swindled, dear hero! It is not in the prairies out yonder, nor is it in the villages of your homeland. It's the cavern within that holds such riches. Getting there is no easy feat, but there is a way: addressing your dragons.

When you come across a dragon on your path and choose to face it instead of fleeing, it will stop trying to eat you. If you can look it straight in the eye, your dragon will submit and reveal the map to your treasure chest. Do not attack or falter, or else it will devour you with ferocious hunger. This map is full of instructions and information, and what it reveals may startle you. It directs you to the forbidden cavern within, which you must enter of your own free will. You must navigate the labyrinth and sail past the sirens. You must destroy the gatekeepers as you reach the inner sanctum. It warns you of the last trap, where most fail. It says that instead of taking the steps upwards towards the sparkling gems, you must jump into the infinitely dark abyss below. The map further reveals that after doing so, there will be a time of total darkness—but do not wavier in your faith! It assures you that soon you will arrive at the other side, and your vision will return. It is here that you will find the treasure which had once been discarded and locked away.

Here is a simple five-step process, referred to as the **A5 Process,** which you can use when you encounter a dragon (a shadow feeling, behavior, or thought) in your daily life:

1. **Awareness**
2. **Acknowledgment**
3. **Allowance**
4. **Annihilation**
5. **Access**

Let's break each of these down and see how it guides you to the riches of your shadow.

1. Awareness

i. Be mindful. Be present in everything you do. Observe your-self from an unbiased and non-judgmental place.

ii. Become aware of what is happening. Notice the feeling of dissonance; you know something is off. What is this about? Is there an agenda, manipulation, story, judgment, lie, ego trip, addiction, or distortion under what you're doing?

iii. Interrupt it when you catch it. Step out of the pattern and see how you are acting out or coming from a story. Stop the behavior immediately if you are clear about where it's com-ing from. Do not finish the sentence, conversation, action— stop it in the middle of whatever you were doing and pause. Do not worry about what anyone else will think. It is better to be in silent integrity than dishonest noise.

2. Acknowledgment

i. See it, look at it, do not avoid it. Listen; do not ignore it.

ii. Feel it. There is always a feeling behind it. Go inside, into your body. Do not search in agony. Let it find you.

iii. Do not deny or discredit. Let it be seen, internally or externally. Initially, you may have to consciously act it out in order for you to become aware of what it really is. Do the consequences merit your discovery?

3. Allowance

i. Allow the feeling to be whatever it wants to be. Do not diminish, push down, shrink, inflate, or dramatize it—allow it to be what it really is.

ii. Do not judge. Do not give it meaning. Report the data.

iii. Keep feeling. Notice any habits otherwise.

4. Annihilation

i. The feeling will take you to the origin. Follow the feeling to illuminate where this suffering is coming from. This will require vulnerability and courage. You will know you've found it as soon as you see something and the feeling amplifies. Go towards it; don't stray and get caught in mind chatter or fantasies.

ii. There may be additional layers that become apparent as you descend and penetrate. You may realize that there was more to it than what was obvious. Keep going deeper.

iii. Once you get there, report what this is really about. The thing you did to trigger this is not the cause: it is the effect of something unresolved within you. Narrate this without drama, psychological inflation, or more suffering.

iv. It is not enough to hover outside of it, look at it, and talk about it. You must go into it and speak from within it. Ensure you are not conning yourself to avoid truly feeling it.

v. Let yourself feel this root cause completely, allowing the shame, guilt, embarrassment, and judgments to arise, but without giving them meaning or making yourself wrong. When you allow yourself to feel these, you will move forward. If you are stuck in judgment, allow yourself to judge, rather than judging the judgment and yourself for being judgmental. All that judging is to prevent you from feeling. Stop the judging, and you stop the defense against the 'bad' things you're protecting yourself from being.

vi. Allow everything, no matter how irrelevant. Feel and surrender into it 100%, not 99.9%—you *must* go all the way through. Do not fight or resist. This is a pivotal moment where you can either end the suffering right now with a new choice, or use this as a reason to keep suffering.

vii. You will eventually penetrate the story. Let it annihilate you. You merely need to overcome the threshold of surrender because the fear of death will stop you. Death can be what it feels like—but what it annihilates is unreal and not who-you-really-are. Rest steadfast in this faith.

viii. The shift does not need to be big or an ordeal. This process supports you through both the extreme and subtle. You will feel it—you shouldn't have to contemplate if there was a shift or not.

5. Access

i. Once you have penetrated the story and felt fully, you will be able to see with true-sight. Before and on the way down, your vision may have been clouded by projection and distorted by fear. Now that you are on the other side, you have newfound clarity.

ii. This clarity, insight, wisdom, growth, learning—whatever form it takes—is now a resource you have access to. It's whatever the shadow was there to teach you.

iii. You are now more in relationship with this aspect of yourself that was previously unconscious. It's easy to slip back into old patterns, so be sure to begin practicing new ways of responding in similar situations.

This is your treasure map. Remember it as **A5: Awareness, Acknowledgment, Allowance, Annihilation, Access**.

Sometimes this process can require a dedicated space and time, or it could only take a moment. It becomes faster and easier as you get into relationship with your shadow. The more you practice this, the less it's a step-by-step process, and the more it becomes your natural way of addressing things. Do not make this into a technique and strategy for more fixing! It's essentially observing, feeling, and telling the truth—in itself a noble way to live.

ENDING THE WAR

The only battle you have is with your ego, and it's of your own doing. The shadow work presented here requires no weapons or shields. You are called not to fight, but to come face-to-face with the worst aspects of yourself. To surrender, let them destroy you, and be reborn defenseless towards your own mind. You will thus vanquish your 'enemy': a fractured-self you long-ago declared war with.

Once you stop fighting, suppressing, avoiding, resisting, and defending against yourself—you can merge with, dissolve into, and integrate your rejected, misappropriated self. You become empowered by the shadow, rather than in opposition to it all the time.

This is an opportunity to see deeper into yourself than you've ever looked before. It is a space without judgment. You are allowed to drop politically correct constructs, cultural norms, and fears of condemnation. Acknowledging and accepting does not equal condoning or bypassing. Remember that just because it *feels* evil does not mean you *are* an evil person.

I offer no hyperbole: staring into your shadow may be the most courageous act of self-love you ever do.

> *"If you gaze long enough into an abyss,*
> *the abyss will gaze back into you."*
> — *Friedrich Nietzsche*

What appears in your shadow is not what you think.

SHADOW IN SERVICE

If you are stuck, and you're afraid of looking at the worst parts of yourself, then beginning to face and embrace your shadow is going to give you access to the vast dimension of resources you've been denying. When in proper relationship, our shadow aspects serve.

What does it mean to be "in proper relationship"? Think about a healthy relationship with another person: we respect them, accept them for who they are, conduct ourselves according to any hierarchy, we have a positive attitude towards each other, we feel safe and at ease, and know where each of us stands with vulnerability and transparency. Think about dysfunctional relationships where there may be: disrespect, fear, uncertainty, drama and chaos, rejection, judgment, misunderstanding, lying, or attacking and defending. We can relate similarly to ideas, the space around us, emotions, archetypes, and just about anything else. We are not 'in a relationship with' an object or idea like we are with a friend or partner, but we are 'in relationship' with it—meaning there's a way in which we relate to it.

Being in proper relationship with our shadow means that we are relating to it in a way that's most appropriate and true. Being 'out of relationship' with our shadow would be to judge it, suppress or deny it, be ignorant of it, try to get rid of it, defend against it, let it run us, or be fearful of it. This is improper because the shadow is part of us, and as we've learned thus far, all of these attitudes against ourselves are futile and lead to suffering. A proper relationship with our shadow would be one that includes communication, understanding, acceptance, discernment, utility, willingness, trust, and love. Most of us don't approach our shadow in these ways, so it's no wonder that it runs us!

The more integrated and functional we become, the more we can be of service to ourselves and those around us. Our range of functionality does not expand from rejection but from acceptance. Once you accept the following (and similar) as true and have embodied this principle, you will possess a rare and powerful relationship with your authentic self.

Your capacity to **create** is the extent of your willingness to **destroy**.

Your capacity to **love** is the extent of your willingness to **hate**.

Your capacity for **courage** is the extent of your willingness to be **vulnerable**.

Your capacity for **freedom** is the extent of your willingness to **restrict**.

When we deny access to a part of our self—including our shadow material—we lose access to all those associated resources. You cannot take away from one without taking away from the other.

Life requires more from us than only being "good boys and girls."

At some point, you may need to do something not nice to defend yourself. Perhaps you may need the furious wrath of Odin to destroy a cancerous project. Or, you may need to feel like a pathetic failure to finally be ready to leave a demeaning job. You may need to betray everyone you love to leave an abusive relationship. Or, you may need to be a heartless asshole to tell some off who's been lying and manipulating.

These are inconceivable if you're trying to be "good"; if you're rejecting your shadow.

Fret not, as you merely need to be *willing* to allow yourself to go there. The willingness enables you to take further steps towards the truth, which may have been obfuscated by your fear. Because even though that's what it *seems* like to you, what you think is "wrong" may actually be something incredibly loving for self and other. What it feels like to you might be the opposite of what it really is—self-love (reverse-wiring).

Protecting yourself is righteous and sane. Destroying a business tumor is healthy. Walking away is standing up for yourself. Betraying abuse is loyalty to safety. Setting a boundary is self-respect and respect for others. As you awaken, the reality of these might not be as "evil" or "mean" as you may have once perceived.

It takes tremendous courage to be willing to do something that feels awful, that only afterward reveals itself to be loving.

APPROPRIATE USE

As you start to acknowledge and dialogue with the shadowy qualities within you, they will begin to lose their nefarious role and dominion over your life. The unconscious becomes conscious. The resources they manage will be at your conscious command. You will make situationally-appropriate choices from a conscious choice, rather than blindly reacting.

Imagine the peaceful warrior:

He does not seek war. He does not pick fights. He lives a life of peace and harmony. He makes love to his wife and raises children. But he also trains in the art of war. He bleeds and bruises. He learns his weapon thoroughly, knowing fully well that it is only meant for one thing—death. He does not hope for death, but he doesn't shy away from it either. Although a sword stays sheathed at his side—he still has one.

And if war comes to him? He does not cower or run—he fights. He fights to defend his family, his home, and himself. He kills and destroys what unrighteously seeks to kill and destroy him. Does he say, "You can't come hurt us; we're only peaceful here!" ...while a sword pierces his lungs and his family gets murdered?

No.

He roars, "You may have free will to come here and do evil, but I also have the same will to stop you—die!" Then he pulls the sword out of his sheath and goes, *SHWUMF!*, stabbing the enemy. The intruder dies, and his family is safe once again. Back into the sheath his sword goes, and on with his life the peaceful warrior goes. His shadow served him because he was in proper relationship with it, rather than judging, avoiding, rejecting, or suppressing it.

This is appropriate, discerning action without shadow-rejection. The shadow can be your ally—a great resource—or your archenemy. Which one it becomes is determined by how you relate to it. If you allow it, your shadow can become one of your greatest assets.

Your shadow is still not what you think.

INTO THE SHADOW TO FIND THE LIGHT OF LIGHTS

In this chapter, I've shared an introduction to practical shadow work you can do every day. No entheogens are required, only great courage. Take the first step and see with new eyes. Don't worry about fixing, changing, or transmuting—simply pivot inwards instead of out and further cultivate your self-awareness.

When I look at what I'd rather not be true about me, sometimes I do it with grace and humor—other times, I end up acting-out worse. I don't try for perfection. I continue to remind myself that I'm not alone and to have compassion. The more I can tell the truth and have compassion for myself, the more empathy and understanding I can have with others. This matters more than climbing any 'levels' of spiritual advancement.

The spiritual practice isn't about rejecting darkness—it's realizing that both the light and dark are love.

Shadow work is not about elimination—it's about integration. It's not about disowning certain dark parts but getting into proper relationship with *all aspects* of ourselves. What remains in the shadow pales in significance compared to our *relationship* with it. You will never defeat all the dragons, and you will never be without darkness. Likewise, you will never be lost, and you will never lose your light, no matter how dim it gets.

DARK NIGHT OF THE SOUL

Sometimes the darkness can seem overwhelming, engulfing us in horror. It can seem futile—hopeless. The light eludes us, and us the light.

"In the middle of the journey of our
life I found myself within a dark woods
where the straight way was lost."
— Dante Alighieri, Inferno

When we are in the depths of our darkness, sometimes that's all we can see. We become deaf and blind to salvation. Like a marionette, we are helplessly danced by all the awful things about us. We only see how we betray, lie, and hurt those we love. We become consumed by the tidal wave of unworthiness, guilt, shame, rejection, hatefulness, and loathing.

We are feeding the night with our demons.

We fall further into the night when we're deep in our cowardice, at the edge of wanting to live. When we are breaking from sorrow, crushed by failure. We fall deeper into darkness when we feel like scum, lower than dirt. When the walls around us are caving in, suffocating us with the gazes of disappointment that shrink-wrap our body. We fall further into the night when we dwell on our incompetence, our mistakes, our undesirableness, our shortcomings, and when we indulge in all the reasons why we don't deserve love, forgiveness, or help.

When we're in this place of darkness, we don't even *want* to see the light. It's more seductive to sink into this pit and let what's wrong with us masticate us than it is to focus on what's holy and right. We dwell in our misery, get off on our self-pity, and indulge in self-loathing. Our addictions to self-abuse make it seem easier to hate ourselves than to love.

The hardest thing we can do when we are in this dark night of the soul is to see our True light. To look unconditional love straight in the eye and see the reflection of how lovable we truly are. To let someone embrace us—and keep holding us, and keep holding us longer without pushing away thinking, "eek, too much love." To allow ourselves to feel unconditional worth amid a swamp of shortcomings. To be treated kindly by the person whom we've just wronged.

For many of us, **shadow work is less about accepting our shadow and more about allowing our light.** It's easy to see how bad we are, how much of a failure we are, how undesirable we are—but how easily we dismiss and deny the evidence of how lovable we are. How hard it can be to accept the idea that there's nothing wrong with us. To allow ourselves to be as wonderful as we truly are. To be gazed upon with eyes that see no imperfection. To be held in arms that know no judgment. How hard it is to let the Divine in to bare witness to our fully-exposed soul without any acknowledgment of our unreal suffering.

We avoid fully penetrating the depths of our shadow—not because we're afraid of the awful things on the other side—but because we're avoiding the unconditional self-love that patiently awaits us there.

This is your shadow. 🐾

JUST STOP

"Stop thinking, and end your problems."
— LAO TZU

When people think of meditation, they tend to think it's about the mind. Stilling the mind, watching the mind, overcoming the mind, but it's actually about *no mind*. Many people get frustrated with meditation because they're using the mind to try to stop the mind. *Good luck!* Likewise, moving forward by trying to unstick the stuckness from the place that got you stuck—will only keep you stuck. It's the insanity of, "If only I do *more* of what isn't working, it'll work." You can't get there from there. This is what you learned at the beginning of the chapter, "An Equation for Suffering."

The problem can't solve the problem it began.

If you've already been trying hard, adding, learning, and starting new things, then doing more of that isn't going to get you unstuck. I'm not suggesting you do or be more, or to achieve new things and set goals. I'm not inferring that you need to become something you are not already. I'm not teaching anything new, only reminding you of what is already True. **There is no fixing because you're not broken. There is no addition because you are not incomplete.** You don't need to try harder, but do less. You don't need to add, but subtract. You don't need to learn, but unlearn. You don't need to start, but to stop.

"It is not a daily increase, but a daily decrease."
— *Bruce Lee*

This healing work is not about perfecting our fantasies, masks, or armoring—nor is it a path to spiritual ascension, transhumanism, or escapism. It's about stopping all the strategies we use to avoid being a vulnerable human. It's not about *overcoming* ourselves but *surrendering* to ourselves. I invite you to surrender to your True Self rather than remain a slave to your egoic self-image. Once you accept that who-you-really-are is enough and there is nothing wrong with you, you'll discover the *serenity of being*. From the place where you're at now, getting to that 'still point of being' requires choice and action in the form of *stopping*. Stopping can be considered the anti-doing, or *undoing*. As you stop doing what causes suffering, drop what isn't really you, and allow everything that *is* you—you will realize how much efforting you've been doing to fight against yourself.

Most importantly, you will get to know yourself for the first time. Most of us have no idea who we really are. This is an opportunity to have a real relationship with your *self*.

Stopping is the path to your True Self.

WHAT IT MEANS TO STOP

How do we know what to stop? Well, we surely don't stop what works. We don't stop what leads to joy, beauty, love, intimacy, connection, gratitude, and any of the other things we truly want in life. It may seem obvious, but how many times have you stopped taking risks or being vulnerable after failing or getting rejected? We stop what's functional and joyous because of the pain we associate with it. Oftentimes we stop doing what works long-term because of short-term pain. We close our hearts off for our entire lives because of one or two heartbreaks. We stop making art and being creative because one group of people made fun of us. We stop being generous because a few people we gave to treated us poorly. It's not that being open-hearted, creative, and generous doesn't work or that they don't lead us to wonderful things—they do. It's that we make other people's projections and cruelty mean something about us and what we're doing. We associate the pain with what we were doing "that caused it." The creativity, love, and generosity didn't themselves *cause* our suffering, but we figure that if we hadn't been open, if we didn't create any art, or we never shared in the first place, we wouldn't have gotten hurt. And so we 'stop' doing all of these to stay safe.

This is the type of 'stopping' that got you here—stuck. This is not the stopping you are looking for. So then, what *is*?

DEFINING THE WORD 'STOP'

Let's first look at two definitions for *stop*:

A. To block, plug, prevent; *"Put your hand over the pipe to stop the water from leaking."*
B. To cease, finish, end, halt; *"She is going to stop smoking."*

The most significant difference between these two is that the first *initiates* an activity, and the second is *the ending* of an activity. The first requires us to take action to stop, and the second is ending action altogether. One is doing, and the other is not-doing. The first (Def-A) requires energy, the second (Def-B) frees energy. The invitation for this chapter is the second, Def-B: the cessation of your suffering by stopping the things you do to block your joy. It is crucial you understand the difference between these two because the power of this entire chapter—nay, the entire book—hinges on the difference.

This philosophy is subtractive, not additive. It's the difference between adding to improve yourself and subtracting to remove detriments. Ending suffering is not about adding pleasure and joy, nor learning 'to love' or 'do happiness'—but in the elimination of what we've learned to do that is preventing our innate joy, connection, and love. Getting unstuck is not about adding 'unstucky habits' or 'stuckless strategies' to your life, but re-moving (subtracting) what you're doing that's keeping you stuck.

Here's what happens:

When we block our light—our love, generosity, humor, and so on—it seems like we're stopping because our light and our gifts are no longer coming through. But what's actually happening is that we're *starting*. We're doing Def-A, which means we are *starting* an action to block, suppress, judge, get self-consciousness, or censor our light. It stops it by actively taking action, not by ceasing action.

These are patterns and coping strategies that we choose to start and actively maintain; they are not shackles we are born with. Think of a child: they have no filter, they're not self-censoring, they are not blocking love to or from anyone... until they learn it. This is one of the primary reasons we love babies so much—they are so easy to love because they *only* know how to allow. It's only as they grow up and start taking on filters and gates (strategies to throttle love) that they start to stop (Def-A) love.

When we are shut down, closed off, numb, or repressed, it's not because we're missing something; it's because we have stopped our natural gifts. We have blocked beauty, love, creativity, or whatever other light from flowing through us. For safety, approval, or self-loathing, we make a choice to stop (Def-A) feeling or doing. We block our-selves from our natural expression. This stopping can be considered *unnatural* because it prevents our nature. This unnatural stopping is what we appear to be doing on the surface, but this is an *action*, and action requires effort and energy. This takes you further and further from your True Self.

We want to end our addiction to these actions that tie up energy and block our light. We want to *cease* blocking, *halt* preventing, and *end* plugging what makes us, *us*. We want to shift from 'stop' (blocking, Def-A) to 'stop' (ceasing, Def-B). This *natural* stopping restores our true nature via subtraction, not addition. This is the 'stopping' suggested in the chapter, "Stop Fixing and Start Living."

You can spend the next seven years learning how to love, or you could just stop doing everything that's preventing your inherent lovability. You can spend six years learning to be more sociable, or you can just stop the judgments, avoidance of feeling, self-censoring, and taking things personally. You can spend three years learning all the tactics to get clients, or you could just stop the stories that you're unworthy and unlovable, the judgments and self-criticism, the self-loathing and rejection, and the resentment.

We are told we need to do, do, do; learn, learn, learn; become, become, become. That's what's easy to sell. It's easy to see quick-fix results. Learning complicated new things seems like progress, even if it eventually leads to more struggle, as we learned in "An Equation for Suffering." It's much harder to sell 'stopping.' People are less interested in removing than adding because +50 still sounds more valuable than -500. We think adding moves us forward, and subtracting takes us backward—but this is the reverse-wiring mentioned in "When Wrong Works."

The more you add, the further you get from your True Self. The more you remove what's not you, the closer you get. This is why stopping is the only way—because it is no longer a doing, but an *undoing*.

What To Stop

Now that you unquestionably understand what it means to 'stop,' I can answer the question "what do I stop?" accurately.

Here is a list of what to stop:

- Stop suffering
- Stop thinking too much
- Stop trying to do it right
- Stop looking for a magic pill
- Stop looking for a way to skip the discomfort
- Stop lying to yourself
- Stop over-analyzing
- Stop trying to fix yourself, others, and the world

- Stop trying to understand everything
- Stop blaming and complaining
- Stop telling the same story over and over
- Stop 'shoulding' all over yourself
- Stop waiting until you're ready
- Stop trying to be perfect
- Stop trying to control everything
- Stop beating yourself up
- Stop judging
- Stop avoiding
- Stop holding your breath
- Stop putting on a show
- Stop cultivating a persona or better mask
- Stop building walls and putting on armor
- Stop the noise and drama
- Stop censoring and throttling
- Stop the addictions
- Stop hiding out and playing small
- Stop distorting reality
- Stop manipulating
- Stop defending and justifying
- Stop living in a fantasy
- Stop being in denial
- Stop trying to be cool or funny or sexy
- Stop letting your ego and arrogance run you
- Stop attacking others and yourself
- Stop suppressing and numbing out
- Stop being codependent or isolated
- Stop making everything about you
- Stop martyring yourself
- Stop abandoning yourself
- Stop withholding and holding others back
- Stop inflating and exaggerating
- Stop gossiping
- Stop using other people to beat yourself up

- Stop trying to be someone you're not
- Stop rejecting love and support
- Stop putting off what you want
- Stop worrying
- Stop poisoning yourself with bad food, ideas, media, etc.
- Stop making it hard
- Stop playing dumb
- Stop competing and comparing
- Stop projecting
- Stop avoiding life
- Stop acting superior
- Stop dissociating from feeling and your body
- Stop making excuses and letting fear run you
- Stop waiting for someone else to rescue you
- Stop fixing yourself

It's a long list. Stop all of it. Any story or behavior that censors, suppresses, denies, or judges you—stop that too.

If earlier in the chapter you thought, "I don't have many things I need to stop," that was your ego. That justification or rebuttal you're probably thinking—**just stop.** It's all suffering. Perhaps a surprising number of these items hit home. If so, that's a good thing. All of these are ways we hold ourselves and others back. Doing these keeps anyone stuck. It's important to find out, not stay in denial.

If you were to completely stop each of these things that you are doing, there is a 0% chance you'd stay stuck. I nearly never say "impossible," but yes: I reckon it would be impossible to stay stuck if you stopped *all* of these. Try it.

If you're looking for the most practical and applicable chapter, this is it. I'm sorry if it's a let-down. It is not fancy. There is no magic pill or sexy formula. There is no ritual, ceremony, or virgin to sacrifice. You don't have to be rich or smart. It's accessible to you in each moment, wherever you go. There is no technique to learn.

You just stop.

It's the simplest, albeit the most powerful tool you have. Do not make the same mistake most people do and underestimate, dismiss, or ignore the simplicity of this. Making the choice to stop in the middle of your suffering is nothing short of a miracle. To be in the middle of defending, attacking, manipulating, lying, justifying, arguing, judging—see the behavior and make a genuine choice to stop it completely then and there—is the single most powerful ability you could develop to get unstuck.

How To Stop

I remember when I'd be in the middle of my drama or story of suffering, and my mentor would tell me to stop. I'd quip back with, "But I don't know how to stop! What do I do?" The answer was always the same: "You just stop." Sometimes it would take a moment, other times a year. It wasn't that stopping itself took that long; it was that it took me a year to get to the place where I was *ready* to stop. Far too often, I see clients use the excuse of 'not knowing how to stop' as a way to remain a victim and not have to change. I've done it myself, so I know the game. Stopping is a choice. It's not something you don't already know how to do. With that said, it can be helpful to explore the nuances and break down the process so that we no longer have the excuse of "But how?!"

As you learned earlier, the stopping we're looking for is the second Def-B definition: ending, ceasing, terminating, canceling, halting. We are not doing, but *undoing*. We are not adding but *subtracting*. Whatever we are thinking or doing, we stop. This requires letting go, not control. If we clamp down and control, we are not stopping but doing something new to block it (a new stopping Def-A). We are *already* in control mode; stopping with more control only creates neurosis. You wind up over-analyzing, obsessing, and being hyper-vigilant about making sure you're stopping correctly. This is not what we want! We want peace, joy, ease—not more stress and anxiety. Stopping is a letting go, a surrendering.

Here's how you stop:

- **Awareness:** You sense there's something else under the surface of what's happening. You become aware of what you're doing and the unconscious stories and behaviors that are running.
- **Choice:** Once you become aware of what you're doing, you have an opportunity to make a choice—to keep doing it, now from a conscious intention—or you stop altogether.
- **Stop:** You make a choice to stop. You let go of attachment and control. You surrender to what may feel like nothingness or death. You go silent. You go still. You end the behavior. You don't do anything, you stop doing, and it undoes itself.
- **Feel:** Once we stop the behavior, everything underneath it—which we were using the behavior to avoid—rises up. Sometimes this is peace, and sometimes it's pain. We may have to stop other stories and protection habits that engage. It is easy to stop (Def-A) feeling—do not do this. Stop blocking and let yourself feel.

Stopping *is* simple; it's only a moment in these four steps. This entire process can occur in a second—or it can take some time to get to the point of surrender and feeling. The letting go, the stopping—it happens in an instant. There is no drama or effort. The fear, avoidance, and struggle leading up to the moment is a different story. It's the process that surrounds stopping—not stopping itself—which requires energy and time.

When we're creating all this hysterical, noisy chaos around "trying so hard to stop," we are fooling ourselves. It's not actually stopping: it's creating a drama. Stopping is easy; it's literally doing nothing. What we really mean when we say "it's hard to stop" is that all the things *around* stopping are hard, like giving up our addictions, penetrating our stories, telling the truth, and facing our shadow. Sometimes we have to stop dozens of chaotic patterns before we are quiet and still enough to get to the root of the distortion we want to stop.

Stopping is not some revelation. It's not something you've never heard before. Yet, it's something so few of us do. Really, all you need to do is stop. This "process" is as simple as possible: you stop doing everything you're doing that's causing you to suffer. This is obviously a lot easier said than done, which is why we're taking an entire chapter to discuss this one topic. It's essential to understand what 'stopping' is and what it looks like when it happens. Without being able to stop, you will never get unstuck or wake up. It is the only way.

You can finish here and practice the mantra "just stop" and get 80% of the benefits from this chapter you need. For that last 20% of mastery, let's explore these steps in-depth.

STEP 1: AWARENESS

The first thing you need before stopping is *awareness*. You need to become aware of the behavior in order to stop it. This requires you to be mindful and cultivate superb self-awareness, meaning you are present and observant of yourself. You are not dissociated, checked-out, numbed-out, or avoidant. You are conscious of what you're thinking, seeing, feeling, and doing. You disengage from autopilot and take control of your steering wheel. Self-awareness moves you from *reactive* to *responsive*. You observe your thoughts, feelings, and behaviors like you give feedback: no judgment, meanings, or stories. Like a camera, you simply watch.

At some point, you will notice something dissonant. You will become aware that you're reacting to a story, trauma, or meaning that isn't real. You will become aware of feelings that don't feel good. You will become aware of destructive or limiting thoughts and words. Whatever it is, you will notice it. This noticing is a witnessing. As you witness your behavior, via yourself or through feedback, it moves from the underworld to the upperworld. That is to say, you make the unconscious conscious, and it no longer runs you.

*"Until you make the unconscious conscious,
it will direct your life and you will call it fate."*
— Carl Gustav Jung

STEP 2: CHOICE

You must make the choice to stop yourself. Nobody else can do it for you. Go inside, make the choice, and take internal action upon it. Choosing is not hoping, wishing, or wanting—you must decide to end the behavior or story and then stop it. There is no non-choice: you either choose to continue or you choose to stop.

Sometimes we don't want to make this choice. We are afraid and addicted. We feel helpless. We are caught in so much self-loathing that we refuse to make the choice to stop. Yet, if we know we must stop, we may manipulate others to do it for us. Thus, we act-out disrespectfully and force others to enforce their boundaries because we lack self-control and self-love. We put the responsibility of stopping on another because we are acting like cowards and victims. It is irresponsible behavior that will keep us stuck.

A good archetype to illustrate this is the 'brat.' This is where someone misbehaves on purpose and gets off on it. It's more than acting out. It's a strategy, a game. The 'brat' enjoys being bad. They test boundaries through disrespect, manipulating the other person to discipline them—to stop them. We think we don't want rules and limits, but we need and seek them, especially as children. The 'brat' archetype resents the masculine figure (often the father) for not setting clear boundaries and letting them get away with things they shouldn't have. This 'brat' despises pushovers they can walk over—even though they constantly push the limits of what they can get away with—because they are really looking for the safety and trust of boundaries. They don't trust themselves to have boundaries, so they are codependent with someone who will 'make' them stop.

What happens when this behavior gets extreme? We see many times the acts of committing a crime and getting arrested or acting violent and getting killed are ways an individual who is suffering uncontrollably gets someone else to stop them. The mythologies of destruction, self-loathing, rage, despair, violation, or any of the other "evil-like" stories have overrun the individual. The person cannot stop themselves. The suffering and disconnection from who-they-really-are and unconditional love become too much for them. This dissonance reaches a point where they see no chance of hope, no possibility of change or redemption, and so they let their stories take control over them. Other people are then forced to stop them, often through violence or legal force. The only things they will allow to stop their suffering are jail, injury, or death. They are begging the space to make them knock it off because they have given up and refuse to do it themselves. This is how addictive our stories can be.

At the same extreme, but making the 'choice' to stop for ourselves is suicide. Suicide is the ultimate stopping—of life. It is the last resort when someone is unable to stop suffering while alive. Again, the dissonance becomes so great, they commit a final act of self-abandonment and use death as a way to stop because they choose not to stop it themselves.

Can you see how much pain, despair, and distortion someone must be in to arrive at either extreme? What we see in this behavior, and in many of the other ways we choose to suffer, is a *cry for help*. It is not something to shame, but a travesty to show great compassion for. Sometimes we want to defend ourselves with judgment against these cries rather than empathize with them. Other times we try to rescue or enable the behavior if we see them as helpless victims. Both reasons are because we don't want to feel the pain in ourselves. This compassion is not only for those at the extreme but for our own cries for help as well.

All types of acting out are forms of suffering, and are caused by suffering. We act out when we're unable to meet our needs, are addicted and unable to stop ourselves, or we've been hurt. These are all forms of feeling powerless, which is at the root of victim mentality. In all three of the prior examples, the behavior is 'stopped,' but it does not result in freedom or joy. It only validates their story of disempowerment and leads to further suffering. This stopping is the kind from Def-A, not Def-B, and so it will not last. However, it may be a 'wake-up call' that leads someone to the real choice, so it can in someway serve. These are the ones who simply won't let themselves have what they want or are unable snap out of it until they hit rock bottom. I don't recommend that approach, though.

You may not be ready to stop—that's okay—but be honest with yourself and own it. If you want to keep suffering, that's your choice; but don't make others responsible for it, and do not act like you want to stop because you feel guilty. It's better to consciously choose to continue the behavior and take responsibility for it than remain ignorant and have it run you. After you make the choice to continue the behavior, pay attention to the effect it has and the results you get from doing it. Letting the behavior play out with mindfulness turns it into an opportunity for *feedback*. While it's not stopping, taking ownership of our behaviors is a step towards it.

STEP 3: STOP

Just as the choice to move your arm is the movement itself, your choice to stop and the stopping itself go hand-in-hand. You cannot choose to stop without stopping—and you cannot stop without making a choice. Separating stopping into 'steps' is a bit of a misnomer, but it's helpful to break down the process *around* stopping.

When you stop suppressing, rejecting, judging, censoring, or whatever it may be, you are ending a behavior, not starting another. **Stopping is a cessation.** You don't *do* anything; you end what you've been doing. When we stop, we go quiet and still. In this silence and stillness, we begin to see and feel what we've been avoiding by running the behavior. There is no need to go and search around your problem and micromanage your process. The stopping allows the undoing. This requires you to let go of attachment to an outcome and the addiction to the behavior. You must let go of control. This is the same control the behavior was trying to exert. This is also the control of what, when, and how much you feel during the process.

Can you imagine trying to control an orgasm? Only letting little bits of pleasure squeeze through in evenly spaced intervals to make sure your body looked just right? It would be disastrous! Control and orgasm are diametrically opposed. Likewise, trying to control your experience of feeling will emotionally constipate you. What you want to do is *surrender*. When you stop, you surrender to whatever is underneath the behavior that will arise once stopped. This is why we don't want to do it: we can't control what comes up. *"What if it's bad, dangerous, or painful? What if it's all this shadow material I've been trying to cover up for years?"* We've become so out of touch with ourselves that we don't even trust our own healing! If you cannot trust, if you cannot have faith—you will struggle to ever truly surrender.

STEP 4: FEEL

Once we stop the behavior, we then discover what it was all about. In that silence and stillness—the apparent void remaining after stopping—we are left with the stories, feelings, and shadow material that fueled it. Many times, this is the reason why we don't want to stop. If our behaviors result from our traumas, meanings, distortions, and stories, we must be left with the cause when we remove the result.

It may move quickly, and in mere seconds you find yourself at peace. You may or may not see what it was about. It can be that easy sometimes. You become aware, choose, stop, and feel in a matter of seconds and get on with your life. There doesn't have to be a big event or a grand realization. Stop and be done with it. Other times what comes up can be confronting. We may be stopping a decades-long myth that has dominated our family for generations. Or, we could be stopping a pattern of walling ourselves off from intimacy. Or, we could be stopping the manipulation we run to get approval from our parents. Or, we could be stopping a story around unworthiness. Or, we could be stopping a behavior of abuse we've used to project our guilt.

These are not all straight forward; we all have different stories, meanings, judgments, emotions, and archetypes at play, even for the same behaviors. There may be guilt, shame, anger, sadness, or pain.

There may be sorrow, grief, loss, or heartache. There may be love, joy, beauty, gratitude. There may be judgments, stories, archetypes, and myths that reveal themselves. You may want to cry, run away, or get violent. Whatever it is, feel it. Feel it completely. Do not act it out, do not make it a drama, but go inside and feel it. It is okay to cry, to do whatever you need to feel it. Even if you have to act out in order to find the truth, stay with it in your body, don't go in your head. You can't "think about how it feels." Feeling happens in the body—which is why we want to dissociate from our bodies so much. It's a spontaneous, organic happening that, ultimately, we can only surrender to.

It may feel terrifying. You may feel anguish and hurt. It may seem as if letting yourself go there will annihilate you, that you will lose yourself. Do not resist it; let yourself surrender to it. Let it destroy you. You've been resisting it your entire life, and it's keeping you stuck. Allow yourself to do whatever it takes to finally feel everything that's coming up. Because you will not die, and you will not be lost. Anything that's True cannot be destroyed, and who-you-really-are is Real and True. The only things that will be destroyed are your illusions because they are unreal. This may feel painful because your ego has identified with them, but it will not *harm* you. *Not* feeling this emotion is what's harming you. Suppressing this feeling for years is what hurts, not surrendering. The self-love of stopping destructive behavior doesn't hurt; it's the ending of the addiction that feels painful.

Once you allow yourself to feel the emotion fully, it will move through you, and you will no longer be at the effect of it. Emotions are literally *energy-in-motion*. Feeling them fully is what allows them to reach their apogee and resolve. Only when we interrupt and suppress what we feel does it become a problem. Be cautious not to stop (Def-A) yourself from feeling, or else you'll wind up back where you started. Contrary to our foolish culture, feeling is not weak, bad, or undesirable. Feeling is natural, healthy, and absolutely necessary. Nearly all of our internal issues occur because we are out of relationship with feeling in some way or another.

The stopping ends it. The *feeling* is what informs you. That's what it's there for!

If you choose not to feel, then perhaps you're not ready to stop. That is okay. Again, be honest with yourself and have compassion. Fooling yourself through this by pretending to feel, or only doing it on the surface, will only weave your web of self-deception wider. You're ready when you're ready. Trust the process.

EXAMPLES OF STOPPING

Let's take a look at how someone would 'stop' in daily life.

EXAMPLE 1

Sally is talking with her family about finances. She becomes aware she's starting to get defensive about her purchases and justifying why she should be allowed to spend her money. So she stops talking. She pauses, goes inside, and feels into what this is about. After a few moments, she recognizes this is the behavior her mother did when her father interrogated her after going shopping.

Sally chooses not to continue this story and stops. The fears of being attacked, ridiculed, and shamed arise. She allows them. She feels the sadness of self-betrayal from having to justify her needs and wants. She spends a few moments to sit with it without having to rush past it.

Sally then reengages with her family and is now aware of how her sibling was 'baiting' her into getting defensive. She no longer engages in the manipulation or justifies, kindly saying "no" to their inquires of spending habits.

EXAMPLE 2

Bob is thinking about how he never meets anyone new. He starts thinking about how he doesn't have many friends, and when he was teased as a kid. He starts feeling sorry for himself but becomes aware he's doing this behavior. He sees that each time he thinks about meeting people, he associates it with being a loser and feels like crap.

Bob has had enough and makes a choice to stop. Panic and anxiety come in, but he no longer wants to run, so he lets them arise. Inner critic voices start campaigning to 'protect' him, saying things such as "If you don't think about solving this, you will be a loser forever" and "See, this feels awful, you need a drink." Bob stops and gets quiet. The pain of rejection moves within his body and intensifies. The fear of being alone begins to bubble up. This time he feels them, rather than judging himself for them and numbing the pain.

Bob cries for the first time in years, feeling great release. He sees a story about wanting to be loved and accepted under the pain. He has stopped making plans that were arranged only to avoid his self-judgment of being lonely. He has stopped using his perceived lack of friends to beat himself up.

EXAMPLE 3

Sally and Bob are having a conversation, and it quickly gets heated. Voices raise, and accusations are made. Bob is attacking, and Sally is getting defensive. Bob sees he is projecting and stops. In the space in which Bob stopped, Sally sees how her martyrdom story is running her at that moment. Sally takes a moment and stops her defensiveness. They both take a few moments to get out of their heads and into their bodies, so that they can feel themselves and each other.

Bob and Sally begin to share how they feel and report the facts without projection, drama, or story. They notice that the argument was not caused by anything real, but by both person's stories. Nothing they were saying had anything to do with what was actually happening in the moment, but the replaying of past traumas. The rest of their conversation was more intimate and meaningful after they stopped letting themselves be ran by their myths and decided to show up presently.

EXAMPLE 4

Sally is at the store buying furniture. She hears her internal judgment start about 'rich people' and high-end furniture. She is aware this is a story about "not feeling enough" and a way to protect herself from feeling guilt. She keeps herself from wealth by criticizing luxury. So Sally stops the judgment. She stops pushing luxury away by stopping all the meanings she gave it, good or bad. She continues shopping without the drama and simply chooses what she wants without justification.

EXAMPLE 5

Bob is in a meeting with colleagues at work discussing new product ideas. Bob sits back and watches the executives and senior-level designers share ideas about what the company should sell next. He is criticizing and judging each one, thinking about how his ideas are better. Yet, he does not speak up. He sits in the background, quiet. He realizes that everyone else is forward and engaged while he is pulled back. He notices he's feeling resentment.

Bob stops judging and criticizing. He notices that he is withholding and competing with the others' ideas. He is afraid they will steal his ideas without credit, or they will mock him for it. He makes the choice to express himself instead of being resentful. Bob stops the withholding and superiority. He feels the fear of ridicule and rejection arise, aware now that's what he was defending against by acting superior in his mind.

Bob leans in and begins to share an idea he had. Stopping the withholding, he notices all this creativity and passion come through that was blocked by the judging and resenting. His boss didn't accept his first idea, but the group didn't attack or embarrass him either. The more Bob began to contribute, the more creativity came through, and collaboration happened—leading to valuable input for their next product. The more he began to share his ideas freely, the more he had people asking for his input.

THE PRESSURE OF
STOPPING ALL AT ONCE

Stopping is the simplest thing, but it's not always easy. It requires no effort in reality, but since we have invested decades of momentum in *doing*, stopping can take a lot of energy. It takes a lot more energy to stop a freight train steaming down the track than one starting from a standstill. It's not that we must do a lot of heavy lifting; it's that we have to face, feel, and heal our stories before we allow ourselves to stop. It's not the stopping itself that requires effort, but everything leading up to it. Just as it took you effort to *do*, it will take initiative to *undo*. The difference is that it takes energy to sustain our 'doings' but frees energy once we have 'undone' them.

We have added so much to improve our persona, are doing so much to fix ourselves, and built up such a narrative—that trying to stop all of it at once is unwise. The space of non-suffering and the void-like-feeling left from a dissolved story or behavior can be disorienting. It's like an addict of fifty years who is dependent on pharmaceuticals, hard drugs, nicotine, and alcohol going cold turkey. We are similarly dependent and addicted to our illusions and suffering. Stopping everything all at once is not only unlikely to succeed, but it can be dangerous.

At our advanced retreats, we make sure participants stay for a few extra days because if they don't have time to reorient and adjust to the normal world, they can take themselves out. When people's false sense of self and life-long stories collapse over the course of a week, it can be like coming down from a psychedelic trip. We take the safety of our participants seriously, even if it's inconvenient. These mythologies and archetypes that run us are more powerful than you can imagine. I say this not to scare or discourage you but to communicate the gravity of this work and the impact it can have on your life. This book is designed to be safe, effective, and approachable for people at many levels of readiness and willingness. You will get precisely what you need, when you need it. Have faith and trust the process—it is wiser than either of our egos.

Doing it all at once is impractical for nearly everyone. This is evident by the infinitesimally small amount of people throughout history who've had an instant, permanent cessation of all suffering and safely sustained it while functioning in society. With that said: do not feel pressure to stop everything, all at once. Do not feel the pressure to have the life of a messiah. There is no race or reward. There is no specialness or status to obtain by grand spiritual events. Most of these goals of 'attainment' and becoming a 'higher vibrational person' are a trap of spiritual elitism. It is important to tell people of our experience to show what is possible, but so often, the ego reaffirms itself, and these revelations get perverted into a 'badge' to brag about. It's not that they aren't valid or worthwhile; it's that most often, they come from a *spiritualized ego* wanting to feel special. This ego veils itself under the guise of spirituality, like a criminal impersonating a detective to stay hidden from the police.

As I mentioned in "The Spiritual Path Is Failing You," the behavior to 'ascend' is often more about a rejection of our humanity than a realization of it. I invite you to let go of attachment—to any of it, by any deadline. It's not that 'attainment' or a fast pace towards awakening itself is a problem, but rather, the neurosis and suffering that we build up around the meaning we give them. You would not believe how much happier, meaningful, functional, and fulfilling clients' lives became after they got off 'the spiritual path.' That's the paradox: it's easier to become enlightened once you stop seeking and desiring enlightenment.

You're ready when you're ready; no advantage is gained from putting pressure on yourself. Relax. Breathe. It is better to attempt a little with integrity and move one step than to try too much, get overwhelmed, and give up. In my own experience, I've found there's a story about "once I get there, then I'll be able to X" running me when I feel this. I feel like "once I stop suffering, then I'll be able to be happy" or "only after I'm fully healed and rich will I be able to relax and enjoy myself." The logic makes sense to our ego, but it never works because you simply cannot get there from there.

> *"Nature does not hurry,*
> *yet everything is accomplished."*
> — *Lao Tzu*

The guideline is this: when it comes up, stop it. If it doesn't come up, don't spend time thinking or worrying about it. If it comes up again, that means you didn't actually stop. Stopping is not pausing until later, and it is not a hiatus until the next time it happens. Nor does it mean coming up with a new story or justification. Stopping means *stop*.

NOT A TECHNIQUE, A WAY OF LIFE

Stopping is not some technique you only do when you're in therapy, meditating, or doing self-work. It's something you'll do, or rather "undo," all the time. It may sound like that will be a lot of work, but this is a flawed perception. This kind of stopping (Def-B) isn't more doing, but *less* doing. You are ending what you already do that takes up subconscious and conscious resources. Stopping is subtractive, not additive, meaning that the more you subtract, the less energy you have tied up. The more you stop, the less you do. It's ultimately less work.

Yes, in the beginning, it will take more effort and willpower to initiate. It may feel like 'work' in the beginning because of existing momentum. This is like any new habit or lifestyle change—and this truly *is* a new lifestyle. Do whatever it takes to make this how you go through life: sticky notes all over your house, alarms, reminders when you pass through doors, at parties and work and in the bedroom, group accountability—nothing is too excessive to get this ingrained. Commit to stopping your stories, addictions, and limiting behaviors as if your life depends on it—because it does.

I've done all of this and more myself until it simply became *who I am*. I don't practice 'mindfulness' at all—I walk through the world aware as my default. I am observing and feeling myself and others on many levels because that's simply who I am. It is effortless *now*. This took years of practice and dedication. I made my entire life about this for four years. It was rough at first, but like everything, the more I was committed, the easier it became. I'm not suggesting you do what I did. I am illustrating that I've done everything I recommend, and it works.

It's not about obsessing or turning this into more neurotic fixing. Fixing is a 'doing,' stopping is an 'undoing.' This is about *committing*. You commit to your True Self instead of your persona. You commit to reality instead of your illusions. You commit to the Truth instead of your stories. You commit to taking responsibility and accountability for your thoughts and actions instead of pretending to be a helpless victim. The way you uphold these commitments is by stopping what you've been doing that interferes with their success.

CONCLUSION

You've now learned everything you never knew you wanted to know about stopping. As repetitive as it may seem to say "stop" so many times in one chapter, you can't hear it enough. Stopping is really *that* important. Stopping our stories, myths, behaviors, attachments, and thoughts that are the root of our suffering is the only way out. Anyone who says you can bypass that and offers a shiny new modality to do it is leading you astray. You can't escape the fact that you can only stop by stopping, and that stopping is your choice alone to make.

The reason stopping fundamentally works is because:

You already have everything you need.

There is nothing wrong with you

You are not broken.

You are inherently enough.

You are inherently lovable.

You are inherently worthy.

You are inherently valuable.

What could you possibly do to become more than all of that? *Nothing.* That's the insanity of "doing more to improve" that this book is inviting you to stop. That's why all the 'doing' only leads to more suffering and struggle: because it's moving you *away* from who you are. It's building up an image, a mask, a persona—a false idol of who-you-ought-to-be for worship and sacrifice—not bringing you closer to your True Self.

This is why stopping is the only way to start getting you back in touch with your Truth. 🦋

ARRIVING TO NOW

*"We shall not cease from exploration, and the
end of all our exploring will be to arrive where we
started and know the place for the first time."*
— T. S. ELIOT

ou may be stuck because you're oriented towards something that doesn't exist. Perhaps you are stuck in the past or stuck waiting for the future. You may be missing, longing, or living in the past and your memories. You may be fantasizing and unable to manifest your dreams and desires. Both of these cause you to miss out on all the joy, beauty, and love only available in the present moment. They cause you to look right past everything you need to get unstuck. This is *an avoidance of the present*, and it ultimately leads to struggle and suffering. Understanding your relationship with your past, present, and future—and making a few shifts to your perspective and habitual way of orienting to life—may be the exact thing you need to get unstuck. Before we explore your past and future, we first need to talk about *now*—the importance of being in the present moment.

The meanings we give our past—our stories—are what prevent us from having a direct experience with the present. At the end of the first chapter, "Your Stucky Story," I mentioned that one way we can "arrive to now" is by letting go of our stories. These stories are what keep us trapped in the past. Our stories bind us to 'what has happened' and create a self-fulfilling narrative that we seek to validate. We take 'what-was' and project it upon 'what-is' and thus can only perceive the moment inaccurately. We get 'stuck in time' and no longer can see what's happening right now. We perceive what's going on within and around us through all these filters, rather than experiencing the moment directly for what it really is. Our stories dissociate us, blocking us from being in the present moment.

You know from the chapter, "The Spiritual Path is Failing You," that our attachment to these stories and a resistance to what-is keeps us stuck, and also that being stuck and suffering are synonymous. You've learned that our stories prevent us from being 'in the now.' This means that stories cannot exist in the present moment. The reason for this is because if stories keep us from the truth and what-is, they cannot be real, and since the present moment is real, stories cannot exist there. Accepting all of this, **we must conclude that we cannot suffer if we are present 'in the now.'** The relevance of this chapter to getting unstuck and waking up is this understanding.

The 'now' is truly the end of suffering.

When we deny what-is, we deny what is *real*. Anything we do from this denial can only create unreal things, and that's exactly what the self-image of the persona is—an image of what's unreal. We impose a distorted image on top of our denial, denying the True Self in the process. We are building a fantasy in the image of an ego—an ego that, based on preexisting distortions, filters, and traumas, already judges and rejects what-is. What's distorted is attempting to fix you with more distortions! It's insanity.

What often happens when people attempt to create a new, more 'positive' narrative or self-image, is that they try to believe something they don't really believe, "fake it 'till they make it," or start living in a make-believe world (again, none of these are real). They layer on "improved" belief systems and strategies to build up a better image—all on top of a preexisting persona. None of this resolves the original error of perception. It's just more of what's not real. This layer-laying takes us further away from what-is and more towards an illusion of how we *wish* things were. Life may look better, but the "improved-self" is still bound to story, belief, and persona—none of which have access to reality (what-is). This creates even more complication and suffering because now the person must interface with reality and the present moment *through* these new, additional layers and filters. However, reality is only found in the *now*.

If, instead of all the adding, improvement, and better images—we stop all the stories and get to the truth of what is real—we would be able to see where we're really at and make a new choice. We cannot make a new choice from a fantasy, only reality. The only way we can change our situation is if we know the truth of what-is. However, truth is only available to us from within reality, not from outside of it. We may see images or references to the truth in our fantasies or through our stories, but we don't have access directly to the symbolic data the truth holds. Everything we need to know is found in the present moment, and it's this raw data that has what we need to get unstuck. Just like a sacred text that has been used as a canvas, completely painted over with an artist's self-portrait—the truth of the moment is covered up with our own images. As pretty as these images we paint may be, they are not real, and they are obfuscating the true information beneath.

Hear ye! Throw your gaudy paintings and imitation artwork into the fire and show up in the world as flesh and blood. Destroy all that isn't real, and whatever you are left with *must be real*. Before moving forward with new creative force, we need to end what no longer serves, rather than hide from the duty of destroying. Destruction is a necessary part of disillusion, as seen in archetypes like Shiva or the Sword of Justice. Instead of making better images, we want to stop painting illusions altogether by getting into relationship with this destructive force. We "become Death, destroyer of worlds"—ending our worlds of fantasy and illusion that we inhabit.

What happens when we do this? When we do everything in the chapter, "Just Stop"? What's in-between the space of stopping and the next doing? There is a void. We feel that this void is like death: empty and nothing. It is—and, it's also the source of life and everything that ever was and can ever be. It's this timeless space, devoid of thought and doing, that we have breath to *be*. It is the moment between doing and undoing, the line-less boundary between the sides of yin and yang, and the transition from the north pole and south pole on a magnet. It is the silence that surrounds our stopping that is of the same essence of *now*. Stopping doesn't mean static, stillness doesn't mean inactive, and silence doesn't mean deaf. This is not about becoming a monk who sits in lotus pose meditating for twelve hours a day. We can live our lives *and* move through the world while remaining present in the now.

The more we drop the masks and illusions of who we want to be, the more we get to live as who-we-really-are. The closer we get to *now*, the closer we get to approaching what is True and real. The timeless forever-now is our access point to Truth and our True Self. It is the still point of being where all time and space converge, bringing the past and future together into this moment. It is this moment where we can show up real.

THE STILL POINT OF CHOICE

Now is all there is. The past and future don't exist except in the present. Since nothing real exists outside of the present moment, what you chose in your past lives now, just as what you will choose in the future lives now. If we want to change our ever-persistent-present (the now), we must change how we *relate* to our past and future. This is our *history* and *vision*. You want to be in relationship with your past, not abandoning, rejecting, or being ran by it. Your history has all the resources, wisdom, and ancestry that you need to carry you forward. You also want to be in relationship with your future by having a vision, rather than moving through the world "blind." This vision of your future is what eventually becomes your 'now.'

The masculine, yang energy of your history comes forth and penetrates into the moment. The feminine, yin energy of your vision receives and opens to the moment. The intercourse of past and future occurs in the now, and it is here where all things are conceived and given birth. This intersection is the only place where we can create anything real, for 'now' is the only time and place that *is* real. *The now* is the meeting point of yin and yang, of the past and future, and of what was and what will be—this nexus is our access to reality. The present moment is the still point, the center of being where you 'get centered.' This is Buddha's 'immovable spot,' as well as the center of *the wheel of fortune.*

As I alluded to in the first chapter, "arriving to now" is to arrive at the center of the wheel of fortune. This is an archetypal symbol that represents the ups and downs of life, the riches and the losses, the cyclical nature of experiences, being caught in the cycle of karma, and living at the effect of the world. Imagine a wheel, like that on a chariot or cart, with an axle the wheel rotates around. This axle is the same still point found at the center of all spinning disks. At the absolute center it is still, and with each degree of movement away from this point, the spin and force become greater and greater until reaching the outer rim, where the brunt of all force is applied. Simply, the farther we go from center, the more turbulent things become. Imagine being a little ant, and you had to choose where on the wheel you had to sleep. Would you pick the center, the edge, or somewhere in-between?

Like an ant on the wheel, the farther *we* are from center, the bigger the effect our circumstances have on us. The farther we get from *now*, from Truth, from silence, from our True Self, from the core of our body, from non-attachment, and from a direct symbolic experience of reality—the more we are prone to get stuck and suffer. The more we let the world and our stories affect us. The more we are caught up in the game of life and the rat race. The more opportunities arise to be victims. The more likely we are to buy into stories of boogeymen, enemies, terrorists, and threats. The more we "get what's coming around" to us. The farther from center we get, the more we become 'uncentered' and 'movable.' We become unstable in life, easily getting tripped up on minor things and are taken out by every new reason to panic, fear, stress, or worry.

"At the still point of the turning world.
Neither flesh nor fleshless;
Neither from nor towards;
at the still point, there the dance is,
But neither arrest nor movement.
And do not call it fixity,
Where past and future are gathered.
Neither movement from nor towards,
Neither ascent nor decline.
Except for the point, the still point,
There would be no dance, and
there is only the dance."
— T. S. Eliot

Most people are on 'the wheel' their entires lives. They live at the effect of their circumstances, unconsciously reacting to highs and lows. They ride the roller coaster of rising and falling success and fortune, attachment and loss, happiness and depression as if that was the only way. You now know that's an illusion—but there is another way. If we can penetrate the stories that bind us to the past and integrate our shadow material, we can release ourselves from the "karma" that keeps us trapped, repeating the same cycles. We can get off 'the wheel' and find the 'immovable spot' within us. This centers us in the present moment. This 'center' allows us to walk through the world unattached and unaffected while remaining fully in feeling and present. This is done without having to be shut off, emotionless, or indifferent. It's from this point—the now—in which we are in proper relationship with our past and future, and where we can access infinite power. Here you can relax into the *serenity of being.*

ARRIVING TO THE PRESENT

Before we take a look at our past and future, we must first arrive to now. Trying to describe 'now' and how to get present is like trying to tell you how to technically move your arm: what neurons to fire, how to select the tendons and muscles, and how to adjust them. It's cumbersome, ugly, and ineffective, inevitably paling in comparison to the grace of your body's movement. As much that I can 'give you reality' from these pages, can I 'give you now.' The best I can offer to get you there is direction—"a finger pointing to the moon."

If you look close enough, you will see that this entire book is a treatise on getting present to life and plugged back into reality. This section will offer a summary of ways to practically implement what we've been learning to get present. When applied correctly, *all* of the concepts in this book are designed to get you to *now*.

Here are some **Practices to Presence:**

- Practice sensuality: the softening and heightening of the senses. Play with flavors, textures, colors, sounds, and aromas.
- Relinquish the *avoidant life* and take up the *heroic life*. Choose to live fully alive, even if it's frightening. Feeling fully alive feels closer to death than the safety of our minds. You must be willing to face 'perceived death' and show up in your body fully. (This doesn't mean being an adrenaline junkie or being reckless in order to feel something.)
- Try new ways of being or moving that you've never done before every day. Do not act on autopilot like a robot. Drive new routes, explore new places, walk in different directions, do things backward, try new foods or music, buy different brands of everything you're used to.
- Slow down. Slow way down. Even slower. Feel each word out of your mouth or through your fingers. Feel each muscle as you move in slow motion.
- Get out of your head and into your body. Feel your way through the space. Move from your core, rather than leading with your head. Relate and connect to the environment and the people in it from feeling, not thought. Exercise

without entertainment and feel your muscles, rather than distracting yourself from discomfort or boredom.

- Stop thinking, doing, judging, assessing, and figuring things out. Experience what's happening without analyzing it or assigning meaning. See things for what they are, not what you understand them to be.
- Feel everything that arises within you rather than avoiding, distracting, or repressing. Stop the eating, entertainment, or anxious ticks that you use to avoid feeling. Face all your emotions. Stop distracting yourself from the stillness and silence of the present moment. You are choosing to disconnect from the present when you use entertainment to avoid boredom or other feelings.
- Do one thing at a time. Don't multitask. Show up to the task or person in front of you. Give each person you're with your undivided attention while you're focusing on them. Don't think or start planning what to say next. Truly listen and feel them.
- Take it deeper: Look people straight in the eyes and maintain soft, genuine eye contact. Connect with them and let them see inside. Feel them and let them feel your presence. Let the world around you two disappear.
- Cut out distractions or any alerts that may pull your attention from what you're doing.
- Stop thinking; quiet your mind. This is the aim of traditional meditations.
- Breathe. Follow your breath into the moment. Drop in and surrender to its rhythms.
- Open your eyes. See the world through the same wonder and awe and captivation as a babe or young animal exploring the world for the first time. What could something be, as if you had never seen it before? Find the beauty and joy in the most trivial of things.
- Relate to things symbolically, rather than using words. Look at an object without labeling it, feel without labeling your

feeling, observe without giving mental narration to what's happening. Speak with feeling, rather than intellectual brain-dumping. Look at scared art through feeling, not a mental understanding or with words.

Do not beat yourself up if you falter; there is no pressure to perform. If you drift out or catch yourself in your head, drift back in gently. It's as easy as a choice. Remember, they're called "practices" for a reason.

Being in the now is not our thought about now, how we're interpreting or perceiving now, or what we're judging about now. *Now* is what's underneath all of that. *Now* is in the ecstasy of the moment chocolate touches your tongue, not how we like it. *Now* is in the sensation of watching snow fall and feeling it fall within ourselves, not the description of how pretty it is. *Now* is in the way your body responds intuitively at peak performance and in the rapture of an audience who is captivated and brought into your movements—not in the mental techniques used to coordinate your body. Thinking about the moment, judging the moment, planning what to do the next moment, analyzing what's happening in the moment, and even *trying* to be in the moment... are not being in the now. These are actions that are looking at 'now' from the outside, not seeing from within it. It's the difference between first-person and third-person perspectives. **If you can 'see now,' you're not present; you're looking *at* the present.**

Here are some further hints for your journey:

- *Now* is a feeling, not a thought
- *Now* is symbolic, not rational
- Presence is from the body, not the mind
- You can't use thoughts to stop thoughts
- As soon as you label, you've lost it
- As soon as you get excited about being present, you've lost it
- It's not found through obtaining or seeking, but stopping and surrendering
- The harder you try, the more you push it away

- If the way to now is complicated and convoluted, it's probably not the way or 'now'
- Write things down, such as plans and ideas, so you don't
  have an excuse to overthink
- Bring your focus 360 degrees around you, inside and outside, feeling and seeing

Your presence is your power, and it requires you to be present,
here, now. It's a gift of tremendous value for yourself and whomever
you share it with. It is the place from which your power to affect the
world emerges. It is where your consciousness is expressing itself at the
edge of eternity. Do not squander it on trivial things—your presence
and attention are finite resources!

WHERE TO FROM NOW?

As I mentioned earlier in the chapter, your history and your vision
meet together 'in the now.' Your body doesn't exist in the past or the
future, and your body is the only place from which you can interface
with the physical world. You cannot show up as your True Self in a
fantasy or a memory. Instead of dwelling in either of these, you want to
be in your body, present, and in relationship with the history behind
you and your vision in front of you. Without an awareness of either
of these, you do not have the resources of your past, nor do you have a
definite place that you're going with them. It's hard to get unstuck and
create the life you want if you don't know the truth of where you're
coming from or where you're going! Getting into proper relationship
with both of these aspects is what we'll be addressing for the remainder
of the chapter.

The only thing that is real is where you're at *now*. Not our stories
about where we're at, nor where we'd like to "positively think" we're
at—but truly what-is, now, in this present moment. Your stories aren't
real because they're about the past. Your fantasies aren't real because
they're in your head. What *is* real is what you're feeling in your body,
what you're experiencing in the moment, the true situation you're

in, and what is legitimately happening around you. If what you're perceiving is distorted due to filters, judgments, stories, or meanings, then what you *think* is happening right now isn't actually what's really happening—it's *a story about what's happening*. I've said this many times, and it needs to be said again here, in the context of 'now.'

If your starting point is inaccurate, you won't be able to get to where you want to go.

If you're starting from a story, you can't get to any place real. Understanding this is pivotal to getting unstuck. If you're starting from a fantasy, from a distorted perception of why you're stuck, or from a place of 'positive denial'—you won't be able to reach your vision in a real way. You may approach another fantasy, you may get to another place of different suffering and struggle, but you won't be able to awaken to your True Self.

You must know and tell the truth about where you've been, where you're at, and where you're going. Otherwise, you're trapped between the walls, unable to access the manifestations of reality. These manifestations can only be obtained *through* reality, which only exists in the *now*. If you're not starting from *now*, you can't get anywhere real. If you want to get unstuck, it requires you to be more honest and real than you've ever been before. What is real is what will set you free. If you're not free *now*, you're not free.

BETWEEN HERE AND NOW

If you want to get somewhere, you need to know two things:

- Where you are now
- Where you want to go

A common mistake I see stuck clients make is that they spend all their time on 'where they want to go,' without knowing the truth about 'where they are now.' They may *think* they know where they are, but they are often in denial or out of relationship with what's really going on. Some are avoiding their shadow, others put layers of 'positivity'

313

over their misery, some are super functional but are playing dumb, and others are afraid to admit their life, relationship, or career isn't fulfilling them anymore. Until they accept what-is, they don't get far. Think about it practically for a minute. It's futile driving to San Diego from New York if you insist on saying you're starting in Los Angeles when you're not. You may have the best map, GPS, driving certification, or travel strategy—but you'll have one helluva time getting to where you want.

If you can be honest about where you're at and where you want to go, things will open up. Be willing to ask the tough questions, or at least hire someone who is, and answer them truthfully. Once you have a grasp of where you're genuinely starting and where you envision going, you are able to build your life around that. Otherwise, you will be spinning your wheels, wondering why years have passed by and nothing in your circumstances have changed much. This is why most of the work I do with clients is about where they are in the moment since what is present is real. If it's occurring now in our session, it's occurring elsewhere in the client's life. I show them where they're at now and reflect the truth of how they're showing up. I help them see how they're embodying their history and their vision. I help them feel what is true, what is fantasy, what is ego, and what is a story. It changes everything, and quite often, they take off quickly. That's what we'll be doing here next.

Up Until Now

Without knowing our history, we are destined to repeat it. The problem is that we have a skewed idea of what happened, and we have a similarly skewed idea of how we show up in life. Begin by getting honest about: what your vision has been, what your values have been, what you've stood for, how you've seen the world, and the choices you've made. The easiest way to determine this is by observing what your life looks like now. We're not looking for perfection or the minutia of every event, but to get to the bottom of what's truly going on in your life. You don't need to compile monotonous lists or use some guru's complex framework: just look around you.

Look at what you prioritize, and you will see your values. Look at what you spend your time and money on, and you will see what's important. Look at where you are in your life, and you will see your past vision. Look at how people treat you, and you will see your character. Listen to your words, and you will know your beliefs. This reveals not how you *imagine* yourself to be but the reality of how you've lived.

> "By their fruits you will know them. Do you
> gather grapes from thorns, or figs from thistles?"
> — Matthew 7:16, Holy Bible

Recall in the chapter, "The Essential External," how our 'manifested results' showed us the reality of our actions. This section is where it applies to your life. If you *think* you value wealth highly but work a minimum wage job and spend all your money on entertainment, you don't. If you *think* your vision was to be a great artist, but you're now ten years into a career as a lawyer without any art—it was not a vision, but a daydream. What your life looks like now is evidence of what you thought, felt, and chose over the past decades. What your life will look like in a decade tells us the truth about what you're choosing *now*. Remember this: **If what you choose happens, then it was a real choice; if it doesn't, you know you never actually, truly chose it.**

This can be a sobering exposé of the undeniable results of our choices. Take care not to give more meanings, create more justifications, or beat yourself up more. You may feel things such as shame, remorse, guilt, disappointment, pride, or gratitude. Feel them. Own them. Take responsibility. You are living the result of your choices; you are not a victim to them. This is your accountability. This is the moment you reclaim your power! You must tell the truth about your choices if you are ever to make better ones. If you deny and avoid them here, you won't heal; you'll shove them deeper into the shadow, or add it to the pile of self-loathing or narcissism.

WHAT YOUR LIFE HAS STOOD FOR

Part I of this book was all about how you got here. Even here in Part II, there are many revelations of how you're showing up in the world. If you've been honest with yourself thus far, each chapter has been revealing a more accurate picture of 'where you are.' You have seen more of what-really-is as you've dropped what-isn't—the stories, meanings, judgments, masks, images, and filters. With that fresh, fertile soil of what-is still in your hands, let's take a look at it from a higher elevation. Observe the bigger picture of where you're at now in your life based on what we've dug up.

Focus on this one question: "What has my life stood for up until now?" These are not your *ideals* of what you value, but your actual values based on the evidence around you. This may have changed over time, so use what's currently in your life. Pay attention to any stories or justifications your choice brings up.

Based on your current situation, have you stood for:

- Scarcity or abundance?
- Beauty or ugliness?
- Efficiency or excess?
- Trust or skepticism?
- Yourself or others?
- Ease and grace or struggle?
- Fighting or surrender?
- Forgiveness or revenge?
- Being right or the Truth?
- Playfulness or seriousness?
- Intimacy or protection?
- Creativity or emulation?
- Fear or courage?
- Bullying or uplifting?
- Freedom or security?
- Comfort or growth?
- Joy or suffering?

- Order or chaos?
- Community or the individual?

There are no right answers. Each one serves a specific purpose at a particular time, and some will vary depending on their context. Even the more 'negative' seeming ones can teach or lead us to something we could not have arrived at otherwise. Remember, everything serves—even what doesn't.

However, this doesn't mean we don't want to move towards greater harmony and functionality. Certain values indeed do lead to greater success and fulfillment compared to others. While we may think it's obvious that aligning with values such as joy, courage, and abundance lead to a better life than suffering, fear, and scarcity—the actual choices many of us make say differently. I invite you to start *actively choosing* joy, beauty, love, play, abundance, truth, and courage. Humanity has shown since time immemorial that these lead to a better life, their worth being self-evident. This work calls you to stand for something worth standing for—and the only thing worth standing for is what's True.

You now have an opportunity to consciously choose for yourself what you stand for. Not only what your culture, family, or history dictates—but what *you* dictate. Will you break out of the bounds of scarcity and difficulty, and instead stand for abundance and ease? Will you let go of the protection and armoring adopted from shutdown friends and family, and instead stand for vulnerability and courage? Will you let go of your colleagues' jealousy and competitiveness and make your life about leading and uplifting others? Will you betray the diseases of your lineage and instead transform your diet and lifestyle, so you and your children may thrive in good health?

You are no longer a victim of your circumstances—now it is your choice.

FROM NOW ON

Approaching the final chapters of this book, you are not the same as you were when we started. As a butterfly emerges from her cocoon, you too will step out of your stucky story and awaken into a new space. As we touched upon in "Just Stop," the other side of stopping can be disorienting. You may have been stuck for a long time and have been so focused on getting unstuck that everything in your life is currently oriented around that. There is time, energy, money all spent on sustaining your stucky story and your attempts at getting out of it. This is the net loss of energy of "Bob's Ladder" discussed in the chapter, "An Equation for Suffering."

By stopping all the things you're doing to stay stuck, you reclaim all the energy tied up in the associated suffering and stuckness. Once the stories have stopped, the fantasies are collapsed, and the addictions to suffering have ceased—what do you do with all that freed up time and energy? Nature abhors a vacuum. Unless you replace it with something meaningful and productive, it will reconfigure. These resources are now free, and like water, will seek level, going wherever there's an easy path. If you have a definite vision, this freed energy will be directed towards creating it. If you don't, this energy will go towards whatever habits or subconscious programs are running. Energy *must* move; that is its nature. It wants to be active. If you aren't guided by a higher purpose, mission, or vision, what's likely to happen is that many of the old, familiar myths will want to reengage. Our libido needs a way to express itself, if not healthily, unhealthily. This is what is meant by the expression, "idle hands are the devil's tools."

DEFINING VISION

In order to get to where you want to go, you need a *vision*. Without a definite vision, you do not have a definite future. After stopping all the stories, the freed up energy is likely to get misdirected again unless you have a vision. Otherwise, you are relegated to take whatever comes at you, living a life of reactivity rather than directed activity. What's the point of getting unstuck when tomorrow you end up back in the same spot? This is why people without vision *return* to being stuck. Our vision gives our creative force direction with the power of will.

What is vision? *Vision* is the embodied future you see for yourself, those in your life, and the world. It is how you direct your consciousness. Vision is what pulls your future towards you. It is the eventual manifestation of what you stand for, who you are, how you live, and what you choose to create. Your **vision** is *what* you envision your life to look like, your **mission** is your *how*, and your **purpose** is your *why*.

Vision is not to be confused with a daydream. This is why people struggle to manifest their desires: they are daydreaming, not choosing. Your vision is not a fantasy that you *hope* will happen; it's what you see when you look forward into your future. Your future is the result of your thoughts, choices, and actions. It is not 'later' in time. It is the inevitable result of what you are embodying *now*. Your vision is not out there, outside of you in a time that doesn't exist—your vision is found within you, *now*. When you eventually get to where you want to be, it will then be considered 'now.' You arrive to *now*, the present moment—you don't arrive to the future.

See your vision by going inside yourself, feeling what is true and genuine to your heart, and visualizing this inner vision projected upon the outer world. We do this all the time anyway unconsciously to distort reality, but when you own it and take over the driver's seat from your subconscious—you can create new worlds. This is the proper use of projection; you are sort of 'hallucinating' reality into being. It's not a fantasy because you are not in your head, dissociated, or avoiding reality; you are present, in your body feeling, and making a choice. It's not a distortion because you still see what-is as what is, without meaning, filters, denial, or story. You're using the same creative force but now unperverted, superimposing your vision upon the world to birth it into being. Instead of painting over what-is with our own images to obscure and deny it, we accept what-is and create something real from it.

REFINING YOUR VISION

Take some time to see what you want your life to look like. What you will be doing, how things will feel, who's there, where you will be, what you're doing after getting unstuck, and so on. Do so in the first person, present tense. Describe it through the senses, not your head. See it and feel it as if it already is, now. Get into it, drop into your body, make it fun and palpable. How you do one thing is how you do anything. This is not some lame 'vision exercise'—this is your life!

Here are some tips:

- The more specific you get, the easier it is to envision and feel—but be careful not to get attached to the specifics! Sometimes it's a feeling you're looking for; how it shows up doesn't matter. The secret is to have a definite vision and move towards it without attachment to outcome. You need the forward momentum and focus of choosing, yet sometimes what you choose will show up and look completely different than you were expecting! This is because everything comes from the symbolic and feeling nature, not what our rational intellect thinks it *should* look like.
- Your vision is not a bunch of goals: it's a symbolic collage of choices. You don't have to figure out how to get there before deciding, you just make a choice now about where you're going, and the details come together along the way. These are descriptions of what you choose your life to look like.
- What you're choosing your 'future' to be, is done now, within you. You choose your vision by owning it *now*, not creating fantasies or hopes for what you would like it to be later. 'Later' never comes. Your vision won't happen unless you choose, which requires you to take action *now*.
- People want to be happy, but take care with this one. Remember what we discussed about suffering and happiness in the chapter, "The Spiritual Path is Failing You." Happiness is great. It's simply not the full experience of being

alive; it's only one note of the symphony. You'd despise a song that only used the C major chord after a few minutes, let alone fifty years. Focus on what brings meaning, purpose, creativity, and fulfillment instead, and the beauty, joy, and pleasure that will come from it.

Here are some prompts to help you further define your vision:

- What do you see for yourself in your vision? For your cells? Your family? Community? The Earth? Humanity? The solar system?
- How big or small are you thinking?
- How value-orientated are you? Do you add or subtract from the world?
- Is life more about having and consuming, or creating and contributing?
- Do you see a lot or a little? Rich or poor? Abundant or struggling? Healthy or sick?
- Does everyone win, or only you? Do you even win, or do you end up losing?
- Is there love, joy, and humor around you? Or drama and chaos?
- Are you alone or surrounded by people that love you? How many people depend or rely on you?
- Have you contributed to humanity or created anything, or merely tried to get by and enjoy the fruits of others?
- Is the world a better place for you having been alive?
- How long do you live for? Who shows up to your funeral?
- What legacy are you leaving your family and the world?
- What will people remember you as and for?

Notice that many of these directly reflect the previous section on what your life has stood for. There are no right or wrong answers. There are no shoulds or shouldn'ts.

It is not for anyone else to decide what scale or level or amount is best for you or what path you should take. You are the only person you have to answer to on your deathbed. You are the one who has to live with regret if you chose to abandon who-you-really-are. You have to be honest with *yourself*. For example, if your vision to live in the forest with your family and dogs on $60K a year makes you happier than a penthouse suite running a business making $20MM a year, you need to have that self-awareness—or else you will end up wasting a lot of your life. Maybe the opposite is true. Perhaps your family wants you to stay in a small town and do what they did, but your heart aches for adventure and enterprise. If you don't follow your heart and find out for yourself, and instead stay to make them happy, you will never know and grow resentful. You must give yourself permission to be true to who-you-really-are—stop waiting for permission from your parents, friends, or society.

The trick is learning what's real and true—and what's settling, suffering, and fantasizing. To know if you're okay with less because that's true, or if it's because of a story or a fantasy of minimalism. To know if you want more and bigger because you need it to support your goals, or because you're ran by a story of inadequacy and proving yourself. This requires us to—as written above the ancient Temple of Apollo at Delphi—"Know Thyself." It's a level of awareness this entire book is helping you to cultivate. Far too often, we fall into line with the desires and visions of others, thinking that's what we want. We fall prey to these stories, identifications, and limitations before even getting a chance to envision a life that comes from authentic choice.

Let's probe deeper and test the integrity of your vision:

- What are your motivations? Why are you doing this, and why this in particular?
- How do you know this will make you happy? Can you be happy now without it?
- Is there a hidden agenda or secondary gain?
- Why are you doing this? Do you even care? Are you having fun or dreading it?

- Do you think it's actually going to happen, or is it only wishful thinking?
- What secret are you hiding from yourself or avoiding?
- Is that what you really want, or what you think you *should* want?
- Is the desire even yours, or someone else's?
- Where are you attached to an outcome? Time frame, details, specific people?
- How does it make you feel to think about being there and the path to it?
- What in that future vision are you not letting yourself have now?
- Who are you manipulating, stepping on, or taking advantage of to get there?
- What are you in denial of? Are you running away from something?
- Do you feel your vision is far away from you in the distance, or here?
- Is this vision all about you, or is it about something greater than yourself?

The key is to answer without judgment. If you can get honest with yourself about where you're at and not take the truth personally, you will be able to make a shift without needing to feel guilty, shameful, or defensive. It's normal when you're completely honest with yourself about these to feel all sorts of 'negative' things. Remember, it's not bad; it's just information—and at least now you know. All feedback is love.

Feel free to adjust your vision as needed. At any moment, you can choose something different if you don't like where you're headed. If you don't care or can't think of anything: just make it up! Moving towards something constructive will yield far better results for your life than staying undecided and stagnate. You'll eventually come across 'your thing' as long as you're moving forward and making new choices.

When you are successful in 'stopping,' you will have freed up energy that needs a place to go. Having a definite vision and focusing on that ensures this energy has a direction to be channeled. It allows your conscious and subconscious resources to align towards a singular vision rather than diffused all over the place, accomplishing nothing. Or worse—going back to being stuck.

If you'd like to go deeper into creating your vision, visit this book's bonus page on my website (andnl.co/aytsb) for a free guide on creating your Lifemap. This is a powerful process similar to what we did here. It offers worksheets with a step-by-step formula for writing down a definite vision—for the remainder of your life. Getting your vision down on paper is no gimmick: it is the first step towards making your vision tangible. 🦋

A New Way
To Move

*"Consciousness is only possible through change;
change is only possible through movement."*
— ALDOUS HUXLEY, The Art of Seeing

tagnation is death; movement is life. Inertness is the
universal sign of death. Nothing can exist without movement. From the swirling of galaxy clusters to the orbit of
electrons around an atom—the building blocks of our
very existence never cease moving.

Everything hums.

There is movement in our thoughts, movement in our emotions,
and movement in our flesh. When we become stagnate in any of these,
movement slows. We get duller and lose wit and memory. We are less
responsive or numbed out. Our muscles weaken and atrophy. Our way
of seeing the world, our degree of empathy, and our joints calcify and
rigidify given enough time.

I've seen the results of both movement and stagnation in people
dear to me. I have never seen chronic stagnation result in anything
desirable. I am convinced that we must keep moving, no matter what.

One of the most peculiar things movement has revealed to me
is that there's a reflection between a person's mental-emotional world

and the way their body shows up in the physical world. It's a tangible manifestation of the principle laid out in the chapter, "A Universal Approach." The (outside) body reflects the (inside) psycho-emotional—and vice versa.

A REAL EXAMPLE

In my own life, I struggled with the idea of being in my body. I spent a good portion of my childhood and young adult life rejecting athleticism because I was bullied by the jocks. Since middle school, I was teased for my lack of sports knowledge or ability. I was so bad, I wasn't even picked in gym class, but lumped in by the coach afterward. When I joined the swim team in my senior year, I was the first person they'd ever seen who kicked his legs and went backward. Yes, I was so bad I literally went backward when I swam—talk about being reverse-wired! I spent years dealing with this humiliation. None of this made me want to *have* a body, let alone play sports or partake in anything athletic.

I detested physical activity and found safety and solace in my mind and intellect. It was a place where I didn't have to face the rejection or limitations of a scrawny frame. I could become superior in my mind and justify it all with the philosophy of "mind over might." But really, it was a way to not have to feel inferior and helpless. So I judged and rejected because I sure as hell didn't want to end up like *them*.

It's how many of us deal with trauma. Unfortunately, this approach has diminishing returns. It always does. It can appear to be safer or less hurtful in the moment, but rejecting any part of ourselves never creates lasting peace and harmony. But we do the best we can do with what we know. And all I knew at the time was pain and suffering, rejection and humiliation.

I thought I was becoming superior to them, but the joke was on me! It was me who suffered and struggled with my fitness-rejection and distorted retaliation. Limits in my flexibility, motion, and mobility of my body were translating to limits in my mindset. I was unhappy with the shape I was in and how weak I was. My body was shut down and locked into old fight or flight patterns. Old childhood stories were getting in the way of new relationships and opportunities as an adult.

When I realized the choices I made as a teenager, I decided to stop rejecting and become athletic for my own good. As I started to be in my body more, strange things would happen. All of a sudden, I'd have old memories or stories pop up out of the blue while I was doing a movement or exercise. It would bring all sorts of feelings that shouldn't logically occur based on my current situation. I began to see how my psychological world was entangled with my physiological world.

I began to feel the things I didn't want to feel, to let myself move through feelings I was suppressing unconsciously for years.

I can't say it was the most fun I've ever had. I won't mollify you—it was uncomfortable facing the reality of how I rejected, deprived, judged, distorted, avoid, and betrayed myself. I wanted to run away many times. I felt some incredibly dark, horrific things. And unexpectedly, a lot of self-love too.

You can imagine how much I learned, healed, and reclaimed in my life from finally feeling all of that. It freed up the stuck energy I was using to avoid facing all of it—like Bob's Ladder and the Equation for Suffering. My life changed. My appearance transformed. Things I struggled with seemed to unstuck themselves.

What's stuck in your life or business is something that's symbolically stuck inside of you.

This is the secret. Moving through the internal stuck feeling will help you move through the external situation because, ultimately, there is no difference. As within, so without. When you unlock it inside you, you unlock it outside of you; there can be no other way. This connection has verifiably demonstrated the practical benefits of getting out of our head firsthand.

Presupposing this is not merely a metaphor—that there is a literal relationship between our model of reality and how it manifests in the body—has been *the* game-changer for my entire therapy model. Everything we learned in "A Universal Approach" is now applied literally to our physical body.

So, how do we do this?

327

How To Become Embodied

Throughout this book, you've read phrases like "how we move through the world" and "moving forward." What you may not have realized at the time was that they were not mere figures of speech—I meant them quite literally. It takes more than new attitudes, beliefs, and purpose to begin showing up in the world in a new way—it requires us to *embody* them.

The only way to embody something is to literally be-in-our-body with it.

One way to attempt this is to change our *body language*.

The idea is that by changing the position and posture of our body, we can affect neurological and emotional changes in ourselves and influence those around us differently. It is a great first step in becoming aware of the power of the body and how the 'body-mind-emotion relationship' affects us. It also helps people out of acute, disempowered states, such as sadness, insecurity, confusion, or fear.

However, this approach is limited because it is not *em*bodied, it's *on*bodied.

It does not take the empowerment from the surface-body into core—it remains superficial. We are not looking to "fake it 'till we make it"—we want to be real about *what-is* so we can make a new choice and create authentic, lasting change. (We'll go into this further in the final chapter, "Above All Else.")

The other way to go about this is to change our *energy*.

I don't necessarily mean it in some esoteric 'aura' way; you don't need to know anything about chakras, etheric bodies, or the sort to grasp this. Look at the word 'energy' as an abstract way of encompassing the following queries of self-awareness:

- How present we are
- How aware we are of each part of our body, or disconnected and pulled-out-of
- How we take up space

- The way our stories and mythologies play through and run us
- What gut reactions or intuitions inform us
- If we can recognize our own agendas and manipulations
- The way we relate to our limbs, physical traits, and self-image
- What awareness we have of the space around us and how we treat it
- If we can discern how things affect us and what our effect on them is
- How we feel, how we feel in our body, and how we feel others
- If we recognize the choices that we're actively making moment-to-moment
- If we expand or contract when interacting with others
- How others respond to us and treat us
- What impressions we give to others

If we can show up in our bodies in a way that fundamentally alters how we manage those—based upon the desired values, characteristics, and results—we are well on our way towards embodying them.

This subtle, elusive 'energy' may be best illustrated with examples. The first phrase shows the "je ne sais quoi" of a situation, whereas the second phrase has no awareness of this intangible 'energy.'

- It's the difference between "letting the beauty come though" and "putting more makeup on."
- It's the difference between "I felt the presence of his body, and the comfort that provided me allowed me to relax on our date" and "it was nice that he paid attention to me the whole date."
- It's the difference between "there's something about her that I can't quite put my finger on..." and "she's weird."
- It's the difference between "I can feel the agony of the artist in his painting" and "this is a sad piece of art."

- It's the difference between "I don't really care about *what* it is you're selling, I know I have to work with *you*" and "sure, I'll buy it."
- It's the difference between "it always feels like he has an agenda" and "I'm not so sure about this guy."
- It's the difference between "everyone lights up when he walks into the room" and "people like having him over."

Notice there's some intangible, non-rational, unconscious factor at play. There is no technique or strategy—it's their *energy*, their *vibe*. There's an awareness of feeling rather than a mere superficial observation.

Through embodiment, it becomes "simply who we are" instead of "what we're trying to do." Rather than thinking about a facade or mask we have to maintain, our body organically reflects the inner changes without much conscious effort.

What happens for folks is that they learn what something is supposed to *look* like, and then they start to mimic it. They copy the appearance *without* the feeling or character that goes along with it. They observe and model (which can be a great way to learn)—but they're only looking at the surface. What they're left with is a two-dimensional photocopy instead of their own multi-dimensional original.

For example:

- They see what 'spiritual' people are doing and then do that to seem spiritual
- They see what 'alphas' look like and how they treat people and then do that to be successful
- They see what their favorite artists or writers do and do that too thinking that is what will make them great
- They see what great speakers say and learn all the speaker tricks and practice doing their performance, thinking that's what will make them influential
- They see what masculine and feminine lovers do and then force all their behaviors to be the "right" polarity

- They see what all the great therapists do and reverse engineer their words and tactics, thinking that doing those will make them better healers

The keyword in each of these is "do." In these examples, they are trying to get somewhere by doing things on the surface, rather than creating the change within to *become*.

People end up *doing* spirituality rather than *being* spiritual. They end up *doing* alpha rather than embodying all the characteristics of a genuine alpha leader. They end up *doing* art and emulating it rather than being an artist. They end up acting, performing, doing manipulative tactics, and putting on a show rather than being someone who's presence and life alone inspires. They end up "doing masculine" or "doing feminine" and forcing this big artificial dance, rather than feeling their own masculinity and femininity and letting that come through. They end up "doing therapy" and "doing tactics" to the client as if they were an experiment, rather than showing up fully present in the moment and creating a space for the real person in front of them to heal.

The result is someone who feels like they:

- Have an agenda or an ulterior motive
- Are doing something *to* you instead of with you
- Are fake, phony, or putting a persona up
- Are putting on a show or performing
- Are trying too hard (to be cool, funny, important)
- Would crumble under pressure outside their artificial environment

It's the difference between an actor who *looks* like he's acting, and an actor who's *being* the character he's portraying. Or the difference between a salesman who's reading a script and taking you through his sales funnel, and the salesman who is listening to your unique problem and offering a solution that will help you best. It's the difference between the original and the cheap knock-off.

This book isn't showing you how to be like me or help mold you into another generic, idolized clone. What you're learning here is how to be more *you* than you've ever been. You do this not by mimicking, but by doing less and allowing yourself to just *be*. You're learning how to show up differently in your body and the world because that's just who you are—not because you're running some technique about what successful people do. We are getting you to stop all the insane things people taught you to do to abandon yourself, your truth, and your body.

A WORD ON THE WORD 'EMBODIMENT'

Embodiment isn't a phrase to throw around to mean, "I'm practicing a new attitude or applying a lesson to my life." Embodiment is to be used specifically when referring to the expression of said quality *within the body*. It is the being of character in one's physicality. It is more like, "This is showing up in the way I rest, move, and inhabit my own body and in the tangible impact I'm having on the space around me." It is the 'below' aspect of "as above, so below." We are taking what is 'above'—our values, beliefs, worldviews, understandings, etc.—and making them so 'below'—in our physicality. This is how we become manifested in the world, rather than getting off to a bunch of theories and fantasies in our mind that lead nowhere.

Imagine the difference between an architect's finished blueprint that applied his design concepts—and the feeling of solidity, strength, and luxury in the massive slabs of white Italian marble under your palm as you touch the wall of the finished erected building. They are markedly different things despite both being about the exact same building.

The body is how we interface with the world around us. If someone chooses to affect our world, action must be taken through the vehicle of the body. Even our thoughts and feelings require a body—this is because consciousness resides in a physical locale. We cannot *only* "think and grow rich," and we cannot *only* transform our 'above' world—we have to take physical action and show up differently in our muscles, in our movement, and in our life on Earth if we want to see change. However, the effect we have upon the world with our body is not only through the gross action of manipulating objects. We are communicating with everything around us, all the time, at subconscious levels. We affect and relate to the space around us without necessarily touching it.

For example, when you move your hands, there is a field-effect it has on the space. It's not only a meat sack that reflects lifeless light as it shakes around—like conventional science would have us believe. Our body is a holographic transducer—there is data, information, and energy that comes through and off of the movement that influences the environment. The purpose, character, quality, feeling, and energy of the intention—plus all our stories, thoughts, myths, and beliefs—combine in our movements, expressions, and physical presence. This presence, or *energy*, communicates to those around us more accurate information about us than our body language or words do.

This is why embodiment is important: it's how we manifest our character. Who we think we are being—and how we're actually showing up in the world—may or may not match. If they do, it is authentic, genuine, and honest, even if it's dysfunctional. If they don't match up, we are incongruent. This incongruence is trouble, even if it produces a functional behavior. Life seems frustrating and confusing to us because we aren't getting what we think we should. What we think we're doing and the results we get don't match up. We may think we're fun and cool, but show up anxious and try-hard, and so without knowing it, we are left without friends wondering what's wrong with us.

Our idea of ourselves may be accurate, but it is not realized without it showing up in our presence. Nothing is real until it's realized. It's only realized when it manifests in physicality, and the way we do that is through our body. It doesn't matter much what you intended or how you think you are. What matters is what you actually *did*. If we think we're athletic, but it's been a decade since we've exercised or played any sport, the proof lies in our activity, not in our idea of ourselves. We can con ourselves for decades thinking we're one way, but if that's not how it's showing up as we move through the world, it ain't true.

What embodiment implies is that this incongruence literally shows up in the body. We can look at the body and see if it matches the narrative or not. How we show up in our body is the result we get, and this gives us the most accurate feedback of what's *really* going on inside. If it's not congruent, we can begin to embody something more functional and honest.

> *"There is more wisdom in your body*
> *than in your deepest philosophy."*
> — Friedrich Nietzsche

Embodiment is how we can take 'above' and match it with 'below.' It's truly "the word made flesh."

A CINESOMATIC PERSPECTIVE

Once I discovered that the "Universal Approach" literally applied to the body, my entire paradigm of self-help, healing, and spiritual development shifted. I stopped practicing all of my former modalities and focused solely on founding *Cinesomatics®* and the *Center for Cinesomatic Development* (cinesomatics.org), which shows how much this rocked me to my core.

If you're not familiar, Cinesomatics is the name of a transformational therapeutic process that utilizes cinematic video technology along with movement to help participants see for themselves the hidden blocks, traumas, archetypes, and stories that hold them back. It's a way for people to see themselves (on-screen) and receive verifiable feedback about their blocks and unconscious patterns.

Witnessing hundreds of folks go through these processes—from everyday self-help enthusiasts to household names—I've seen firsthand how "what is happening in the person, is happening in the person's life." I've seen how trauma reconfigures and distorts the body. I've seen how timeless mythological archetypes play through generations of family members. I've seen how the smallest shifts in the way someone relates to something adds zeros to their income or attracts a wonderful new person into their life.

There is a cornucopia of information available to us in this shadowed somatic world. It reveals more than I could have ever imagined—and it was always there, but I didn't have the eyes to see. Most of us shut out the data and choose not to look, then forget it's even there.

For example, how someone walks through the room can reveal more about how they show up in the world than any resume ever could. How someone shakes their hands can reveal the way they relate to men and women, and the masculine and feminine. How someone demonstrates giving and receiving symbolically with their body can reveal the subconscious blocks and strategies used when literally giving and receiving in their life.

It all maps out. There are clear correlations between those who are functional, joyous, and gracious—and those who are dysfunctional, struggling, and miserable—in the feeling of their movements. It may not always show up apples-to-apples, but it does relate.

Everyone is different, and because there is no right or wrong way to embody an archetype, we don't rely on body language cues or superficial stereotypes that claim how someone *should* be. Instead, we go into what the person *feels* like. We use what's called "feeling-based awareness" rather than intellectual analysis, checklists, or standardized tests to intuitively observe each person as an individual, in the moment. It sure drives the academics crazy—but it gets tremendous results, and that's what matters.

The video component of this work tends to steal the show because there is nothing else out there like it. No longer do we have to take a guru's word for what he sees in us—we can see how we are showing up on the screen with our own eyes. It's the ultimate feedback mechanism. You get to see for yourself how your stories, ways of relating, approaches to life, and shadow material affect the space. You get to see how you embody certain archetypes, lead and follow, respond to the masculine and feminine, and so much more.

While at times incredibly confronting, it is a true lifesaver for those of us who easily con and lie to ourselves. The reason being that it presents indisputable evidence of our ruse on screen for us and anyone else to see. The video doesn't judge, lie, manipulate, or get sucked into our stories or agendas—it reports the data without distortion. This accurate reflection then allows us to see our own distortions when compared with it. The 'interference' pattern, or the dissonance between them, reveals where we are incongruent. This awareness is usually the beginning of the end of the story since we can no longer deny it.

This methodology illustrates how our stories show up in the body, and it speaks to cutting-edge (albeit unconventional) ways for helping us heal. The upcoming section will give you an opportunity to implement what you've read thus far with a powerful somatic exercise. It's time to get into your body and discover a new way to move out of your stucky story.

THE EMBODIED-STORY EXERCISE

Earlier in this chapter, you learned all about embodiment and how our beliefs, worldviews, stories, perceptions, strategies, and blocks manifest in the body. How our inner-world reflects in our outer-world. Reading about movement and embodiment is one thing—moving and feeling it in your body is something totally different. What use is theory if we can't apply it and experience it for ourselves?

In this section, you will have a chance to take everything you've learned in this book and put it to use in a single exercise. You will get to experience the concepts you've been reading about *somatically*, meaning that you will be using your body to do so. This somatic approach will help you begin to embody the theory and concepts in ways words simply cannot offer.

> *"Nothing ever becomes real 'til it is experienced."*
> — John Keats

This exercise provides the physical realization of the chapters you have read thus far.

You will be able to experience for yourself how concepts such as reverse-wiring, "how you do one thing is how you do anything," embodiment, stories, and shadow show up in your body. Through the movements in this exercise, you will get to put everything you've learned into practice. It will give you a tangible, empirical experience to work with and physically see, rather than a nebulous mental concept in your head. What you'll be doing is a simplified version of our basic Cinesomatic movement work. It has been adapted to be done alone without any facilitation.

If you want a new result in your life, you need to make new choices; to do things in a new way. The best way to move through your stuck situations is to actually move in a new way! The internal resources you unlock by practicing movement patterns also unlock their corresponding patterns of neural activity and of seeing the world. If your pattern of seeing the world is not serving you any longer, perhaps finding a new way to move in your body can help you think differently. **This is the practical application of what we discussed in "A Universal Approach"; find what patterns are stuck in the body and then use the body to make a change in the patterns elsewhere in your life.**

The most confronting and liberating aspect of this approach is that by moving and being in our bodies, all the stuck and repressed feelings, memories, and stories begin to dislodge and arise for us to deal with. This is the physical layer of our shadow. For example, have you ever been in a deep stretch or yoga pose, and all of a sudden, a memory or emotion comes rushing up out of nowhere? This is why: unresolved stories and emotions get stuck in our body. Everything affects everything else; we are holographic. As you embark further on this journey, you will be presented with opportunities to face, feel, and heal things you don't even remember are in there. They will often arise at the thresholds between your old way of being and a new way. I invite you to face them, as you learned to do so in the past chapters.

Each chapter in this book is a doorway, not a final destination. This exercise is a foot-in-the-door to a new way of living. There is more that awaits you once you walk through. As soon as you truly grasp the implications of this exercise and the philosophy behind it, everything will be different for you from that point on.

THE EXERCISE: INTRODUCTION

First, you will explore being in your body and how conceptual ideas are represented symbolically within your body. You will get a reference point for feeling empowered and what it looks like to embody it through movement. You will then watch your video (if you chose to record it) and review some questions to reflect.

Second, you will do the same thing, but this time you will embody your 'stucky story.' You will get to experience how your idea of being stuck is represented symbolically in your body. You will be able to compare how an empowering movement and a disempowered 'stuck' movement differ in feeling and manifestation. You will then watch your video and review some questions to reflect.

Third and lastly, you will start back in the stucky story and then have a chance to experience reverse-wiring in your body (if that's related to you being stuck). You will then explore a new way to move altogether. This new way of moving is to discover a way out of being stuck *through the body*, rather than by thought or 'doing' in the world. You will then watch your video, review some questions to reflect, and then conclude the exercise.

This exercise is an exploration of embodiment, not an assessment. There is no "answer" to be found at the end of this exercise. If done earnestly and with self-awareness, the movements and questions will give you new reference points, perspectives, and feedback about yourself in a way you've never done before. **This particular exercise is about *experiencing*, not diagnosing.**

EXERCISE OUTLINE

Part I: Reference Point for Empowerment
- Empowered Movement: Discover how concepts and archetypes appear in the body
- Review Set A: Reflect upon questions

Part II: Reference Point for Being Stuck
- Stucky Movement: Discover how your stucky story lives in your body
- Review Set B: Reflect, shift, and have new awareness by answering questions

Part III: A New Way to Move
- Stucky Movement (2nd): Move from the stucky story again
- Opposite Movement: Discover a somatic way out of being stuck or reverse-wiring
- New Movement: Find a way to move out of the stucky story
- Review Set C: Reflect, shift, and have new awareness by answering questions

In total, there will be five (5) actual movements to perform, and three (3) sets of questions to review. The review sets are found at the end of the instruction section.

EXERCISE OVERVIEW

Objectives
- Experience the physical realization of the theories learned
- Discover how mental stories show up in the physical body
- Explore a new way to move through your stucky story

What You'll Need
- Private, standing-space with room to move freely

- Something to record video of yourself, or if not, a full-length mirror (optional, but recommended)
- Pen and paper for answering questions (optional, but recommended)

Physical Demand
- Low: Ability to stand and move the body (adaptable to sitting)

Estimated Time
- Set aside 90 minutes; it may take less

THE EXERCISE: PREPARATION

PRELIMINARY NOTES

Follow the instructions. Read through all the instructions first before starting so you get an idea of what you'll be doing. This includes everything up until the end of "The Exercise: Instructions." Do not read the conclusion or review sets before starting.

Make sure to keep your eyes open and pay attention to what's going on internally and with your body. Be aware of how you're approaching the exercise and answering the questions.

There is no speaking during the exercise. Do not use words or sounds while moving.

If you are revisiting and repeating this exercise, Part I can be omitted, as its purpose is to introduce you to expressing stories, archetypes, and conceptual ideas through the body.

SETTING UP

1. Find a private space for moving where you can stand and move.

2. Make sure you have your book and pen and paper if you wish to write down answers.

3. Get your camera (or any video recording device) set up to film your entire body. Make sure you have room above your head and feet in the video. Alternatively, find a mirror (that doesn't require you to hold it); a full-length one is preferred. You will stand in front of the mirror, facing it to see yourself from head to toe. *(Neither are necessary to benefit from the exercise, but they are helpful in seeing what you're doing. A video recording can be especially powerful for review, as we do in the Cinesomatic workshops.)*

4. If using video: when you're ready to begin each Part (I, II, III), start recording. When you finish each part, stop the recording before going on to the review set. You will also want a way to watch and play back the videos after each part. At the end, you will wind up with three (3) videos, one for each part.

DECIDING ON WHAT TO FOCUS ON

Before beginning, decide what you want to work on. You will need two (2) concepts: an empowering one and a stucky one. These will be referenced in the exercise instructions as we go with the labels used below.

Empowered Concept: Think of something that's working really well for you in life, a quality that's well cultivated, or one of your strong suits. This can be something abstract, such as 'problem-solving' or something literal like 'being a good mother.' Whatever you pick, make it simple and empowering for you.

Some examples are:

- Excelling at school
- Confidence in doing your job
- Being creative
- Performance in a sport or art
- Motherhood or fatherhood, caregiver, or partner

- Selling something

Stucky Concept: Think of something specific you're struggling with, ideally the 'stucky story' you've had in mind throughout this book. Make sure it's something you can put into a few words. Keep it simple. You don't need all the details of your story; pick one main thing. Here are some examples:

- Being unappreciated at work
- Keep attracting the same kind of people
- Not being able to close sales
- Fear of approaching people
- Not feeling confident in your body
- Plateaued at a certain income level
- Nobody listens to you
- Feeling overwhelmed in business

Before getting into Part I, you should be all set up and ready to go with your space and equipment, and have both your "Empowered Concept" and "Stucky Concept" decided. For example, "being creative" and "unable to talk to new people" would be the two things selected to work on, respectively.

Let's begin!

THE EXERCISE: INSTRUCTIONS

PART I: REFERENCE POINT FOR EMPOWERMENT

Step 1 — Stand & Center

What to Do: [Start recording] Stand up in your space and get situated, facing the mirror or camera (if applicable). Take 1-2 minutes to center yourself, become present, and aware of your body.

Explanation: This is to get settled into the exercise and tune-in to yourself. Bring awareness to your breath. Bring awareness to each part of your body. Bring awareness to how you feel. Relax and drop into your body. Keep your eyes open and be aware of any tics, fidgeting, swaying, anxiety, etc. Do not analyze, try to fix, or change anything you're doing. Just notice.

Step 2 — Feeling the "Empowered Concept" in Your Body

What to Do: Bring to mind the "Empowered Concept" that you decided on before you began. Go into the *feeling* of this concept. Feel this in your body, rather than thinking about it. Take up to a minute (or as long as needed) to get this feeling.

Explanation: You are taking a mental concept that is empowering for you and bringing into your body. You do this by going into the *feeling* of it. You want to associate in the first-person perspective. If it's a literal behavior, imagine doing it, but feel the action rather than going into your head. If it's a concept, say 'creativity,' go into what it's like to feel or be creative.

Step 3 — The "Empowered Movement"

What to Do: From this feeling, allow it to express itself through your body and movement silently. Through movement, convey your "Empowered Concept." You want the feeling to move you, rather than thinking of logical ways to demonstrate it. Use the first thing that comes up. Take 1-3 minutes to explore the movement and pay attention to what you're doing. (If using a mirror, look at it to observe yourself.) [This will be referred to as the "Empowered Movement"]

Explanation: Now that you've got your "Empowered Concept" internalized as a feeling, you want to express it through the movement of the body. You are looking to take a concept and represent it symbolically through gesture, movement, feeling within your body. It's similar to miming, or the game charades, when you convey an impression of an idea, concept, or feeling using gestures and movements without words. It's not about mimicking the behavior or acting out a memory. It's about letting the feeling move you, even if it doesn't make sense or look "right."

Step 4 — Review

What to Do: [Stop recording] You may stop, sit down, and take a moment to relax. If you're filming, be sure to stop your video recording and prepare it for review. Take some time to reflect with "Review Set A" located at the end of the instruction section. Once you have finished reflecting on the questions, come back to your space and proceed to Part II.

PART II: REFERENCE POINT FOR BEING STUCK

Step 5 — Stand & Center

What to Do: [Start recording] Stand up in your space and get situated as before in Part I. See if you can stop any tics or movement you noticed from last time. Take up to 3 minutes to stop, get still, and center in the present moment.

Step 6 — Feeling the "Stucky Concept" in Your Body

What to Do: Bring to mind the "Stucky Concept" that you decided on before you began. Go into the *feeling* of this concept. Feel this in your body, rather than thinking about it. Take up to a minute (or as long as needed) in order to get this feeling.

Explanation: This is identical to Part I, except with the other 'concept' you decided to use. You are turning your "Stucky Concept" from an idea into a feeling. This brings it from the mental realm into the physical realm so you can express it through your body. The same suggestions apply as before. Notice how different this one feels compared to the first.

Step 7 — Stucky Movement

What to Do: From this feeling, allow it to express itself through your body and movement silently. Through movement, convey your "Stucky Concept." You want the feeling to move you, rather than thinking of logical ways to demonstrate it. Use the first thing that comes up. Take 1-3 minutes to explore the movement and pay attention to what you're doing. (If using a mirror, look at it to observe yourself.) [This will be referred to as the "Stucky Movement"]

Explanation: This is identical to Part I, except with the other 'concept' you decided to use. You are now getting a comparison between something that empowers you and something that disempowers you, and how you've internalized these symbolically and have embodied them. The same explanation of miming and charades applies here too. Let the feeling of the story move you.

Step 8 — Review

What to Do: [Stop recording] You may stop, sit down, and take a moment to relax. If you're filming, be sure to stop your video recording and prepare it for review. Take some time to reflect with "Review Set B" located at the end of the instruction section. Once you have finished reflecting on the questions, come back to your space and proceed to Part III.

PART III: A NEW WAY TO MOVE

Note: Steps 10 & 11 are done in tandem.

Step 9 — Stand & Center

What to Do: [Start recording] Stand up in your space and get situated as both times before. Take up to a minute to center.

Step 10 — Stucky Movement (2nd)

What to Do: Take a minute to get back into the "Stucky Movement" you did from Part II. Feel into what this was again, and express the same "Stucky Concept" through movement from last time. DO NOT STOP the movement to transition to the next step (11).

Explanation: You want to get back to the same "Stucky Movement" from the previous part because, in the next step, you will transition to the next movement from this one.

Step 11 — Opposite Movement

What to Do: While you are still doing the "Stucky Movement" from Step 10, *begin doing the opposite*. Whatever "do the opposite" means to you (as long as it's still a movement), move the opposite way from how you were just moving. Once you've got it, keep doing this for

1-3 minutes and then stop. Pay attention to how this feels and looks. [This will be referred to as the "Opposite Movement"]

Explanation: While you are moving from the energy of your "Stucky Concept," you do the opposite of what that movement is. People can interpret "opposite" in many ways, and it is purposely left vague and up to you because it needs to reflect how *you* perceive the world. It may feel weird, awkward, confusing, or uncertain—that's normal. Notice what this looks like to you in the mirror or by feeling and observing yourself. Does it look more functional or better to you than the "Stucky Movement"? If so, you may be dealing with a reverse-wiring!

Step 12 — New Movement

What to Do: You are going to find a new way to move that isn't as 'stuck.' Go into the idea and feeling of your "Stucky Concept" as you have prior, and this time, rather than doing the movement as you would naturally do, find a *new* way to express it with your body. Find a way to "solve it" through a different movement—a gesture or movement which conveys this in the body—that you've never, ever done before. Give yourself up to 5 minutes to explore and experiment. [This will be referred to as the "New Movement"]

Explanation: If you found that the last step produced a movement ("Opposite Movement") that looked less stuck than before ("Stucky Movement"), you are free to continue doing that here and explore deeper. If not, or if you would like to explore something new, you may use this step to play and experiment. This is an opportunity to move your body in a way that it's never moved before. See if you can find a movement that would symbolically represent what it would be like to be unstuck compared to the "Stucky Concept." Let your body move you into a movement that *feels* better. You are free to try multiple things until something 'clicks.' If nothing does, that is okay.

Stop at the 5-minute mark.

Example: If your "Stucky Movement" was bashing yourself on the head, perhaps bringing your palms from your head to the sky instead would represent something different from being stuck and feel better than hitting yourself.

Step 13 — Review

What to Do: [Stop recording] You may stop, sit down, and take a moment to relax. You are done with movement. If you're filming, be sure to stop your video recording and prepare it for the final review. Take some time to reflect with "Review Set C" located at the end of the instruction section. Once you have finished reflecting on the questions, you are finished. There is no need to come back here. Continue right on from the last question to the chapter conclusion.

GUIDED AUDIO BONUS

There is a free audio recording for the instructional part of this exercise available on my website for your convenience. You can listen to me give instructions if you prefer to follow along with voice instead of reading. It does not include the review sets or explanations, only what to do. You can find it on the bonuses page of my website (andnl.co/aytsb). This bonuses page is also linked at the end of this book.

THE EXERCISE: REVIEW SETS

If you recorded your movements, replay your video and watch for each review set. You may use the video to help you answer the questions. Questions that pertain only to video playback are labeled with [video].

REVIEW SET A (PART I)

a. How still were you when you started to stand and center? Were there any tics, anxiety, or unease that arose as you stood still? Did this anxiety continue into the other parts of the exercise?

b. Did you feel embarrassed, silly, stupid, or shy in expressing yourself with your body?

c. Were you really feeling, or were you in your head thinking about what it felt like?

d. Were you analyzing yourself, or were you present in the now?

e. Did you exaggerate, act it out, or turn it into a drama or performance?

f. Did you do it halfheartedly or take it seriously?

g. How much space did you take up with your body in the room?

h. Were you worried about what people might think if they saw you doing this?

i. Did the "Empowered Movement" feel familiar and natural, or foreign and difficult?

j. Did any emotions arise? What were they, and how intense?

k. If there were people there, how would they respond to the feeling you're conveying?

l. [video] What do you see as you watch yourself moving?

m. [video] What judgments, stories, meanings, or feelings come up as you watch?

n. [video] If you were a stranger looking at this movement and had to guess what it was trying to symbolize (like charades), what would you call it?

349

o. [video] Notice your vision. Where is it? Down, forward, up?
    Did you follow the instructions to keep them open or not? Can
    you feel your future in your vision?

REVIEW SET B (PART II)

a. Did you notice any difference between the first time you stood
    to center and the second when you were invited to stop any
    tics? Was there any new anxiety or less compared to last time?
b. Did the "Stucky Movement" feel familiar and natural, or for-
    eign and difficult?
c. Were you really feeling, or were you in your head thinking about
    what it felt like?
d. Were you analyzing yourself, or were you present in the now?
e. Did you exaggerate, act it out, or turn it into a drama or
    performance?
f. What did you notice that was different from the "Empowered
    Movement" in Part I and your "Stucky Movement" in this part?
    Any of the below:

    • Emotions
    • Thoughts
    • Stories
    • Feeling
    • Energy
    • Attitude
    • Body language
    • Body movements
    • Posture
    • Direction, scale, speed
    • Breath
    • Tension

g. Imagine meeting someone who portrayed the same feeling
    as your "Stucky Movement." What real-world results would

a movement like this translate to? Would this show up in a business, factory, relationship, household, etc. as any of the following:

- Functional or dysfunctional
- Joy or suffering
- Productive or not productive
- Inviting or isolating
- Generous or selfish
- Creative or rational
- Efficient or cumbersome
- Loving or fearful
- A lot of money or little wealth
- Fun or serious
- Allows beauty or perverts it
- Easy or hard
- Masculine, feminine, both, or neither
- Large vision or no future

h. What results are you getting in your own life that match any of those you listed in the previous question?
i. Could you see any movements that remind you of your parents or caregivers?
j. What did you learn about how you are in your everyday life from the way you moved your body so far?
k. Could you notice any similarities or differences between your right and left sides while moving? Front and back of your body? The top and bottom of your body?
l. [video] What do you see as you watch yourself moving?
m. [video] Look at yourself on video. If this was a stranger, what kind of person would this be? Describe how much money they make, what their friends and family are like, what kind of house they live in, what career they have, what the sex is like, what clothes they might wear, etc. Just report the details.

n. [video] What judgments, stories, meanings, or feelings come up as you watch? Do you see any shadow aspects of yourself running?

o. [video] Where was your vision this time? Any differences between this and the prior?

p. [video] Does this movement appear to be taking responsibility or not? Accountability or not? Is it powerful or powerless? Notice if you see any 'victim mentality' running.

q. [video] Imagining this was another person, is the movement making it all about them, or are there 'other people' symbolically involved in the movement (giving, communicating, interacting, etc.)? Does this person seem caught up in their own world, or are they 'plugged-in' or 'connected' to the space around them?

REVIEW SET C (PART III)

a. Certain parts of the instructions were left open for interpretation *on purpose*. Did you struggle with any specific part of them?

b. Were you trying to do any or all of the exercise "right"?

c. Were you letting the feeling guide you to doing it "opposite," or were you in your head thinking about what it should look like?

d. Were you in your head, or were you present in your body?

e. What did you notice that was different from the "Stucky Movement" when you began Part III and your "Opposite Movement"? Did anything get "reversed"? Any of the below:

- Emotions
- Thoughts
- Stories
- Feeling
- Energy
- Attitude
- Body language
- Body movements

- Posture
- Direction, scale, speed
- Breath
- Tension

f. Do any of these changes feel better or worse or indifferent?

g. Which of the three movements did you find to be the most functional? ("Stucky Movement", "Opposite Movement", "New Movement")

h. Imagine meeting someone who portrayed the same feeling as your "Opposite Movement." What real-world results would a movement like this translate to? Would this show up in a business, factory, relationship, household, etc. as any of the following:

- Functional or dysfunctional
- Joy or suffering
- Productive or not productive
- Inviting or isolating
- Generous or selfish
- Creative or rational
- Efficient or cumbersome
- Loving or fearful
- A lot of money or little wealth
- Fun or serious
- Allows beauty or perverts it
- Easy or hard
- Masculine, feminine, both, neither
- Large vision or no future

i. Are any of these you listed more functional than what you answered in the corresponding question for Part II, your "Stucky Movement"? (Review Set B, question 'g')

j. When you did the "Opposite Movement," did you find that it felt any better, lighter, or freer? Did you find it odd, uncomfortable, or wrong? Could this potentially be a reverse-wiring as discussed in the chapter, "When Wrong Works"?

k. What did you discover in the "New Movement" compared to how you are stuck in real life with your "Stucky Concept"? Remember, this is all *symbolic*, not literal.

l. [video] What differences do you see watching yourself between all the movements?

m. [video] Look at yourself moving the "Opposite Movement" and/or "New Movement" on video. If this was a stranger, what kind of person would this be? Would they be more or less successful, happy, etc., than the person you identified in the last Review Set B, question 'm'.

n. [video] What judgments, stories, meanings, or feelings come up as you watch?

o. [video] Look at yourself and your vision between the movements? Can you notice any differences or similarities?

p. [video] Look at yourself in the context of the space. What is your relationship with it, and how does it change as your movement changes? How would someone else relate to these behaviors without knowing your intentions?

q. Were you judging the instructions or yourself during the process?

r. Did you approach this as you were playing or testing?

s. Did you let yourself have fun, or did you make it hard?

t. Were you looking to change anything, or were you looking to know the truth?

u. Were you curious or skeptical?

v. Did you like or dislike the exercise or any particular parts?

w. Did you dismiss and skip the exercise altogether? What are you avoiding?

CONCLUSION

You've completed the Embodied-Story Exercise! While it's still fresh in your mind, write down your top three takeaways from this exercise.

This is an exercise that makes the mind-body-emotion connection tangible. You got to see firsthand how stories and archetypes are represented in the body, not only in thought. You were able to see how each of the chapters practically applied here, through the movements themselves or what was revealed by the review questions. Were you able to see how all the concepts like being present, stopping, feedback, embodiment, avoidance, and being in your head applied here?

Check in with how you're feeling after completing the exercise.

There is no right or wrong, or value judgment about yourself to make from this. There is not a grade or diagnosis, pass or fail. What this means about you is found within the data of the movement and your answers. If you're feeling let-down or discouraged, notice what attachments to specific outcomes you had. For example: Were you looking for this to save you or reveal the grand answer to your problems? Were you looking to do it right and get confirmation? Were you secretly hoping for some analysis that would enable you to stay stuck? What you were looking to get from this is how you set similar expectations in life.

Again, this was not an exercise—this was your life! How you do one thing is how you do anything. The way you approached this, or even judged and skipped it, is affecting other areas of your life. This book and the exercises within are not separate from you and your life. If you are honest with yourself in answering the questions and take a look at how you approached this and what happened, you will have everything you need to know about why you're still stuck. It's all here. Look at your "Stucky Movement" on video. Look at the answers from the review sets. Take the time to see how all of this relates to your life. Start to look for patterns and similarities in other things you do. For example: If someone arrived at this exercise with a victim mentality, they'd look to this to save them as they've looked to books or teachers or healers to save them prior.

You can revisit this exercise as often as you'd like with other stucky stories and archetypes. It's a great practice for exploring all the concepts of this book at once. I'd also recommend practicing your "New Movement" for a few weeks or months until that is the default you go to for your old "Stucky Concept." You're basically 'rewiring' your nervous system with a feeling and somatic interpretation that's more functional, writing over the old 'program.' Do not be concerned about doing it right or messing yourself up by doing it wrong. Get in your body, move, and have fun exploring embodiment!

A note for the skeptics and skippers: If you haven't done this, I can respect your choice. I know for some folks this "body movement stuff" looks bizarre. I get it, I really do. I thought it was the stupidest thing ever—until I tried it myself, and everything in my life turned around. This book will still help you if you don't do this exercise, but please don't cheat yourself. Judge it and discard it if you want to—but give it an earnest try first. It's better to try something and leave it than think you know better and miss out.

Remember, how you do one thing... 🦋

Above All Else

"Rather than love, than money,
than fame, give me truth."
— Henry David Thoreau

hroughout the preceding seventeen chapters of this book, you have learned why you're still stuck and how to change that. It can be a lot to digest, remember, and implement. Every chapter is essential and relevant—that's why these concepts have made it into the book. Even so, it can be helpful to distill the philosophy down to its quintessence, so you have something simple to focus on. A 'north star' if you will.

As you arrive towards the conclusion of the book, I'd like to offer **The Five Tenets**. If put above all else, these will guide you steadfast through the inevitable challenges of life. There are many virtues equally as important—such as **love, beauty, joy, play, and gratitude**—that bestow great value. I'd recommend making those what you stand for as well. Yet this book is about getting unstuck, so the tenets here reflect that purpose.

We have addressed or at least touched upon each of these, so you are already familiar with them. Their inclusion here shows how paramount they are to your success and why they bear repeating or elaboration.

The **Five Tenets** are:

- **Stopping**
- **Feeling**
- **Truth**
- **Responsibility**
- **Choice**

Not only is this a list, but it tells you exactly how to get unstuck! When read as a sentence, they reveal the instructions: **Stop, feel, tell the truth, take responsibility, and make a new choice.**

Memorize this phrase; write it until it's ingrained into your brain; put notes of each word around your house to remind you. Make it your new mantra. It is so dense with instruction that you could even meditate on it. Whenever you're experiencing some sort of chaos, struggle, or problem, use this phrase to get unstuck.

1. **Stopping:** Whatever you're doing, stop. Stop the stories. Stop over-thinking. Stop the addiction. Stop dramatizing. Stop avoiding. Stop suffering. Remember the massive list I gave in the chapter, "Just Stop"? Stop whichever of those apply. Without stopping, you can't proceed with much efficacy.

2. **Feeling:** Get out of your head, drop into your body, and feel. Feel whatever is there without judgment, completely. Feel everything you don't want to feel. Feel yourself and feel others. Feel what you're picking up intuitively. Do not suppress your emotions, nor act them out. Feel what's truly underneath the stories, avoidances, and drama you just stopped.

3. **Truth:** Tell the truth to yourself and others. This requires you to be able to see the truth first. Look with the eyes of your True Self. Look beyond the surface and observe

without judgment or meaning to see what-is. Do not lie to avoid; do not deny and go into fantasy. Make Truth the most important thing—not what you want to believe or would be good—but what is real and true.

4. **Responsibility:** Accept and surrender to what-is, not what should or could have been. Do not blame, do not be a victim. Take responsibility for your life and the world around you. Own what you've done. Take ownership of as much as you can effectively be of service to. Let go of the desire to harbor shame or resentment. Focus on what is within your control and what you can do about it now.

5. **Choice:** You are not a victim because you have the power to choose. Don't ask others to choose for you, don't be undecided, and don't live in a fantasy. If you don't like the results you're getting, make a new choice; or at least consciously own the same choice so that it's not running you unconsciously. Don't hope, wish, or want—choose it and move to fulfill it. Choice isn't merely a thought; it's backed by action!

Follow the instructions, and you will prevail in any stucky situation. I have written each of these words profusely throughout this book. It's not that I don't like variety. It's that these particular words are consequential and used to convey precise meanings. These aren't words you don't know already, but the way I've used them carries a different depth than how they get thrown around. Perhaps you've come to understand their richness better through the context of the chapters, or maybe all the pieces aren't quite filled in yet. In leaving you with these Five Tenets, I'd like to expand upon them so you may benefit from their richness.

This will not be a closing chapter, but your final ascent. This chapter is the longest in the book. However, it is divided into each of the Five Tenets, making it easy to pace yourself. You may desire to rush to finish, but relax into it and take your time. There's still a lot here for you.

STOPPING

As we've discussed countless times, much of what will help you is not found in doing more, being more, adding more—but from stopping. Stopping is the most important step in change because without stopping what's not working, you will end up sabotaging whatever new actions you take. If your boat is filling up with water, it doesn't matter how good you are at scooping or what high-tech buckets you have. Nothing will change until you stop the leak! If you make more money but don't stop the scarcity or unworthiness stories, you're eventually going to subconsciously find a way to dump all that money.

When we stop doing, we find stillness and silence. It's in this void of stopping that we can allow what-is to arise. We fear that on the other side of stopping is nothing. Though, it is within this space of 'nothing' that we are able to receive everything we need.

Stopping is so instrumental to your getting unstuck, we've devoted an entire chapter to stopping, "Just Stop." Thus we will not go into it in-depth here. However, this is an essential one of the five, and I encourage you to read that chapter in tandem with the other four found here when reviewing the book. You will also notice how many concepts crossover between these two chapters.

FEELING

As you move through this work and daily life, many things will arise for you to feel. Some of these you will judge as "good feelings," and others you may deem "bad feelings." Whatever the feeling is, you only have two choices when you face it: allow yourself to feel it or to resist it. If you choose to **feel**, your life will be in accord with the Tao, and you will find peace. It may be hard, intense, and painful at times—but it will be real, and you will emerge with new wisdom. If you choose to **resist**, you will go against the flow of life and will be ran by what you avoid.

You may start to feel something uncomfortable and quickly think, "This sucks! I don't want to feel like this. Andrew is a sadist. I'll just go back to my avoidant life... it wasn't *that* bad."

That's the thinking that got you into this mess to begin with. We have been conditioned to think that 'feeling bad' is a bad thing. We are taught to stop doing something if it feels bad, or if we are feeling a bad emotion, to stop that too. It makes sense, right? Why would we want to feel bad? It's not an unreasonable pathology, but that doesn't make it any less detrimental. The problem with refusing to feel something we perceive as bad is that it's a denial of what-is, which can only lead to suffering. Feeling 'bad' or any of the 'negative emotions' is just as necessary and informative as the 'good' feeling emotions. It's a *good thing* to let yourself feel whatever is genuine, even if it's 'bad.' It may seem easier to numb, avoid, and deny than to feel what's awful and terrifying—but this choice will result in suffering. There will be no freedom until it's fully felt.

Allowing yourself to feel *is* allowing life to unfold. Resisting any genuine feeling is a resistance to life. This is where so many of the healing modalities and positivity folks get it completely wrong. They pervert the shadow and miss what feeling is all about.

It's not about feeling good—it's about *feeling*.

Feeling is not about feeling 'bad.' Feeling is not about feeling 'good.' Feeling is not about judging or assigning meanings, picking and choosing, denying or avoiding. Making what we feel into something 'positive' or 'negative' distorts reality. Doing this turns it into a story *about* feeling, rather than actually feeling what-is. Feeling is none of this. Feeling is about *feeling.* We want to feel all of it, completely, without making it good or bad, right or wrong.

If you make this healing work about *only* feeling good, you are already judging and giving meaning to what you feel. This is not feeling, but assessing. This *parsing of feeling* is a mental process that leads to a loss of all the love and information the 'bad feeling' is there to give you. When we do this, we do not experience what's real, and so we can't be informed by the truth. The feeling itself is information; it is not an enemy. We feel to let our subconscious inform us—not judge what we feel and change it, fix it, or clear it. We are not looking for some ideal feeling we can obtain, or a shadow aspect to kill off, but to fully feel.

Feeling is the purpose of healing, not a 'strategy' to improve ourselves. *Feeling itself* is why and how we heal; we aren't trying to 'feel good' through healing. If you focus on arriving at what's after feeling, you're making healing about the wrong thing and will delude yourself.

Feeling is not about:

- Distorting things positively and attacking anything perceived as 'negative'
- Spinning things negatively to be a victim and indulge in self-loathing
- Rushing through to the happy part at the end
- Having someone take our pain away
- Eventually ascending to a magical place
- Deleting our shadow material
- Faking feeling to not have to feel
- Coning ourselves with, "I've already dealt with that"
- Making it mean something
- Dramatizing, inflating or deflating, or being hysterical
- Needing it to hurt or be hard to be valuable (no pain, no gain)
- Letting it run us, acting it out, or reacting to it
- Manipulating the space with it for attention or a pity party
- Indulging in the suffering or self-punishment

Do not fall into the trap of using 'feeling' as a strategy to suffer more! All of these things are not feeling and only make things worse. *Feeling* is truly feeling whatever is coming up for you that's real and experiencing it for what it genuinely is. It's not about acting it out or turning it into an event. We want to stop all of this so we can 'arrive to now' and be with what-is. Feeling everything authentically is the way there. Feeling is the way to Truth and the path of the *heroic life*.

FACING YOUR FEELINGS IN LIFE

It is no use locking yourself up in your house for a decade to face all your feelings before you permit yourself to live life! You cannot find freedom through imprisonment, but that's what we do when we put off our joy until we are 'healed.' That's not what this book is about. Remember, we want to stop fixing and start living, not use this work as a reason to isolate and suffer further. You will have plenty of opportunities in daily life to penetrate your stories and feel what's real. There will be two categories of 'feelings' you will encounter: *live feelings* and *triggered feelings*. **Live feelings** are what you feel based on the present moment of what-is. **Triggered feelings** are old, unresolved emotions that get reactivated due to what's happening now. They are both real; the only difference is their validity to the present moment.

Remember: 'Feelings' are about what we genuinely *feel*—it's not the same as when people talk about their "feelings" in common use. Revisit the chapter "When Intellect Slows You Down" for a refresher on the difference.

Live feelings are what we feel because of something that's happening now. They are new, based on the present. All you have to do is feel them completely. That's it. You allow them instead of judging and resisting them. You face them instead of avoiding them. You feel them fully instead of pushing them down. As you let yourself feel fully and stay with it, eventually it will move through you. This feeling has data for you. It's there to inform you. Listen. Pay attention. This is how it resolves. What happens if we don't do this and instead say, "Nope! No thanks, not now!" and shut it down? These *live feelings* then turn into potential *triggered feelings* at a later time. Ignoring a feeling doesn't delete it. Instead, the energy gets trapped, awaiting a future opportunity to be fully felt.

In our work together, "getting triggered" is not a bad thing—it's a sign pointing towards what needs healing. What that phrase really means is that something is happening now that has resonance with unresolved shadow material, and we subconsciously associate it with the situation in front of us. We then project and think it's *that* person

363

or thing in front of us—it's not. That person or thing is merely aggravating something far bigger inside of us. Instead of letting this run us or using it as an excuse to play victim, we want to permanently resolve and collapse the trigger within ourselves—not attack our projected symbol of it in the external world. It's not about what's happening now, but a story of what has happened.

Getting triggered is not about anyone else—it's about *us*.

For example: Somebody says something to us about our outfit, and we get upset. It wasn't anything mean, but for some reason, it really bothered us. Unbeknownst to them, we grew up in a house where our siblings constantly teased us about our clothes. We got triggered because of the comment, but we didn't realize that what we were really feeling was the anger, humiliation, judgment, shame, and rejection of our siblings. All that was still there in our unconscious, waiting for its chance to be heard. Was it their fault? Do we point the finger at them and force them to change? Do we make a law that makes it a crime to talk to people about their clothing? No. We go inside and use it as an opportunity to heal the deeper trauma. We use this as a chance to reclaim our power and be *less* in victimhood.

When we are mindful and self-aware, we *want* to know our triggers! This is how we heal in real time, in real life. Once we are aware of its origin, we can collapse these triggers by going inside and penetrating their source.

Choose to *"face, feel, heal"* instead of *"avoid, react, fear."*

When we allow ourselves to finally feel what's at the heart of our triggers, the energy moves through us, resolves, and integrates as wisdom. Unless we allow this process to unfold, the emotions are still there, waiting to be seen, acknowledged, and felt. It's from this underworld that they run us. These unresolved feelings pop up any chance they get, often when we're low on energy and don't have the bandwidth to keep them suppressed.

If you'd like step-by-step instructions on how to do this, follow the same **A5 Process** outlined in the chapter, "Dragons and Their Treasures."

"But won't feeling all of this hurt? There's a reason why I don't want to feel it."

There is a difference between something being truly harmful and something being terrifying, painful, and uncomfortable as a step towards healing. Nothing I'm suggesting is harmful. It may feel awful. It may frighten you. It may be the hardest thing you've ever done. But if followed correctly, it can only heal.

If you are on the precipice of healing, I say *go in, dear one.* Lean into the fear and face the pain you're avoiding. Let yourself see the horrific consequences of your actions and dance with the demons that haunt you. Let the truth annihilate all that suffers within you. No, it probably won't feel pleasurable at first. No, it may not be nice or fun in the beginning. No, it might not match your fantasy. But it is real—and what is real is all we have. This is your liberation.

GOING INSANE

When we are 'in feeling,' we can not only feel ourselves, but we can "feel" others too. When others are in feeling, it's easy to "feel" them. We don't *need* to ask how they are feeling in order to know because what they're feeling is apparent. *They* are feeling it, so *we* can feel it—but only if we're in feeling too. There is intimacy, connection, and vast amounts of symbolic data being exchanged at the subconscious level. We can feel them, and they can feel us, without even having to ask. We are open, and they are open. We are present in the now, and so are they. We exist at the same "wavelength," and so we can communicate hyper-effectively, almost like we're reading each other's minds. This is called *having access.* Common phrases to 'have access to someone' are when we say it feels like "we can reach them" or "we can get through to them."

In contrast, when we are *not* feeling, people lose access to us. They don't know what we feel because we won't even let ourselves know. It's also another strategy we use to stay safe and hide our vulnerabilities. We hide out by turning off our feeling so that people don't know what's going on inside for us. The people who live in fear, who tend to be dishonest or inauthentic, and who are insecure, love this strategy. It's incredible what we can do. We regulate our energy to prevent any data we don't want to be seen from "leaking out," ensuring others only see us how we want them to see us. We do this psychologically and emotionally within ourselves, as well as with our 'public persona.' How we only allow certain "approved" aspects of ourselves to come through in videos, photos, writing, and other media. This is related to the narcissistic image discussed in the chapter, "The Most Important Person."

Stopping (Def-A) feeling to protect ourselves seems like an efficient strategy, right? Perhaps. It may work—but only at the highest costs. The problem with shutting off feeling is this: **if you can't feel, you're insane.** You have no access to reality because you cannot experience reality through the egoic mind: you must experience it through feeling. You can only access what-is through *now*, and now can only be felt, not thought about. If you're thinking about now, you're not present. To be able to truly feel in reality is sanity. This is why we have the body, and it's why all these attempts at leaving the body to avoid feeling—spiritual or otherwise—can be dangerous.

People want to experience emotions without having to actually *feel* them. You can see this with people getting excited and depressed, going hysterical and being addicted to drama, and then numbing themselves with alcohol, drugs, sex, shopping, entertainment, and pharmaceuticals in order not to feel—or even *to* feel. Some are so numb and repressed, so dissociated from who they are, so desperate to feel something... anything... that they are willing to do the craziest things to get that 'hit'—even self-sabotage and nosedive towards rock-bottom. The thing they're avoiding most—being alone with themselves, getting still and silent—is what would provide the space to finally begin feeling something genuine. It's all their shadow material in the stillness and silence that they're avoiding. This is what they are terrified of feeling, but at least it's real. Feeling what's real is what will bring them back to sanity—it is the only authentic way out of their suffering.

This is how powerful the avoidance of feeling is. *Feeling* is your lifeline to sanity, reality, and truth. We can let ourselves feel everything we've been avoiding and move forward, or we can push down even harder. It's up to us. We have the freedom to choose truth and feeling. We also have the freedom to repress and dissociate to a non-feeling place and continue conning ourselves. That's the beautiful part: we all have the choice, and there is no right answer.

Whatever you choose, you can't mess it up—it's your life. Remember, everything serves, even what doesn't. Everything is eventually a path home. The real question then becomes, how much unnecessary suffering do you want to live with?

TRUTH

If you seek enlightenment, make Truth the most important thing, and truth the next.

Truth with a capital 'T' is the ultimate truth of truths, highest order of orders, most real of all of reality. It is the *eternal truth*. Being eternal, it rests outside of duality, and therefore cannot have an opposite. It is immutable and supersedes all else. It is Love, and it is Divine. Truth emerges into our level of existence symbolically, archetypically, and mythologically. It is our *understanding* of Truth, not Truth itself, that is rational. It governs our reality mathematically, which we come to know through the sciences as numbers, formulas, geometry, patterns, and waves. It's something that tickles us when we drop into those mystical, intimate moments in the stillness and silence. It is the quantum backdrop of the universe—the guiding force of True Justice for all of consciousness.

Truth with a lowercase 't' is the truth of everyday life. The truth that we speak and write in the physical world. This lesser truth exists in order of duality, so it does have an opposite: the lie. We align with truth with the oaths we take, the agreements that we hold, and the promises we make. We stand for truth when we stop corruption and deceit. This truth helps us become more accurate and real, as we learn and correct our ideas when we ascertain them to be incorrect. We look for facts, evidence, and tangible proof of our ideas and endeavors because that's how we know it's real.

However, facts are not the Truth. Evidence is not Truth. "Facts" may change over time, or they may be subjective. Talking about the truth is like looking at a menu; you get the concept of the meal but not the food itself. The only thing that is the Truth is the Truth. What we consider 'true' or 'our truth' based on our limited knowledge of the universe may or may not reflect *the* Truth. Truth goes beyond all. The mystics sought a direct experience of Truth—of the divine—not merely words or ideas about it. Throughout history, we see this archetypal journey in the Arthurian grail quests, medieval alchemists, and behind the secrets of the ancient mystery schools.

What would your life look like if you, too, valued the truth and Truth above all else? What would you have to change in your life? All the way to the most seemingly insignificant distortions. From white lies to monstrous lies, they are all equally not-the-truth. If you lie in the bedroom, you'll lie in the boardroom. If you lie to yourself, you'll lie to another. How you deny the truth one way is how you'll deny the truth other ways. The more you can tell the truth about yourself and others, the faster things move and the freer you get. You cannot get unstuck by trying to lie and fake your way out of it. You will not reach genuine success and fulfillment if you are not genuine! How you do one thing...

You can hide the truth for a while, but you can't hide from the truth forever. Deception requires energy to sustain it; the truth does not. Truth stands on its own; lies need to be held up. This is why life becomes so much easier when you tell the truth and more complicated when you lie. You might as well start with the truth because eventually, the truth is always revealed. This is how we know truth is the orientation of the Tao.

> "Three things cannot be long hidden:
> the sun, the moon, and the truth."
> — Buddha

SPEAKING THE TRUTH

When I was young, I was a compulsive liar. This pattern arose mainly from the fear of getting punished. I wasn't the most well-behaved, so my tendency to lie about things became a habit. When I was twenty, I realized I was lying about all sorts of benign things, completely unnecessarily—things like how my day was going or how I felt. I lied to myself, too, just to cover up my guilt, inadequacies, and shortcomings. Lie after lie to manage the cognitive dissonance between my fantasies and the evidence before me.

One day I was reading something about lying and it *clicked*. I remember the 'choice point' to stop lying and start telling the truth. Since then, my life has worked a lot better. Imagine that! I've been far from perfect, but I prioritize being as honest and authentic as possible in everything I do and have that standard for those in my life. I falter, but I am continually reorienting myself to not only what's true, but Truth itself. Truth is held above all else. This is why getting feedback is crucial because it calls us out on our self-deceptions and illuminates where we may have gone dark. This is what we discussed in the chapter, "The Essential External."

Being able to hear the truth and speak the truth about *ourselves* is only half of it. We need to be willing to speak the truth about what we see in the world and in others. There are two significant challenges we face in doing this. The first is with our filters of perception and projection. This takes time to resolve and occurs through all the healing we've discussed in this book. The second is in withholding our true self-expression and withholding feedback.

> "Bad men need nothing more to compass their ends,
> than that good men should look on and do nothing."
> — John Stuart Mill

There are times when we are afraid to tell the truth or express ourselves, or we have determined it's simply unwise. If it's because of an irrational fear, it is up to you to have the courage to do it anyway.

Speaking your truth in the face of fear and adversity is the pinnacle of meaningful expression and freeing in itself. If you're speaking out against something dangerous, you must decide if the consequences are worth it relative to what you stand for.

Other times we withhold because we think people can't handle it. It's none of our business what someone can handle or not. We withhold our beauty, gifts, ideas, femininity or masculinity, and power because we presume we're "too much" for people. We withhold our feedback because we think they can't handle the truth. How arrogant we are! It is not gracious; it's a power trip. If we speak the Truth and express ourselves fully, we have done all that we can do. This means doing so without any agendas, manipulations, attachment to outcomes, being ran by our stories, or attacking. If we do this with integrity, the rest of it is out of our hands. Who do we think we are accepting or rejecting for another what we offer? What right do we have to say what someone else can handle or if they should like or dislike us? It's none of our business what people think—especially of us! We cannot control how people take it, even though we may try to control through manipulation or influence. We can still express ourselves authentically and present the truth so that they can hear us—but as soon as we start holding back, pulling punches, mollycoddling, censoring, or diluting—we are doing them and us a disservice.

Aside from certain instances of appropriateness, such as with children or being under oath, we have no right to "protect someone from the truth." It is a complete act of superiority and arrogance. We are holding them and ourselves back. We may even find that deep under our *conscious* intentions, we are secretly jealous, competitive, or spiteful and are doing it on purpose. This is why it's so important that we feel and get in touch with what's real and true for ourselves beyond our stories and persona. We want to be of service to those around us—not unwittingly hold them back. Remember: there's nobody else out there. What you do to yourself, you're doing to others—and what you're doing to others, you're doing to yourself. As within, so without, as we learned in the chapter, "A Universal Approach."

Make a choice to put Truth above all else and live by it the best you can.

UNCOMPROMISING HONESTY

If you want to know the truth and be free, you must ask the hard questions few want to ask. You must be willing to get uncomfortable and vulnerable with others and yourself. You must do it first; do not wait for anyone else to offer you the truth. Whatever is broadcasted in the world for you to believe will keep you asleep. If you want to know the Truth, it must arise from within and of your own accord. You must ask and choose to know the Truth; it cannot be force-fed to you.

Here are some questions to get you started:

- What are you lying to others about? To yourself?
- What do you want to be lied to about to feel better?
- How are you manipulating others?
- What are you inflating or exaggerating?
- What are you pretending to be or have?
- What would you do if there were no laws or consequences?
- What don't you want others to know about you?
- What personal secrets do you hold that nobody else knows?

The last two are great icebreakers to open up and create more trust and intimacy.

Ask the second to last one like this: "What's one thing you don't want me to know about you? Here, I'll go first. What I don't want you to know about me is that I..." You can go as lighthearted or deep as you want to depending on the context and your rapport. Although, the more vulnerable you are, the deeper the intimacy and trust, and the more open you will be. If you've got some great rapport, a bonus question is: "What's one judgment you have about me?" You can do likewise with the last question about secrets, making it fun or sexy, or using it more therapeutically.

We all have things we hide from the world and ourselves. Secrets, experiences, dreams, fetishes, fantasies, guilts—acknowledge them and let them out. Do so appropriately, of course, in a safe container with those that won't judge or try to fix you but simply *witness*. Let your deepest, darkest (or lightest) truths be expressed and witnessed. It is liberating. Your secrets are keeping you stuck! I know it isn't easy to confront, but life is easier on the other side. Reaching freedom requires us to face and feel the terror and annihilation we're avoiding by keeping these hidden. When you stop rejecting yourself and all your shadow material, you stop rejecting others and judging theirs. This defense against rejection and destruction will drop the less you need to keep secrets. It will also allow you to start letting people in—all the way in. The resulting vulnerability is what allows for intimacy, and it's the only way you'll be able to experience acceptance from yourself and others.

I remember telling people close to me about the times as a kid I stole, lied about everything, cheated in school, picked my nose and wiped it on the pews in church, shameful sexual experiences, and all sorts of other 'awful' things. I thought these would make me look like a horrible, dishonest person. I thought people would look down at me with disgust and not trust me anymore. Yet... that's the opposite of what happened. They felt closer and trusted me more—a reversed-result. Not only that, but *they* began to open up and share their related experiences. Rather than rejecting each other, we laughed and cried about them together. It was not only healing for me, but it gave *them* permission to look at what they had been repressing. What was most beautiful was that they got to see their reflection of compassion in me: that they were still lovable and accepted regardless of their experience. They saw that they were not alone, and whatever happened from sharing was not the deathblow of rejection they had thought. It's what I got to experience from them, too.

As we touched upon in the chapter, "Your Life Is Not About You," it's not only about you and your fears and struggles. You don't realize how your withholding is also holding others back. Your choices to keep the truth hidden hold us all back. You not wanting it to be about your issues makes it about you and your cowardice. Instead, grabbing the reigns of terror and riding your shame and embarrassment into the abyss of vulnerability is what makes your life about something more than yourself. This willingness to go first, lead, and make a stand for the truth is *transcendence*—and it is the hallmark of bravery. Your courage to lay witness your healing process can be the permission slip someone else needs to be courageous and share. We cannot heal if we keep our secrets locked away in shame and guilt. Let your ghosts out and be free. You'll free others as you do.

This Truth is your gift.

RESPONSIBILITY

In the chapter, "The Victim Trap," we talked about responsibility in reference to taking ownership of the circumstance, rather than blaming others. This sense of responsibility relates to ending our victim mentality and taking ownership of our power. There's another type of responsibility alluded to in the chapter, "Your Life's Not About You," where we take on 'external' responsibility beyond our own. This sense of responsibility is about stewardship and leadership (as in taking charge of the situation and leading). It's the subtle difference between being responsible *for* and being responsible *to*.

In the following section on 'stewardship,' it's *to* (I am responsible *to* my family). In the last section referring to 'reclamation,' it's *for* (I am responsible *for* this happening). The sections will be broken up into further subsections, indicated by a colon.

RESPONSIBILITY AS STEWARDSHIP

This sense of responsibility is that of duty, pride, and caretaking. It is that of being a steward and leader of the space you inhabit, internally and externally. It is an expansion of self to include others in our responsibility. It differs from the 'reclamation' version of responsibility in a few nuanced ways. First, there is an indifference to victimhood because there is no implication that we have given any power away or feel helpless. Second, this is not solely self-responsibility, as we can 'take a sense of ownership' of the world around us in service to it. Finally, it's unrelated to any guilt or blame projections, as ownership isn't *for* something we did or didn't do, but *to* someone or something.

A mentor I once worked for tells a story that illustrates 'responsibility as stewardship' perfectly. At the time, he was a twenty-something engineer who began working at a copper plant. When he started, he wore a suit to work every day even though he wasn't close to an executive position. His fellows laughed at him, mockingly. It was no matter—because, in his mind, he acted as if it was *his* factory. Not in an entitled, bullying way, but in an "I'm responsible for this" way. If he saw something that needed to be done, he did it and stayed late if he had to. If it needed fixing, he figured out how to fix it. While others walked past something because it wasn't their job, he would take the five minutes to do it. He didn't wait for permission or to be told; he just did it as if it was his own house.

His managers took notice and promoted him, seeing that he could handle more responsibilities. Within two years, he was running the entire plant. He took their output from $3 million to $30 million with his ideas and innovations... why *wouldn't* they let him run it?

He once told me, "Run the business as if it was yours because someday it might be." He wasn't necessarily referring to me and his business, but the principle by which this section is inspired. Maybe you don't have a business, but a family, household, community, or job. What would happen if you genuinely took a similar mentality on? Notice what stories come up right away! This attitude towards taking ownership will not only help you get unstuck, but serve you in achieving great success.

RESPONSIBILITY AS STEWARDSHIP: *YOUR KINGDOM*

Imagine being the king (or queen) of a kingdom. Let's assume you are a fair, just, and beloved ruler. You rule over the lands and govern the folk within your domain. In exchange for prosperous commerce, fertile lands, knights for protection, and governance, the peasants and noblemen submit to your authority. You have your castle, court, and every duty that goes along with it. You must meet with representatives and hear pleas and complaints. You must tend to the politics and religious ceremonies. You must inspire and lead the troops into the battlefield to defend your people. You must forgo the mundane and trivial. If something happens to the kingdom, it is your choice how to respond—and your head if it fails. Yet, you have absolute freedom and power. You can fulfill your vision for yourself, your family, and your kingdom and implement all your desires. Under your rule, you can make your land the greatest in the nation, lifting all your citizens to elevated safety, joy, and prosperity. You get to influence and affect the destiny of thousands of people, for better or for worse.

Now see your own life this way. How would your life look like if you owned what was yours as if it belonged to royalty? What would your home look like if it were to be fit for a king and queen? How would it feel to treat yourself royally? What if you walked through the world as a king in his kingdom? How would you see yourself and the world differently? What sense of ownership for the space around you would you have that you don't now? How much bigger would your life become to support this way of showing up in the world? This is not about becoming an egomaniac but embodying the responsibility and leadership of this archetype for yourself. To become the king or queen of your own life and show up with nobility.

Take the throne, your majesty—it's thy birthright! This is not a fantasy. You have access to the power of the king and queen archetypes for your own life.

As you've seen in "The Victim Trap," taking this level of ownership of what we do and how we live our lives isn't a walk in the park. There are many people who want to be king or queen—have high status and power positions—but don't want to accept the responsibility, account-ability, and sacrifices that go with it. They want the glory without the grit, the freedom without the constraint, the pleasures without the problems. If you want freedom and a life of meaning and fulfillment, it requires you to not only *take* responsibility, but *take on* responsibility.

If you don't, that's fine. There's nothing wrong with not claiming your crown. I'm simply here to let you know you have one and what it takes to consecrate your nobility.

> *"From everyone who has been given much, much*
> *will be demanded; and from the one who has been*
> *entrusted with much, much more will be asked."*
> — *Luke 12:48, Holy Bible*

RESPONSIBILITY AS STEWARDSHIP: *A BURDEN?*

"How does taking on more responsibility get me unstuck? Won't that weigh me down even more?"

It's a common idea that taking on more responsibility is adding an additional burden to our lives. This is a mythology of the 'minimalists of life' who try to get by doing as little as possible. It's a philosophy of, "How can I do, take on, and contribute as little as possible and extract the most from everything? How can I get away with as much as possible before having to be accountable or responsible to anyone?" The premise is that it makes for a simpler life, and it may, but 'simpler' doesn't mean easier or freer. This mythology was a reverse-wiring that took me from a six-figure software business to living out of my car, with literally pennies in the bank. I wasn't allowing a life of less, I was rejecting a life of more. I was trying to escape responsibility in order to have an easier life, but that's the exact opposite of what happened.

More responsibility is *not* a burden! Scarcity, hunger, poverty, sickness, fear, and suffering are burdens. It's a distortion of reality to see just and righteous work as a curse. Those who struggle most don't have work, a house, a family, a mission, or responsibilities to take care of. We get it backward. For example, look at being homeless or jobless. People think it's "freeing" not having the cares of society, but it's not. It's a prison being stuck in survival mode and constantly being on the go figuring out ways to pay for things. Each night worrying about where you're going to sleep or eat, or how to afford basic necessities. There's no freedom in that. There's no actualization in that. It's constant survival mode.

I know because I've been there. As I mentioned, I chose to be homeless and live in my car in LA because my software company closed, and I didn't want to go back to "employee life" because I had entrepreneurial freedom for so long. I was "willing to do whatever it took" for my dreams... but instead of getting a job to support myself, I took it to mean "try and start a business from my car." Talk about a fantasy! The "freedom" that comes from avoiding responsibility is not the type of freedom I'd recommend.

RESPONSIBILITY AS STEWARDSHIP: *FIRST, AN ORDERED HOME*

Before becoming responsible *to* anything else, take responsibility *for* yourself and your existing possessions. Literally and metaphorically, make sure your home is in proper order before trying to address someone else's home. The relationship you have with your internal space is reflected in the space where you live. How you're relating to that 'internal' space of your home will reflect what you're going to do in the world. Are you going to bring your dysfunction and chaos, or your grace and order, into the lives and businesses of others? How you do one thing is how you do anything.

Too many people with distorted ideas of themselves, and a shadow they're out of relationship with, go out into the world in an attempt to change it. This is *irresponsible*. What's unresolved in the subconscious gets projected upon the space as something that needs "fixing" or "saving" in the world. The person sees a problem 'out there' that needs solving when it's really something 'in here' that needs resolution.

The victim mentality wants to be saved, and so it projects this outwards. A "powerful person" with a victim mentality becomes a 'savior' to others. These pseudo-saviors may think they're being benevolent, but none of us need "saving"—we are fully capable adults. This is the arrogance and superiority of a victim; they project their helplessness upon others because that's what they secretly feel about themselves. These "powerful victims" haven't found true empowerment. They're in reaction-formation to their victimhood, enacting their fantasy of power upon the world because of their resources.

This potential pitfall is why it's imperative that we take responsibility for our own 'home' before we start preaching to the world. This is why we take ownership of our shadow material instead of pushing it down: because what we avoid runs us. Of course, we're not perfect and will have plenty of opportunities to discover more and transform along the way. It's not about preventing ourselves from helping others until we're 'ready' or 'perfect,' but making sure what we're putting out into the world is actually of service to others and ourselves—not our ego, shadow, or trauma. Often the best way to be of service and lead others is by healing and leading yourself. Being of service to the world is more about who you *are* than what you *do*. Take responsibility of this first, and things will naturally find their way to your just, right, true, and capable hands.

> "Yesterday I was clever, so I wanted to change the world. Today I am wise, so I am changing myself."
> — Rumi

RESPONSIBILITY AS STEWARDSHIP: *SERVICE TO THE WORLD*

Once you have your own estate in order, you can begin taking ownership of the greater problems of the world. The more responsibility we take for what's happening in the world, the more power we have in changing it. Think about the most celebrated entrepreneurs and philanthropists. What do they do, really? They find a massive problem and dedicate their lives to solve it or donate resources to someone who is—all in hopes of making the world a better place. Their life is not about them or the money, but what they can do with their resources to improve the human condition. **They take ownership of the problem, not**

because it's their fault or because they caused it, but because that's the only way they can start to change it. They take responsibility of the problem in order to find a solution, not blame themselves or others. It's no longer an ephemeral, abstract issue plaguing humanity, but something "of theirs" they have the power to begin addressing. Compare this to the victim mentality of "it's not my fault, not my job, not my problem" and how little it produces for the person or in the world, and you'll see how taking responsibility is paramount to success.

You don't have to be rich or a genius inventor to do this. Begin by taking ownership of as much as you can, whatever is within your means. Start with where you're at, with what you have, even if it's only a small room, a bed, food, and this book. If you handle what you already have well, you will be provided with more. We each embody a certain energetic level of how much responsibility we can be trusted with. As we embody each level and become comfortable with that range, we can then increase and take on more. We can literally see this express itself in each person's movement in the Cinesomatic work, and it's quite apparent who runs a big business and who is struggling to pay rent—it all gets revealed through the way they embody themselves and the space. It is said that success leaves clues; well, success also leaves "clues" in the body, mind, and energy of someone and can be a reference point for high functionality.

As your energetic range of what you can take on expands, you bump into the 'bounds of your stories' that determine your limits. If you're not in proper relationship with your shadow and you still have these stories running you, they will wreak havoc. In this circumstance, when we take on more than we're able to sustain—be it money, love, joy, beauty, or freedom—we will find a way to dump it. You see this when people get unstuck and things start going incredibly well for them, but their myths reach an upper limit to feeling good and having life be easy—and *CRASH!*—they take themselves out. Once, when this occurred with me, it was an actual car crash that took me out. It doesn't have to be a literal crash, of course. Any kind of self-sabotage is fair game for our ego to use to keep us "in check."

Here are some practical examples:

- If we are shown too much love and affection, we will dismiss it.
- If we suddenly win $100 million, we will be as poor as we were beforehand in five years.
- If we take a position we don't believe we deserve or can't handle, we will then self-sabotage and mess up in order to get fired.
- If we meet someone we feel is "out of our league," we will act out and push them away.
- If we are used to suffering and struggle, and then we start letting life be easy, we will find ways to create drama and problems.

Most of these are all subconscious reactions. We don't realize this is going when things go awry, but there's always an explanation for why we take ourselves out (self-sabotage).

You need to crawl before you walk, walk before you run, and run before you try out for the Olympics. Taking on responsibility is similar. We need to acclimate to our range and embody it, not merely read about it in a book and think we've 'got it.' It doesn't have to take a long time. People take decades to do what can be done in months because of their stories. This work accelerates that process authentically and sustainably. You can learn your lessons after hitting rock-bottom over and over again—or you can stop all that and begin to penetrate the stories, face your shadow, and apply everything else in this book so you can keep expanding without taking yourself out.

RESPONSIBILITY AS RECLAMATION

Tip: A quick review of the chapter, "The Victim Trap," can be helpful before continuing to this section dealing with victim mentality.

Reclamation is about reclaiming what is rightfully ours. We take back what was lost and own it again. When we are being victims, we feel helpless and powerless, so the reclamation is our sense of power. The only way we can reclaim our power is by recognizing and accepting that *we made the choice to give it away*. In this context, taking responsibility means owning this choice, stopping the self-betrayal, choosing to be empowered and embodying that power. It is our ability to respond with ownership that empowers us. This is our "response-ability."

It's through taking responsibility and being held accountable that power is regained. It can only be taken back by the stopping of giving it away. It is not reclaimable through fighting, stealing, regulations, or winning against another. The victim relying on indignation feels that someone else is holding their power over them, and they must fight to take it back. In actuality, nobody can hold another's power; it's merely projected and relinquished. Our power never really 'goes' anywhere—like some magical flask of one's essence—rather, it's chronically dissociated from.

The reclamation of power is done *within* the individual themselves, not in a battle against anything external. **The only war is an internal war, which gets projected upon the world.** Perhaps the circumstance is unfair and disadvantageous, but blaming and attacking it will not get one closer to peace and inner power. We addressed this in "The Victim Trap." This course of blame will only further perpetuate the story that the person is helpless, and the circumstance has ultimate power over them. The war needs to end *inside* before it ever ends *outside*. Even if the war outside is won, it will never bring about freedom or power if it is not first won within.

We must find our part in the current circumstance in order to break the cycle and learn from it, or else we are destined to repeat it. The same pattern of victimization will reoccur with different clothes and faces, but it's the same story. Victims indulge and find identity in these cycles, even building status and communities around them. One thing is to come together and support; another is to become codependent, enabling, and hold each other back. The person choosing a heroic life refuses to be a victim, breaks these cycles so that they don't continue to happen, and doesn't base their sense of self on their circumstance. This is triumphant and truly righteous, and all people want to do is rage against it with justification!

RESPONSIBILITY AS RECLAMATION: *FREEDOM THROUGH OWNERSHIP*

Taking responsibility doesn't sound fun or sexy. It's easy to dismiss as something you already know. It's not some magical transformational technique. There's no proprietary ten-step program to sell. You just, as my grandpa would say, "man-up." However, it isn't necessarily the tough, hard burden or shameful act that we may think. Many of us are missing the joy found in taking responsibility. Yes, *joy*. We find it a weighty or solemn act. What we fail to comprehend is that this ownership is *for* us, not against us. It is not a burden or a sign of guilt: it is a path to liberation and healing. When you understand that taking responsibility is a *benefit for you*, rather than a sort of self-incrimination, you will free yourself from the need to defend and become outraged.

Being responsible doesn't mean you *caused* it. It means you *own* what happened. People feel that taking responsibility means they are at fault or are to blame, which is not the case. The logic of 'fault' requires blame. It dictates that if *they* take responsibility, it somehow acquits the *other* of what they did, which is not the case either. We want to phase out this 'either-or' mentality. Taking personal responsibility doesn't affect another—that's what makes it *personal*. Owning our part doesn't excuse the other person for their actions. The other person is *still* held accountable and responsible for their choices and will ultimately have to answer for what they did. However, that burden is not ours to carry.

Most quests for justice and revenge do not end the way we think; we're never quite fulfilled from them. The void we're trying to fill was never in the hands of our enemies. It's through this distorted perception of revenge that the victim can't see the True fairness and righteousness that comes with sovereign self-responsibility but instead looks upon it with contempt.

*"Fool that I am,' said he, 'that I did not tear out
my heart the day I resolved to revenge myself'."*
— Alexandre Dumas, The Count of Monte Cristo

If we want to be free from victimhood; if we want to be free from
our stucky stories; if we want to be free from the bounds of scarcity,
struggle, and suffering—we must take complete ownership. We must
accept responsibility for every choice in our life if we are to be free of
what binds us to suffering and illusion. The more freedom we choose
to have in our life, the more responsibility we must *take* and *take on*.
This freedom comes through reclamation *and* stewardship.

Absolute freedom requires absolute responsibility.

How much freedom and power do you have over your circumstances? If our situation thus far has been someone else's fault, then
we're also saying we had no power over it. If we had no power doing it,
we surely don't have any power to *undo* it. If we don't assume responsibility, we relinquish choice and are thus powerless. Being a victim is
not freedom. Our happiness and peace are held hostage by those we
blame—not because they're bad and stole it from us—but because
we have given them the key. We've not only made them responsible
for whatever we're blaming them for, but for its resolution too—and
then we have the audacity to demonize and attack them! All this does
is create suffering and keep us stuck.

**The more you own what happens in your life... the more of
your life you own, rather than *it* owning *you!***

When we hold someone else responsible for our suffering, we are
simultaneously holding them responsible for our *joy*. In this game, we
can only be happy and at peace when *they* allow us to be. We think
we're taking the easy way out, but we become prisoners. We give up
our freedom to avoid responsibility and then implore the world to do
it for us. Waiting for justice or for the world to change in order to get
unstuck is a losing game. Waiting for your circumstance to change in
order to be unstuck is a prison. At any moment, you can take the key
back, unlock your cell, and find freedom again. The only thing between
you and doing that is a choice—and the rage, hatred, sorrow, revenge,

despair, and helplessness underneath it. It's a choice only you can make and a feeling only you can feel—nobody else can do it for you.

You are responsible for where you're at in life. *You* are responsible for what you choose. *You* are responsible for how you perceive. *You* are responsible for feeling. *You* are responsible for getting unstuck.

If you are still stuck, it's because on some level, that's what *you* are choosing.

CHOICE

The deciding factor of everything in your life can be summarized in one word: *choice*. Until you make a new choice and act on it, nothing will change. You cannot merely hope, daydream, fantasize, or desire and think it so—you must *choose* it. How do you know if you've done this? If you *think* you've made a new choice, but nothing has changed, you didn't actually make a new choice. The feedback you get from the evidence around you is the proof of choice. Thinking, assuming, stating, and proclaiming is not enough because we are great at conning ourselves. This highlights the importance of what you learned in the chapter, "The Essential External."

Most folks don't consciously choose; they are ran by their myths, shadow material, and further unconscious programs. This is why it's so easily defended with, "But I didn't choose that!", because they legitimately aren't conscious of the choice. While this is fair, it's dangerously easy to use this as an excuse to play the victim and act helpless to our own mind. Not being aware of the choice and blaming it on a subconscious part of ourselves doesn't excuse us from the responsibility. Our subconscious is still *us;* thus, it is still us who made the choice. A choice we make in the shadows and hide from ourselves is not any less of a choice than one we proclaim aloud to the world.

Yet, we don't feel the same sense of empowerment when we are ran by these *shadow choices*. We cannot reclaim our power and get unstuck if we remain ignorant or disown our unconscious choices, nor if we deny our conscious ones. Indeed, the degree of accountability we are held to regarding these unconscious choices versus the ones we make conscious is less. Yet, the purpose of this book is to help you awaken to a higher order of living, so the idea is to eliminate any excuse we have to claim ignorance. The reason for this is because the more you own your choices, the more you are able to consciously steer your life.

An easy way to discover our choices (or non-choices) is by paying attention to what we say. The words we use define our world. Whether we speak them aloud or say them to ourselves in thought, we are constructing our own version of the world with words. There are may 'tells' which expose the truth of our conviction. Feel the difference in certainty each of these phrases conveys. Say each one aloud and feel the response in your body:

- It's impossible
- It never will
- It won't
- I can't
- It didn't
- It was supposed to
- It could
- It might
- I hope
- I'd like to
- I want
- It's probable
- It's likely
- I think it will
- It hasn't yet
- It will
- It is happening
- I have
- It is
- It did
- I had

Which ones feel weakest or strongest? Which feel like justifications? Which feel certain or uncertain? Which feel more real or less likely to happen? Which words do you find yourself using to describe your vision? Did any stories, judgments, or images arise; any past situations where you've used these? Can you feel which are more likely to be a fantasy or a choice, which ones will lead to success, and which feel like victim mentality?

Let's go further and apply this to your stucky story. Add on whatever your vision is after getting unstuck to each one of these and do it again. For example, "I hope to have a relationship. I'd like to have a relationship. I will have a relationship." and so on. You can use this exercise for anything in life you're looking to create and see which phrase resonates most—this shows you where you're at with it. You are looking to get to the place where it feels authentic and congruent to speak it from the most certain phrases.

If you want more certainty in your life, be more certain in your choices!

Start by using stronger words. Not only which words you use, but take stronger ownership of the words themselves and remain accountable to what you say. Holding yourself accountable creates the conditions for your success—it doesn't turn your failure into a punishment! This is another reverse-wiring. The reality is that we will be more likely to reach our vision by holding ourselves accountable than if we are avoiding consequences. If your words are weak, uncertain, or excusable—what do you think the outcome will be? We use weak words to avoid committing. Stop using 'weasel language'! We are afraid to take responsibility and accountability because we don't believe it—we don't believe it because we haven't owned the choice!

Weak words create weak results. If you want things to happen, don't give yourself wiggle room for them *not* to happen. It's the classic parable of "burning your ships" in order to ensure victory or die trying.

Words alone are not enough—you must take action. Yet, words are the first thing we bring into existence from thought. This is why writing and speaking the truth and our vision is so important: we are literally using 'the word' to create 'something from nothing.' This is one of the secrets of the ages. Your words set precedence for your choices, so make them as powerful as they can be. Do not worry about looking foolish or wrong—people won't "get it," and that's okay. Keep your proclamations to yourself or within your team that shares the vision until it's manifested.

MAKING IT HARD

If you look at highly functional people, they are extraordinarily quick at making optimal choices. They make a choice and do it. If they don't like the results, they simply choose something else. Highly functional people don't complain because they are not victims; they know they are the ones who picked. There's no nonsense. People who are struggling in life have great difficulty making effective choices and doing so right away. It's not a coincidence.

Choice itself is easy: *you just choose it.*

That's it. It doesn't require all this extra heavy lifting and drama many like to associate with making a choice. It doesn't require us to figure out everything beforehand, to know the odds of future outcomes, or what people say we're able to do. A choice is the choice itself; it is not all the noise around it. All the stories, forecasting, deliberating, fear, and excuses? They slow us down because they are not required to make a choice.

I invite you to let go of all the drama around choosing.

Just stop.

Get out of your head. It's all an attachment to outcome and scarcity mentality. Here's a great question to ask yourself to know if you're in scarcity, "If I added two zeros to my income, would I still be spending all this time researching, analyzing, debating, and worrying?" If the answer is yes, then either you are dealing with something at the scale of people's lives, or you have other mythologies running you. If the answer is no, then stop and choose. If you don't like the meal, throw or give it away and get something else. If you don't like the trip, change it. If you don't like the house, move. If the person isn't what you wanted, end the relationship. For the typical person, none of it is life or death.

Yes, there will be consequences, and you are accountable to them, but the speed at which you move through a majority of your life, and the extra time and peace it brings, will more than make up for it.

We create all these fake-choices and half-choices (none of which are actual choices) that keep us stuck in limbo. It's paralysis. Make a choice and get on with your life and deal with it. It's much more functional than taking ten times the amount of time to find the perfect thing and then being anxious worrying if it was the best decision. If this is your behavior, you're squandering your life on things that don't matter. Your ego is trying to convince you and justify why they are so important, but it's just another way to suffer needlessly. Choose and move forward. This behavior is slowing your entire life down.

The 'how' may take a lot of time, but the choice doesn't require a 'how' before being made. One of the biggest hangups of choosing is the notion that we *have* to figure out how we can do it, or if it's even possible beforehand. This is the biggest cause of the 'failure to launch' for any vision I've seen. People are afraid to choose something without the external certainty of its success. They need to know how it's possible, what the guarantee is, and all the details of the plan before deciding if they're going to pursue it. This is the best way to never make your dreams come true.

Do not wait until there's proof to start. Start in order to find the proof. Start in order to find the 'how.'

The certainty is *internal*. You make the choice first, and then everything you need to make it happen will come into being. It may take some time for inventions and discoveries to be made, or resources to align, or the market to be right, but if you don't make the choice now, then when in five years those things happen (if they even do because perhaps you're an essential component in their happening) you won't be ready. You have to choose *now* and own that choice before ever being concerned with the 'how' or 'when.'

A META EXAMPLE OF CHOICE

A perfect demonstration of this is *Awaken to Your True Self* itself. All the concepts I've shared *in* the book are what I've had to implement to *create* the book. It's a book for me as much as it is one for you.

What you're reading has been a decade in the making. I chose to be a writer a decade ago when I started writing about personal development, having had no interest in writing before. I hated English class in school, and thought writing essays were the worst. It has taken me ten years to learn, experience, acquire, build, embody, test, fail, reinvent, and transform into what was required for this book to be *this book*. Creating the book itself took two years to arrive at this final form after two iterations that flopped. You would not be reading this right now if I did not make the choice ten years ago to start, or two years ago and "fail." There are still unknowns about this book as I write it, but I have a vision, a plan, and will figure it out as I need to.

I take action on whatever is in my control now and surrender and have faith in the rest. I allow it to unfold without attachment to the outcome while still focusing on my vision and taking relentless action. I have structures that support me staying on track but am open to listening to where *it* wants to go, rather than forcing it where my ego thinks it should. The book is informing me what it wants to be. My job is to get out of the way and use my gifts to bring that forth. I follow the feeling while using my mind to connect the dots and plan. At first, I thought this was meant to be a free, twenty-page document... *it* wanted otherwise! Since my allegiance is to truth and feeling above all else—not my ego—I trust it, even if it doesn't match what I pictured. As I see it unfold over time, I consistently see that it never fails me. It is the union and acceptance of both masculine and feminine, yin and yang approaches—a middle path between doing *and* allowing, not either-or.

You will move much faster by choosing first and figuring it out as you go, than you would by attempting everything upfront in order to be perfectly ready. Even if you don't know what you want, choose *something* and start. The more you choose, try, and learn, the more experience and data you get on the way to figuring out where you want to go. Deal with the failures as you go and learn on the fly, and readjust as necessary. You can change your vision and trajectory of life at any moment, no matter how far down the path you are. There will be repercussions, but you can always change your mind. Agility and adaptability are essential for us to survive and thrive in the world which evolves around us.

I started with building computers because I was curious and nerdy, and now I write and teach spirituality and therapy—two seemingly dissimilar fields. Yet everything I learned about technology at fourteen, I still use today in my business. And not only do I use it, but my work also requires it! I could not be doing what I'm doing now in this field if I didn't choose to get into technology and design back then.

> "You can't connect the dots looking forward; you can only connect them looking backward. So you have to trust that the dots will somehow connect in your future. You have to trust in something—your gut, destiny, life, karma, whatever. This approach has never let me down, and it has made all the difference in my life."
> — Steve Jobs

JUST ANOTHER FANTASY?

There have been many things in my life that I wanted but never actually chose. These are things that never showed up in the physical world despite how much I focused on them. I wanted them so bad, but because they didn't happen, I knew the truth was that I wasn't *choosing* them. Often, I was afraid and in denial or trapped in an egoic fantasy. The road to writing and publishing this book has been paved with a trail of non-choices and dramatic fantasies—a decade of them.

There was no secret technique, no clearing method, and no blessing from a guru that created this book. After a decade, the only true difference between this book existing or not was the choice for it to exist.

That choice *includes* work. I have referred to myself as an author and to this book as "the book I wrote" and "my book" as if it was already done... well before it was published. Writing these words now, I have unwavering certainty that I've chosen this book. I can feel it with every cell of my body. I can promise with 100% knowing that this book *is*. Not only do I feel it absolutely, but I've invested thousands of hours on it, have a date for release, and a publisher ready to print it.

I *feel* it; I *own* it; I am *taking action*. I have *embodied* the choice.

It is not a fantasy in my head, a hope, or a dream. My words weren't lies, nor were they delusions. None of these were so because I have *also* decided, taken ownership, created a vision, prioritized it, oriented my life to it, taken dedicated daily action towards it, and have poured myself into creating the book. I am still writing these words, but the book is already done inside. I can see it, and I can feel it. I am writing the book knowing that it already is a published book—I'm just working towards it until time catches up with what I already know to be true. It is unquestionable to me. Death itself could not stop this book from being published. As trusting of the Sun rising tomorrow, am I sure of this book becoming a book.

And yet...

The ultimate proof is in the result. The only way to know for certain that I made the choice is if you're actually holding this book in your hands. This is the tangible proof that it was a choice rather than another fantasy. Otherwise, I could have chosen something like: "an almost book," "an unfinished manuscript," "a lot of hard work for nothing," "time practicing writing and preparing for a different book," "wasting time to prove I'm a failure," or "more evidence for my story of suffering." I could easily have had the *fantasy* of a book but subconsciously be choosing a different vision that undermines it.

We *think* we're choosing the goal, and we *think* that we're envisioning it, but sometimes we're really not at all. Maybe we're thinking more about how it will crash and burn, or perhaps we're choosing a learning experience instead of immediate success. Maybe we are secretly focusing on what the failure or rejection feels like, not the vision of successful manifestation. This distinction is extremely nuanced and subtle, and requires us to have a high level of self-awareness and integrity. It can be a slippery slope between fantasy and choice, where a few missteps can send us tumbling down a cliff of self-sabotage and devastation. If we want our vision to come true, we must be honest with ourselves about what we're *really* doing and what shadow material may be running us. Everything in this book will help you do that.

A classic example of this is when someone gets caught up in their "big idea." They start hyping up their plans to start a new business, how they're going to change the world, getting themselves all motivated and excited, and a few months later... they're back at their nine-to-five job, never to talk about it again. This pattern isn't about failure or trying and someone doing their best; it's a story about the insidious nature of pseudo-choices. Can you guess what this person *really* chose? What they actually chose was to "get hyped and attempt a fantasy, not commit to it 100%, validate their stucky story, and go back to their job as a failsafe." We know that was their choice because *that's what happened* instead of a business opening.

What we have chosen is what actually *happens*, not what we *expect* to happen.

This is why telling the truth and getting feedback will help you get unstuck. Feedback is the litmus test of choice. You need to know the reality of the choices you're making before having to wait years to find out the hard way. This is what getting formal feedback does: it saves you decades of struggle. Once you can trust that you can tell the difference between "what you want to happen" and "what you choose to happen," as well as the difference between "being in a fantasy" and "being at choice," your confidence will become unshakable. To do so, you have to be willing to *feel* in order to make this distinction; it's not something done by an intellectual algorithm. As you regain trust in your ability to discern, feel, listen to your intuition, and make real choices—your trust in life and others will be lifted too. This is foundational to a successful *heroic life*.

YOU CHOSE TO STILL BE STUCK

Your life will change when you make a new choice and take action upon it. That choice can only be made *now*, and it's made in an instant. You are the only one who can make it. It is this awesome power of choice that allows you to change your circumstance. Choice is what gets you unstuck. Choice is what gets you everything in your vision. No matter how low you feel or how bad you think you have it, someone who had it worse has risen and prevailed. It wasn't by accident—they chose to. If they can do it, so can you.

If you're stuck, you now know that was a choice. Being stuck is a choice!

...and it may have been precisely what you needed. There's nothing wrong with being stuck—hell, that's what led you to this book. Remember that everything serves, even what doesn't. Everything is working out *for you*, even if you can't see it that way for another decade. Accept where you're at, recognize what you've needed to learn, and then make a new choice—or don't. There are no 'wrong' choices, but they all have their consequences. Trust yourself and trust the process. Surrender to what you can't control, accept what is, and change what's in your hands to change... which is a lot more than you think.

The door has been opened, but only *you* can walk through it. The choice is yours—now and always. 🦎

CONCLUSION

ou've made it to the end of the book—but this is just the beginning of your journey. It is not uncommon for people to get their breakthrough only from an epiphany they have while reading. However, it's much more common for people to get their breakthrough by **consistently applying what they learned in their everyday life.** In some way or another, as an acorn or a forest, every reason for you still being stuck can be found in this book. Knowing the reason is only part of it; the rest is up to you. There's no getting unstuck without the choice, and that requires commitment and action. If you want the results, you need the resolve.

If you're feeling overwhelmed, uncertain, or fearful—that is normal. In the introduction, I prefaced that this book may be confronting. Whatever you're feeling, it's okay. It's part of the process. All it means is that you're moving towards a greater way of showing up in the world. Do not back away from the foreign land; step forward into the unknown—that's where your life lies! It's hard to shut your eyes to the truth once you've seen it—you can't un-know what you've learned. That is authentic awakening. There may be a lot to go through; keep moving forward. One day at a time, one 'stop' at a time.

These ideas are not regulated only to getting unstuck—they are universally helpful no matter what you're going through, especially if you're already thriving! Rereading this when everything in your life is working great will reveal even more secrets. The principles and insights within these pages offer more than a mere "get unstuck book."

It's a **relationship** book, not because it talks about sex or dating, but because it shifts the way you relate to everything in your life. It's a book about **hope**, not because it's full of motivational stories, but because it shows you that *you* have the power to change your situation. It's a **business** book, not because we talk about business or money, but because it reveals how the shadow aspects in your life hold you back in your career too. It's a **spiritual** book, not because we talk about religion and metaphysical powers, but because it reveals the divinity of humanity itself. It's a **self-help** book, not because it's about personal development or improving, but because it shows you how to drop the persona and stop fixing altogether. It's a **performance art** book, not because it teaches about acting, music, or dance, but because it illuminates an authentic way of being, rather than living our life performing for approval, acting out, or trying to 'do.'

Whatever you're dealing with—no matter what genre, topic, culture, situation, or level—this book *will* apply, and it *will* help you.

Book Summary

Everything you needed to know about why you were still stuck and what is required to get unstuck is within this book. Not only unstuck from a situation, but how to start waking up from your illusions and become self-realized. I hope you've found value in the depth and breadth of topics and saw their relevance to your situation. If you haven't had your breakthrough yet, keep applying these concepts daily and reread the book until you do. It's all in here. We have covered a lot of ground, and if you followed the advice in the Introduction, you took some time to get through it. Now is the time for a final review, summarizing our journey together in one place.

PART I SUMMARY

In Part I, each of the chapters presented a unique angle on how you got to be stuck. This part was heavier on the 'why' and less on the 'how.' The chapters also introduced—or retaught you in a different light—fundamental concepts and principles for piercing the illusions of your struggle. This first half helped you make sure you *knew* where and why you were stuck, not where you *guessed* you were stuck.

In **Chapter One**, you learned that what you considered "being stuck" was actually a *story* about being stuck. You were able to recognize that stories about you and your life are not the Truth, but narratives about your interpretation of them. You learned that this work is not about changing the meaning of a story to be positive or labeling things as 'good' or 'bad,' but about stopping the judgments and stories altogether. Finally, you were able to imagine what your life would look like if you had amnesia, and all your stories about your limitations were gone.

In **Chapter Two**, you learned about change and where it happens. This was revealed in The Hierarchy of Change: identity, feeling, belief, attitude, behavior. You then came to know something beyond these levels, and even beyond change: your True Self. You learned about personas, which are the masks and images we present to the world. You also got to choose between a real apple pie or an artificially flavored apple treat. Finally, you discovered that the doorway to creating profound change in your life is vulnerability, which is the reason we hide behind our personas to begin with.

In **Chapter Three**, you learned the equation for suffering. Through math examples and Bob's Ladder, this equation revealed that the very action of looking for a solution to an unreal problem was responsible for creating the problem. You were able to recognize any secondary gains you may have for wanting to stay stuck. The power of identification became apparent when you saw "The Hiccup Man" make his entire life about his stucky story. You learned that the truth requires no defense, and anything we feel defensive about is in someway a lie. Finally, you faced a desperate ego that clings on to its identification with struggle and suffering.

In **Chapter Four**, you learned how intellect slows you down and the benefits of not being in your head. We went over the different types of intellectual personalities that can struggle despite being so smart. You studied the various intellectual traps and the advantages of non-intellect. We defined 'intellect' and 'intelligence' and the differences between the two. You were able to determine if you were in your head or in feeling. We went into the pain of the egoic intellectual and their superiority as protection. Finally, I invited you to trust in a greater intelligence than your ego and begin developing your intuition.

In **Chapter Five**, you learned all about 'the most important person' in self-help, detailing narcissism in depth. We explored the narcissistic image, self-betrayal, what's unreal, and our addiction to being unlovable. We discussed how the narcissist tries to meet their own needs and their struggle with letting others in, like when they won't accept gifts or help. There was an example of Bob and his subtle narcissistic behaviors, as well as how we use weasel language to avoid accountability. Finally, you learned about narcissistic supply and objectification, and why all of this keeps you stuck.

In **Chapter Six**, you learned about the typical spiritual path and why it's failing you if you're stuck. We discussed suffering: what it is, what it looks like, and how you suffer. We went over the trap of a 'spiritualized ego' and trying to 'ascend' to avoid being human. Finally, we touched upon your divinity and "tat tvam asi"—the recognition that 'you are it.'

In **Chapter Seven**, you learned all about the victim mentality. Introducing the topic, we first established what a victim was in this context and got on the same page with definitions of responsibility, shame, guilt, etc. We then identified the victim persona and the common strategies used to stay stuck in victimhood. Next, you learned about how we play the blame game and give our power away, even if we blame ourselves. The illusion of innocence showed you that we have a part to play in all circumstances. Finally, you learned the way to reclaim your power is to stop giving it away, starting with taking responsibility and accountability for everything in your life.

In **Chapter Eight**, you learned about how we avoid life and the ways avoidance keeps you stuck. We started with where this avoidance comes from: a distrust in life. We went deeper into the origins of this mistrust and why it causes us to avoid life. You learned that an avoidance of feeling is the basis of all avoidance and at the root of anxiety. We explored twenty-one significant ways in which you may be avoiding life and why they keep you stuck. I asserted that we tend to avoid the very thing that would move us forward. You learned about fantasies and how to determine if you're living in one. Finally, I invited you to live the heroic life rather than an avoidant one.

In **Chapter Nine**, you learned how to start living your life instead of fixing it. I shared my story of warts and how I wanted to fix everything in my life and the distortions that caused. We went over the fixing-addictions and flawed premises that caused much of my past suffering. Finally, I invited you to realize the truth about your True Self: that you are enough, you are lovable, you are not broken, and you have everything you need.

PART II SUMMARY

In Part II, you began to learn new ways of moving forward in your life. Not only 'why,' but 'what' and 'how' to do something about it. New or more deeply defined concepts that redefined how to live without being stuck. Ways of seeing the world, yourself, and your transformational journey that fundamentally shifted the way you relate to life. Whichever reasons for being stuck that weren't revealed or resolved in Part I were done so in Part II.

In **Chapter Ten**, you learned that "how you do one thing is how you do anything." We covered scientific understanding of the Big Bang all the way to mystical principles of the Mysteries, illustrating the fundamental principle of "as above, so below." We then dove deeper into how the microcosm mirrors the macrocosm and the practical application of inside-outside, perception-projection. You learned a form of 'alchemy,' where changing something internal affects the outer, and the outer the inner. We went deeper into symbolic awareness and the need for purification. Finally, we looked at some practical examples and ways to shift your stucky story by shifting something similar elsewhere.

In **Chapter Eleven**, you learned about reversed-results and how we get reverse-wired. We looked at examples of this phenomenon and how we miss these distortions because they're within our chain of perception. I shared a personal story of suppressing my smile and gave examples of how we can become reverse-wired. You learned how to determine if some aspect of yourself is reverse-wired and how self-love can feel awful if we've been avoiding it our whole lives. I explained why you might need to 'betray' your stories and culture. Finally, we addressed perfectionism and the path of doing things wrong and messing it all up.

In **Chapter Twelve**, you learned about the necessity of feedback and the two ways in which it comes: from others and from the manifested results in our life. You learned what proper feedback looks like and how to give and receive it. We went over how our results give us the data we need to escape our own personal hell. I asserted that all feedback is love, that feedback itself is not positive or negative, good or bad. You were able to see how we defend against the truth and why it's so hard for us to listen. Finally, we expanded further into why the truth requires no defense and why it may feel painful when we hear it.

In **Chapter Thirteen**, you learned about how to make your life about something greater than yourself and your stucky story. I shared my story and what I had realized about my self-centeredness. You learned to identify how you may be making things about you, what that means, and why it negatively affects you and others. We went over how meeting our needs from a distorted place and "not letting it be about us" keeps us stuck. I shared my experience with holding the group back and how you can show up to serve the space rather than take away from it. I offered ways in which you can make things in your life about something greater than oneself to get unstuck. Finally, you learned about the martyr archetype and were left with a set of powerful questions to live by.

In **Chapter Fourteen**, you learned about the shadow and how to relate to yours in a new way. You received a crash-course on the unfolding of one becoming enlightened. We then explored the ideas of illumination and how we as humans typically deal with our shadow material: by trying to get rid of what we judge. From here, there was a shift in the way we relate to our shadow: I invited you to begin witnessing it rather than rejecting it. I asserted that our shadow was the best parts of us, which the ego threw away. You learned the "A5 Process" for facing any shadow material that arises throughout your day, rather than avoiding or denying it. I shared the peaceful warrior example, and you explored the appropriate uses of our shadow aspects when we are in proper relationship with them. You realized that both the light and dark are love. Finally, we dove into the dark night of the soul, where you discovered that your deepest shadow work may not be in the darkness, but in the light.

In **Chapter Fifteen**, you learned everything you never knew you wanted to know about stopping. I asserted that your work is not in doing more but in stopping more, which is the path to your True Self. We covered the dangers and pressure of trying to stop all at once, including the impossibility of suffering your way to joy. You learned the two definitions of 'stop' and that this work is subtractive rather than additive—that it's an undoing, not a doing. I provided an extensive list of things to stop in order to get unstuck. You learned how to stop by having awareness, choosing, stopping, and feeling. Finally, I gave examples of how to practically apply this with a warning about turning 'stopping' into another technique.

In **Chapter Sixteen**, you learned about being present in the now and how to create a vision. We defined "being in the now" and how to get present. You learned about the still point of choice, the wheel of fortune, and the illusion of past and future. You identified what you've stood for and the choices you've made by looking at your present life. Finally, you learned to create a definite vision to ensure all the freed energy from your stucky story has a productive place to go.

In **Chapter Seventeen**, you learned a new way to move through your stucky story. We explored the idea of "as above, so below" applied to our mind and body, plus the subtle shifts of energy that make all the difference. You learned what embodiment really is and the difference between 'doing' and 'being.' You discovered that how you move in your body symbolically represents how you move through life. Finally, you did the "Embodied-Story Exercise," where you got to apply all the theories in the book in an experiential movement, in the style of Cinesomatics.

In **Chapter Eighteen**, you learned about The Five Tenets and went into further detail about each topic. You were given an instructional phrase, or mantra, to get unstuck: "Stop, feel, tell the truth, take responsibility, and make a new choice." I asserted that it was not about feeling good, but *feeling*. We covered getting triggered, rescuing, and going insane. We explored the differences between Truth with a big 'T' and truth with a little 't'. I invited you to speak the truth and be uncompromisingly honest. You learned about responsibility as both stewardship and reclamation. That absolute freedom requires absolute responsibility. We went over choice and how powerful our words are. You learned why we make it hard for ourselves and how to know if your choice is real or a fantasy. Finally, we concluded with the realization that still being stuck is a choice—one that you have the power to change.

FINALE

I encourage you to reread this book at least once a year. Put it in your calendar right now if you have any doubts about returning. You will have changed and grown and encountered new challenges, and each time you read this book, you will discover new things that you weren't at a place to see before. As you continue to apply the concepts and drop the filters, you will discover layer upon layer of riches—not only in this book but in many of the great texts as well. Perhaps, even some within yourself.

The only useful things are those that are used. I invite you to take what you've read and benefit as much as possible from it. If you don't apply anything you've learned, you may not find the book too useful. If you didn't learn much yet choose to apply many of the principles revealed within, you might find it exceptionally useful. Perhaps this book will serve you as a conversation-starter on your coffee table or during your commute. Maybe the apocalypse arrives, and you use the paper to keep yourself warm. Or perhaps you get stuck in the snow and put the book under your tire to get literally unstuck. I would love that.

Whatever use you have for this book, I am grateful you trusted me with your purchase and for your time exploring these concepts with me.

We will conclude with words from Joseph Campbell:

> "The first step to the knowledge of the wonder and mystery of life is the recognition of the monstrous nature of the earthly human realm as well as its glory, the realization that this is just how it is and that it cannot and will not be changed. Those who think they know how the universe could have been had they created it, without pain, without sorrow, without time, without death, are unfit for illumination.

> "The agony of breaking through personal limitations is the agony of spiritual growth. Art, literature, myth and cult, philosophy, and ascetic disciplines are instruments to help the individual past his limiting horizons into spheres of ever-expanding realization. As he crosses threshold after threshold, conquering dragon after dragon, the stature of the divinity that he summons to his highest wish increases, until it subsumes the cosmos. Finally, the mind breaks the bounding sphere of the cosmos to a realization transcending all experiences of form—all symbolizations, all divinities: a realization of the ineluctable void."

And my final words to you:

You have everything you need already. There is nothing wrong with you. You are worthy. You are lovable. You are enough. There is nothing to fix, only new choices to be made.

Go forth fully-alive and be who-you-really-are, for the heroic life is what humanity calls forth from within you. Break through your stories, filters, and images and awaken to your True Self. 🦋

Postscript

Thank you for taking time out of your day to read this. There are a million other things you could have done, but you chose this—it's an honor. It's my desire that you're walking away from this more aware than you were before. More you than you were before. Less stuck than you were before. Right now may be the beginning of an entirely new way of approaching transformation—and perhaps life—so have compassion with yourself. This book's results don't end when you finish reading; the awareness you've gained will continue to blossom over the months and years ahead. It's a process to surrender to, not force to go faster.

If you've enjoyed this material and want to expand further into similar topics, I think you'd get a lot out of my other work. I offer advanced workshops, private and group sessions, and training programs to aid in your unfoldment. We explore things such as: dream analysis, movement diagnostics, symbolism, enlightenment, archetypes, intuition development, feedback, ego death, reverse-wiring, shadow work, true-sight, somatic resourcefulness—everything else discussed in this book—and more. At the time of publishing, I currently facilitate all classes directly. Please visit my website for programs, dates, and availability. I'd love to see you in our groups or at an upcoming talk!

As an independent author, your reviews and shares of the book are incredibly important. If you've received value from this book, I'd be grateful for anything you do to rate and review. Study groups are also a great way to learn further and share these ideas. Together, we can help more people wake up and get unstuck.

For speaking or media opportunities, events, book signings, interviews, or to promote this book as an affiliate, please contact me through my website. You may reach out to my publisher for bulk orders at publishing@metaheal.com

Sign up for my newsletter at: **andrewdaniel.org**

BONUSES

There are free bonuses available at my website as auxiliary resources for this book. These include the audio recording for the Embodied-Story Exercise, the Lifemap™ process, access to questions and answers about the book, virtual book club access, and more.

Visit this link to access your bonuses: **andnl.co/aytsb**

Legal Disclaimer: These are bonus gifts and not a part of the book or your purchase. The author reserves the right to remove or modify some or all without notice.

Acknowledgments

This book required tremendous work over two years, and I am grateful for everything and everyone that enabled me to get it published. I am thankful for the experiences in my life and everyone who taught me what I know now. I am grateful for the shoulders of giants I stand upon and the poets, mystics, philosophers, alchemists, truth-seekers, and revolutionaries that have risked everything to live and die by the Truth. I am grateful for everyone who contributed to this book, in all forms over the years. It would not have been possible without a few dear people to me.

I'd like to give special thanks to my dad, Robert, who has also devoted a great deal of time and effort in not only encouraging me and this book but brainstorming and editing it as well. You can thank him for a better book.

Thank you to my mother, Kimberly, for giving birth to me and raising me, including her encouragement with this book, and for subjecting herself to testing the movement exercise—twice.

I'd also like to thank my sister, Aryn, for her proofread, helpful suggestions, and conversations around the book.

Thank you as a whole to my family for their belief in me and this book, and mostly for putting up with me talking only about this project for the last six months! Including my brother Aidan and my grandpa Jim for their love and support.

Thank you to Federica for her encouragement, belief, feedback, and impetus to write this version of the book.

Thanks to my friends over the years who have believed in me.

Thank you to all my clients, readers, and students over the last decade. Without people that cared to read what I wrote, I wouldn't be here!

Thank you for getting this book and reading it, and most importantly, for using it to heal and help yourself and others.

ACKNOWLEDGMENT FOR MY INFLUENCES

I am deeply appreciative for Karl Wolfe and everything he has helped me see and become. You would not have most of this book without him either. He was a man who changed many people's lives and likely saved mine. I am grateful to have worked with, and been mentored by, a true master, and before his passing, a friend and colleague.

I would also like to acknowledge Joseph Campbell and Alan Watts for their contributions to the world, which have greatly influenced my work as well.

About the Author

Andrew Daniel is an entrepreneur, author, and spiritual teacher. As the founder of Cinesomatics®, he facilitates advanced workshops utilizing his video-movement technology as Director at the Center for Cinesomatic Development.

Andrew's interest in design and programming at a young age led him to code a particle and physics engine by eighteen. This was his entrance into the world of entrepreneurship, and for seven years, his products were used by top Fortune 100 companies and reached millions. During the latter part of this time, he began writing about personal development on his blog while embarking upon his healing journey. After an awakening, his career shifted completely to transformational work. His first teaching, *Holistic Sex (Mindvalley, 2014)*, became the definitive philosophy for holistically reconciling the schism between sexuality, spirituality, and the sexes.

As a pioneer in the field of embodied transformation, Andrew works in his private practice with clients and teaches publicly on a wide array of topics through books, online programs, and at his internationally held workshops designed to help those on the path of genuine awakening.

Learn more about Andrew at **andrewdaniel.org** and Cinesomatics at **cinesomatics.org**

Obimus tenebras ut lucem lucum inveniamus.